Cambridge Lower Sec~~ondary~~
Complete
Global Perspectives

Karem Roitman
Rory Blackstock
Nazim Qureshi
Vijay Shetty

Oxford excellence for Cambridge Lower Secondary

OXFORD

OXFORD
UNIVERSITY PRESS

Great Clarendon Street, Oxford, OX2 6DP, United Kingdom

Oxford University Press is a department of the University of Oxford.

It furthers the University's objective of excellence in research, scholarship, and education by publishing worldwide. Oxford is a registered trade mark of Oxford University Press in the UK and in certain other countries

© Oxford University Press 2021

The moral rights of the author have been asserted

First published in 2021

All rights reserved. No part of this publication may be reproduced, stored in a retrieval system, or transmitted, in any form or by any means, without the prior permission in writing of Oxford University Press, or as expressly permitted by law, by licence or under terms agreed with the appropriate reprographics rights organization. Enquiries concerning reproduction outside the scope of the above should be sent to the Rights Department, Oxford University Press, at the address above.

You must not circulate this work in any other form and you must impose this same condition on any acquirer

British Library Cataloguing in Publication Data

Data available

978-1-38-200874-7

10 9 8 7 6 5 4 3

Paper used in the production of this book is a natural, recyclable product made from wood grown in sustainable forests.

The manufacturing process conforms to the environmental regulations of the country of origin.

Printed in India by Gopsons Papers Ltd., Sivakasi

Acknowledgements

The publisher would like to thank the following for permissions to use copyright material:

Moeller, Karla, "How are humans different from other animals?", Ask a Biologist, https://askabiologist.asu.edu

"Real stories from refugees: Doaa's story", adapted from World Economic Forum, www.weforum.org

"Real stories from refugees: Emmanuel's story", adapted from World Economic Forum, www.weforum.org

Trivedi, Ayushi, "Women are secret weapon in better water management", World Resources Institute, www.wri.org

"Surprising statistics about global food consumption", One, www. one.org

"Statistics on sustainability", Sustainability Management School, https://sumas.ch/sustainability-statistics

"Do not be lazy, let us fight for this Rwanda", adapted from a translation of radio RTLM's transcripts of 15 May 1994, for the United Nations International Criminal Tribunal for Rwanda, Montreal Institute for Genocide and Human Rights Studies, http://migs.concordia.ca

Duncan, Arne, "Civic learning and engagement must become staples of American education", Home Room, https://blog.ed.gov

"The way you see colour depends on what language you speak", The Conversation, https://theconversation.com

"MLA style guide", University of Washington, Library Guides, https://guides.lib.uw.edu

All other texts written by the author.

Cover artwork by: Amelia Flower

p8: Naeblys/Shutterstock; p10: Jimmie48 Photography/Shutterstock; p12l: Salparadis/Shutterstock; p12r: andreiuc88/Shutterstock; p16: galacticus/Shutterstock; p24: Kailash Kumar/123RF; p25r: Rick & Nora Bowers/Alamy Stock Photo; p25l: Auscape International Pty Ltd/Alamy Stock Photo; p25b: World History Archive/Alamy Stock Photo; p26: SoumenNath/Shutterstock; p28: DM7/Shutterstock; p30: EFE News Agency/Alamy Stock Photo; p32: ArtisticPhoto/Shutterstock; p46: MicroOne/Shutterstock; p49: madpixblue/Shutterstock; p51: Lightspring/Shutterstock; p56b: International Telecommunication Union; p56t: Duolingo, Inc: https://blog.duolingo.com/which-countries-study-which-languages-and-what-can-we-learn-from-it/; p59: GL Archive/Alamy Stock Photo; p61: galacticus/Shutterstock; p68: Dima Zahar/123RF; p72: Ian Cuming/Ikon Images/Science Photo Library; p74: Rawpixel.com/Shutterstock; p81 Istvan Csak/Shutterstock; p118: Africa Studio/Shutterstock; p122: Hum Images/Alamy Stock Photo; p128: Pamela Maxwell/123RF; p141: Greg McNevin/Alamy Stock Photo; p155: © World Food Programme 2020; p164l: History and Art Collection/Alamy Stock Photo; p164r: Keith Corrigan/Alamy Stock Photo; p167: AB Forces News Collection/Alamy Stock Photo; p182: Travelpixs/Shutterstock; p183: Carolyn Jenkins/Alamy Stock Photo; p184l: Fischer, Ed/CartoonStock; p184r: Allenby, Kendra/Cartoon Collections; p192: Ondrej Prosicky/Shutterstock; p193: Matteo Pessini/Alamy Stock Photo; p197l: Nicram Sabod/Shutterstock; p197r: Panos Karas/Shutterstock; p207: AnnaStills/Shutterstock; p215: Rawpixel.com/Shutterstock; p236: sitayi/Shutterstock; p244: Frank Hoensch/Getty Images; p262: freepik.com; p272: Navino Evans/Wikimedia Commons.

All other photos provided by Shutterstock & OUP

All artwork by: Aptara

Index compiled by LNS Indexing

Although we have made every effort to trace and contact all copyright holders before publication this has not been possible in all cases. If notified, the publisher will rectify any errors or omissions at the earliest opportunity.

Links to third party websites are provided by Oxford in good faith and for information only. Oxford disclaims any responsibility for the materials contained in any third party website referenced in this work.

Contents

Welcome to Global Perspectives   4

Year 7

Challenge 1 What makes us human?   16
Challenge 2 Diplomacy and national traditions   32
Challenge 3 Globalization   46
Challenge 4 Education   68
Challenge 5 Seeking refuge   84
Challenge 6 Employment   100
End of Year 7   116
Citing sources   118

Year 8

Challenge 1 Water crisis   122
Challenge 2 Migration   136
Challenge 3 Beliefs about food   150
Challenge 4 Looking at the future   164
Challenge 5 Trade and aid   178
Challenge 6 Sustainability   192
Challenge 7 Making a difference   206
End of Year 8   216

Year 9

Challenge 1 Disease and health   220
Challenge 2 Conflict resolution   234
Challenge 3 Sports for all   248
Challenge 4 Languages   262
Challenge 5 Writing your report   278
Reflection   292

Economic appendix   294
Writing appendix   296
MLA guide   298
Index   301

Welcome to Global Perspectives

Introduction

Global Perspectives is a course like no other. In this course, you will acquire the tools you need to explore what *you* are interested in. You will be taught how to carefully judge what you hear from the media, politicians, and groups who want to convince you or sell you things. Through this course you will grow as a critical thinker, as a creative investigator, and as a powerful communicator. This course is not about memorizing content – although you will encounter fascinating facts and information that you are likely to remember – this course is about learning, practising, and improving the skills needed to collect, analyse, and use information in the most powerful way.

Purpose of this book

This book has been designed to help you to develop specific **key skills**:

- Research
- Evaluation
- Collaboration
- Analysis
- Reflection
- Communication

You will learn about each of these skills as you explore a variety of fun 'Challenges'. This book will provide you with a multitude of exercises that will help you to understand and work on each skill. You can also use these exercises with other topics that interest you.

As you work through the exercises in this book, you will learn how to undertake research, how to analyse and evaluate research findings, how to work with others to find and present solutions to problems, and how to reflect on your learning and work. Most importantly, you will learn to see topics from a variety of perspectives. Thus, you will learn about how your personal interests affect, and are affected by, local, national, and even global issues. You will also practise seeing issues from the perspective of other people, making you aware of the many sides of any problem.

Structure of the book

Years

This book is divided into Years 7, 8, and 9. As you move through the years, activities will become more challenging and you will work more independently. This will help you prepare to undertake your own research project in Year 9. We start Year 7 with a special discussion on perspectives, which we will be using throughout the book.

Challenges

Each year covers multiple 'Challenges'. Each challenge will help you to explore one of the topics in the Global Perspectives curriculum, such as education, food and agriculture or Globalization, through fun exercises.

Key skills

The exercises in each challenge will help you to develop the **key skills** mentioned on the previous page. The skill being covered will be clearly stated at the top of each section. The learning objectives of each chapter will be discussed in the introduction of each challenge and listed in the Table of Contents on pages 2–3.

Extension activities

At the end of each challenge, we will provide a series of **extension options** that allow you to take your research further and/or to link it with other areas of your studies, including maths, literature, history, geography, arts, sciences, and philosophy.

You can use this book:

- linearly – by working through all the challenges systematically to develop and sharpen your critical thinking and research skills

- by skill – by choosing areas that sharpen a particular skill

- by topic – by choosing challenges that you find particularly interesting.

Whichever you decide, we are sure that you will enjoy the journey and grow as a global thinker and researcher.

Welcome to Global Perspectives!

The six key skills

As you work through this book you will be seeing these characters to remind you of what skill you are working on:

Research

Hello! You can call me *curious*. Or creative! I am always asking questions! I will try to inspire you to follow your creativity to new research areas. I will teach you to ask questions, to find information, and I will give you tools to keep track of what you find.

Analysis

I am Professor Analysis. Getting information is good, but it is only once you analyse the information that you can do something with it! I will guide you to interpret data, synthesize arguments, find evidence, and understand causes and consequences. As we understand, interpret and use data, we will come up with solutions for problems posed in the challenges.

Evaluation

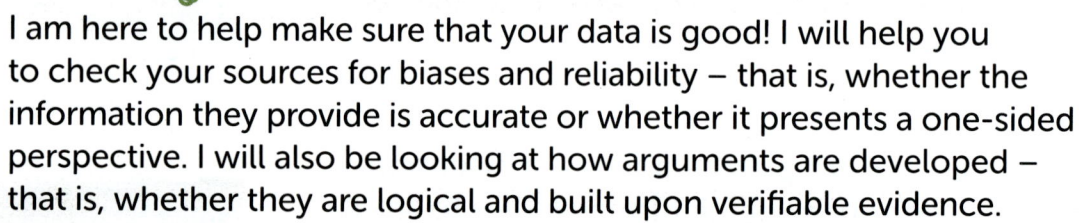

I am here to help make sure that your data is good! I will help you to check your sources for biases and reliability – that is, whether the information they provide is accurate or whether it presents a one-sided perspective. I will also be looking at how arguments are developed – that is, whether they are logical and built upon verifiable evidence.

Communication

Call me Chatterbox. I like to talk, and write, and sing, and make videos – and so much more! I am here to help you share your findings with different audiences so that others can understand your reasoning and be convinced by your arguments.

Collaboration

I am a people-person. I will help you find ways to work constructively with your peers.

Reflection

I am the deep one in the group. I like to sit back and think about what we have done, what we have learnt, what we might be missing, and how it has affected us. Learning is about *you* as a person. I am here to help you become a reflective, deep learner.

Perspectives

Wait! There are six skills, but I am also very important. I am here to help you see the topics and ideas we speak about from different points of view. In particular, I want you to see how issues that affect an individual person (personal) might also affect your neighbourhood or city (local), your country (national), or the world (global).

In each challenge in this book you will encounter several of these characters. As you explore fascinating topics you will have the opportunity to research, analyse, evaluate, reflect, collaborate, and communicate in a great many ways. You will have exercises to practise with, group activities and games to enjoy, and opportunities to put your research into action. Remember, you can always take these skills, and the exercises we propose, and use them to research your own interests. Make Global Perspectives yours!

Topics

The exercises this book presents will teach you skills you can use to research and understand any topic. Make the book yours! Take the research exercises in the topic of Employment (Challenge 6), for example, and use them to research pollution. Exercises are interchangeable between topics. To help you use the exercises in this book for any topic, we have included a table that lists all the exercises by the skills they focus on at the end of the book.

Challenges and issues

Within each challenge presented in Global Perspectives there are various **issues** you can decide to focus on. An issue is a particular problem within a larger topic. For example, when looking at the topic of **environmental change**, one issue to look at is **plastic pollution**, another is **greenhouse gases**. When looking at the topic of **work**, one issue is **fair pay**, another is **unemployment**. As you research different issues we encourage you to think critically about what has caused these problems and think about some possible solutions.

Perspectives: Global, National, Local and Personal

Anything you can think of – from your shoes to the weather, from your favourite sports team to international peace negotiations – can be looked at from various perspectives:

- global
- national
- local
- personal.

You can start any research or investigation from any of these perspectives.

You can think of these perspectives as the 'distance' you see a topic from. Let's think of one topic – *sport* – and 'see' it from each perspective.

From a **global perspective**, you are looking at a topic as though you are sitting in the International Space Station, looking down at Earth and realizing how everything is interconnected – we are all part of one big globe.

At this level, you might notice global or international leagues for a sport. Some enquiry questions at this perspective, or level of analysis, might include:

- Who are the greatest players in the world?
- Who are the greatest players in history?
- What are the international rules for the sport?
- How do sports promote global unity?

From a **national perspective**, you are focused closer in, at the level of a country. You are thinking in terms of state power, national boundaries, national laws.

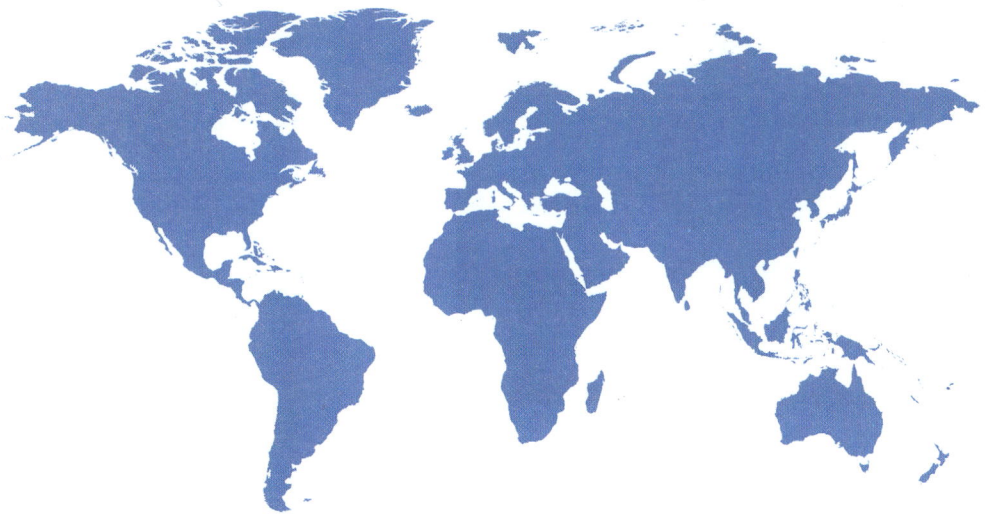

At this level, you might think about your country's sports leagues, the main players your country has, the most famous player in your country's history. You might enquire:

- How are sports funded in your country and who benefits from different sport activities?
- What is the most popular sport in your country?
- Who are your country's main rivals in different sports?

From a **local perspective**, you are looking at sports at the level of your local community.

At this level, you might think about your local — school or neighbourhood — sports team.

- Who runs it?
- Is it linked with other groups like religions or ethnicities?
- How is it funded?
- How do local leagues affect their communities?

From a **personal perspective**, your focus is even narrower. Here, you are thinking about individuals. Thinking about sport at this level you might be thinking about the biography of a particular player. Or you might be thinking about what sport *you* play.

- Why do you like a particular sport?
- What do you need to be a better sportsperson?
- How has sport affected your life?

Using perspectives to understand an issue

If you want to understand the impact of any decision you make, or the many sides of a problem you are interested in, then it is worth thinking through each perspective. Let's take an example: the impact of buying a packet of ready-cut fruits in the supermarket – conveniently packaged in plastic to keep them fresh.

Looking at each perspective will give us different insights that help us answer the question, 'What is the impact of buying pre-packaged fruit?'.

Personal: You might find pre-packaged fruit convenient to take with you to school. Or you might wonder why pre-cut fruit is needed at all. If you are disabled and struggle to cut fruit, you might find these the only way to eat certain fruits.

Local: If the fruit is from your city, local farmers might benefit when these packages are bought. However, if it is not from your city, then by buying it you are perhaps buying less from local farmers, who might then become poorer. The packet of fruit will also affect your local environment when thrown away – how much trash can your city cope with before it runs out of space? If you throw it on the ground – not that you should! – you will add to the pollution of your hometown and the plastic might end up in a local river, hurting fish and local birds.

National: Looking at this from a national perspective, you might consider whether the fruit is grown in your country. If you are buying it from another country (importing it), you are paying to bring it into your country. You might also consider the impact on the culture: if you are bringing in exotic fruits, your population is getting used to food that is not native to you, that is not seasonal.

Global: The pollution from the cars and/or planes transporting the fruit does not stay within your country: it contributes to global environmental changes. The rubbish that ends up in rivers and lakes enters the local ecosystem. However, this ecosystem is connected to the global environment. The plastic you threw away in, say, São Paulo, might end up in the stomach of a dolphin in Florida.

It is important to understand that *perspectives overlap and interact*. What affects you as a person will also affect your community, your country, and even the world. In the same way, a global problem – such as global warming – is not just global, it affects you as a person, and what you do as an individual will affect the world. You can analyse each perspective separately, but you need to remember that they are **interconnected** and **overlap**.

Why do we need multiple perspectives?

There is an old saying, "Don't miss the forest for the trees." This means you should not miss the big picture by focusing only on the details. In truth, it would also not be a good idea to miss the details by only looking at the big picture!

By considering personal, local, national, and global perspectives, you can see the forest *and* the trees.

If you stand very close to a tree, you can study the texture and colour of the bark, smell it, feel its shade.

But you cannot see the shape of the tree until you stand a bit further back. Then you can see how tall the tree is, how far it spreads, whether its top branches are different, whether it bears fruit.

You have to stand even further back to realize that the tree is in a large forest, and to understand the nature of the forest.

If you always look at a forest from a distance, you will never learn about the individual trees. If you only look at one tree, you will not understand how it connects to others, how ecosystems form and work. You need to look very closely *and* you need to look from afar.

Personal, local, national, global – they are pieces of a complex puzzle. You need all of them to understand the full picture.

Each perspective is complex. Don't think that a local perspective is less complicated than a global perspective, or vice versa. Each perspective is simply different and can, therefore, show you different aspects of an issue. Moreover, you often need to see different sides of a problem to try to find a solution. Being able to change your perspective is a very powerful tool. You can use this tool whether you work in politics, in business, in sports – or even just to understand tensions and changes among your friends.

1 Using perspectives

Read this short story, then try to see what different perspectives are included in it. Think about how these different perspectives give you a more complete understanding of what is causing the problem.

Tim was sad. He had lost his school's racing event. He blamed the state of the path where he had to train: there were holes and weeds sprouting all over the place. Why couldn't the school fix it? His mom was also upset. But she was angry at the government. Every year they gave less money to schools, so the schools could barely afford books, much less could they afford to maintain the sport grounds. Tim's sister meanwhile was listening to the news. The price of oil, their country's main export good, had dropped again. This meant more poverty for all. Tim's dad blamed himself; he thought he should spend more time with Tim but was just too busy working to be able to help. And he had to work long shifts to be able to pay the bills.

Discuss:

- Who uses a local perspective?
- Who uses a national perspective?
- Who uses a global perspective?
- Who uses a personal perspective?
- Can you see how these are interconnected?

Challenge:

If you wanted to fix Tim's problem what solution would you come up with if you only spoke to Tim? If you only spoke to his mother? If you only spoke to his father? Does coming up with a good solution require you to look at a problem through multiple perspectives? Why or why not?

2 Perspectives on your identity

Multiple perspectives can also be used to help you understand *who you are*.

Try to answer each of these questions with a partner. Take turns asking and answering the questions:

1. Imagine that a Martian asks you who you are. What would you answer?

2. Imagine that you are in an airport and meet someone from another country. They ask you who you are. What would you reply?

3. Imagine your partner is the cousin of a school friend. They ask you who you are. What would you answer?

As you think through your answers it is very likely you did not answer the same thing for every question in Exercise 2. You are always *you*, but who you are, how you think, and how you present your identity, is affected by the perspective you are using.

When you use a global perspective, you might mention you are from Earth! When you meet someone from another country, you are likely to mention your nationality, and maybe your city. When you meet someone who knows your friends and local area, you might mention your family, your neighbourhood, your sport team and other local information. All of these are components of your identity. All of them are you. All of them are true. But different components are more relevant, or more important, in different contexts, in different perspectives.

3 Perspectives to understand others

You can also use different perspectives to understand others, including your classmates. When you wonder why a person acts as they do, try to understand their personal background, their local background, their national background. Each of these might give you insights into what they believe and why they act as they do. Try the following questions to practise understanding others from different perspectives.

1. Look up the biography of a famous politician, celebrity, or sportsperson. Try to understand who they are from a global, a national, and a personal perspective.

2. Interview someone you know – it could be a friend or a family member. Try to see them from a different perspective. Try to learn something new about them.

3. Look up the story of Martin Luther King. How do you think his skin colour affected his choices? What about his religion? How do you think his nationality affected his life?

 ## 4 Discussing perspectives

Use the following questions to hold a discussion as a class or in small groups. See if you can come up with other questions about perspectives.

1. Which perspective do you think is easiest for you to use?

2. Do you usually think of problems in a global, national, or personal perspective?

3. Do you think politicians should think about problems using one perspective more than the others? Why or why not?

 ## 5 Thinking further about your identity

Draw yourself! Make a self-portrait of yourself where you write in all the different parts of your identity. Use Exercise 2 to think about the many parts that make up who you are. Here are a few ideas to get you started. Think about what you look like, the music you listen to, the communities you belong to, the beliefs you hold. You could use magazines to find pictures or words that represent you and add them to your portrait.

Year 7

Challenge 1
What makes us human?

1.1 Humanity

Think about the following questions. You can try to answer them individually or discuss them with others in your class.

1. Do you think humans are the most important creatures on Earth? Why or why not?

2. If we could plug all your memories and feelings into a computer, would that computer be human?

3. If we can add robotic components to humans – link their brains to a computer, change their bones for titanium rods, make them able to hold their breath under water for hours – would they still be human?

Challenge overview

Imagine you are walking down the road when, suddenly, a bright green light blinds you. You cover your eyes until the light disappears. Slowly you open your eyes and before you is a strange creature. It has no eyes, but you are sure it can see you. It has no mouth, but you hear its voice. It is not solid, but you can feel it moving. It is an alien.

The alien is a Year 7 student from the planet *Glomatron*. It is researching different life forms. You can sense it is looking at you with curiosity. It wants to understand you.

You point at yourself and say, "Human!". The alien keeps looking at you quizzically. It takes out an intergalactic dictionary and is busy for a few minutes. Then somehow it communicates into your brain the following information: 'HUMAN. Interesting word, but it is not in my dictionary. Tell me more. "HUMAN". Human edible? Human dangerous? Should I destroy human?'

This is your first challenge. We need to come up with an explanation of what a 'human' is for the alien. Where will you start?

What skills will you develop?

In this challenge you will work on developing the following skills:

Research 1: Getting started
→ You will look at strategies to approach a new topic. You will learn the power of 'free thinking' and thinking of opposites.

Research 2: Choosing a research question
→ You will look at how to create good questions to lead your research.

Collaboration: Working as a team
→ You will look at how to work well as a team.

Analysis 1: Recognizing arguments
→ You will work at recognizing arguments used to support a position.

Analysis 2: Checking the evidence
→ You will look at how evidence is used to support an argument.

Communication: Debating the answer
→ You will work with a group to argue for a position in a debate. You will work on presenting your argument clearly, and on judging others' arguments carefully.

Taking it further
→ This section will give you a lot of ideas to take your learning further, connecting it with other subjects and expanding your understanding.

Research 1
Getting started

Free thinking

One of the most powerful tools when you are starting a new piece of research is **free thinking**. It can feel scary to start to think and research something new, but letting your mind think freely can help you realize that you already have some ideas, some interests, and some questions to follow!

In this challenge, as you start thinking about what makes us humans and how to explain what humans are, you could start by writing *everything* that comes to your mind when you think about **humans**.

The important thing here is to let your mind come up with ideas freely, think of it like a *storm!* Let everything that comes to your mind come! Don't try to filter ideas or use only 'good ones'. While thinking freely, just let your brain explore and don't judge yourself – everything that comes gets written down. You might be surprised with what comes to your mind. You might also be surprised by the connections you can make with this 'rain' later. So don't stop the storm!

1.2a Free thinking

Take out a piece of paper and write everything that comes to your mind as you answer the question: **What is a human?**

1.2b Group discussion

Try thinking freely as a group. The same rule applies – encourage everyone to say anything that comes to their mind, as silly as it might seem. Write it all out, no judgements, no criticism. You might be surprised. An idea or word that seems completely unrelated to the topic might lead to interesting questions, insights, and paths of discovery.

Year 7 Challenge 1

Thinking about opposites

Sometimes we get stuck and need other ways to answer a question. A trick is to ask the opposite. For example, rather than thinking about *what makes us human*, try thinking about *what makes non-humans*.

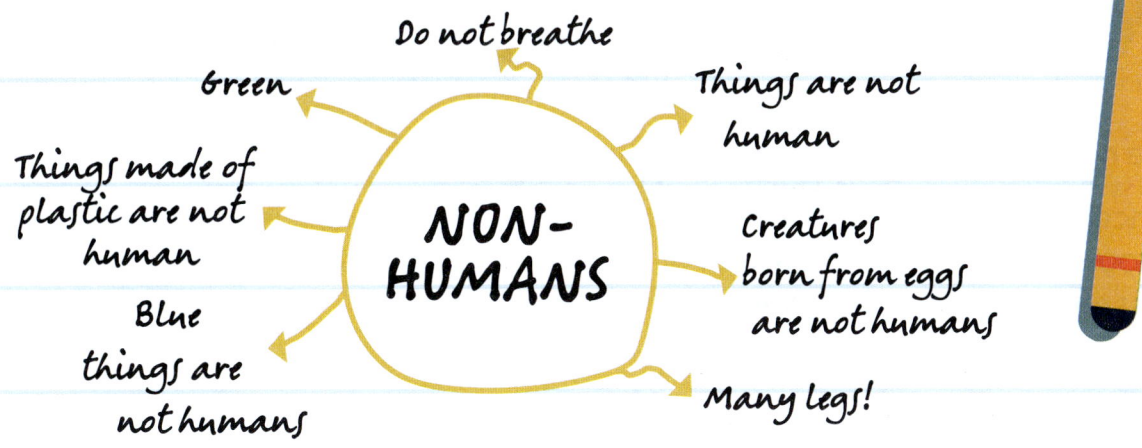

Remember

The point of these exercises is to start thinking about a new topic creatively.

- Perhaps this is a new area you have never thought about, so you are not sure where to start. Free thinking can give you some ideas to follow.

- Perhaps this is an area you have thought about a lot and cannot imagine how to create a new, fun project from it. Free thinking can help you come up with new angles on an idea.

- Maybe you feel a bit overwhelmed by the topic. Free thinking can help you get all your ideas, questions, and even worries out there.

Expanding your free thinking

You can draw or paint in your notes. There is no reason to use only words!

You can write/draw each idea on a sticky note and later move the notes around to organize them.

You can use different colours to organize your ideas. For example:

- **Blue** for logical ideas
- **Green** for emotional ideas
- **Red** for strange ideas
- **Purple** for ideas you feel uncertain about

Once you have spent some time letting your mind 'rain ideas', take a step back and see what you have found. Look at what you have written. Do any patterns jump out? Does anything now seem missing? Is anything particularly interesting to you?

19

Research 2
Choosing a research question

We now move to a **critical part** of any research: *asking questions*.

Once we have spent some time thinking about our topic, it is time to choose a question to research. For example, what questions should you research to explain to an alien what humans are?

Good research questions

Some questions are better for research than others. Some questions will lead you away from the topic you are interested in. Other questions are so large you will find yourself lost in too many answers, too much information, too many possible paths.

Good research questions are focused, clear, and unbiased.

Poor research questions usually fall within one of these categories:

- **Too broad**. Questions in this category are so big you will feel a bit overwhelmed and find that you have too many options.

- **Too narrow**. These are questions that do not answer the whole topic you are interested in. They might be answered by a simple 'yes' or 'no', giving you very little, or no new, insight.

- **Irrelevant**. These are questions that are not about your present topic. They will take your research in the wrong direction.

- **Biased or leading**. These are questions that *force* you toward a specific answer, rather than helping you see an issue from many different points of view.

- **Unrealistic**. These are questions we simply cannot answer with the information available to us.

1.3 Good questions

Look through the questions below. Using the categories on the previous page decide whether each question is a good or a poor research question and why. Discuss your decisions with your peers.

1. What are humans?
2. Why do humans like sugar?
3. Do all humans wear black shoes?
4. What makes humans different from other animals?
5. How are humans different from machines?
6. Why do humans exist?
7. How do humans floss their teeth?
8. Do humans live in a galaxy?
9. Is it important for humans to be vegetarians?

Bullseye

When thinking about research questions, it sometimes helps to think of a bullseye.

The bullseye is the topic you want to learn about. The further you get from the bullseye, the further you are getting from the purpose of your research. Whenever you are doing research and start coming up with questions, it is a good idea to ask yourself, 'Am I getting closer or further from the bullseye?'

*To get a good question you need to remember what you are trying to find out. That is the **aim** of your research. That is the bullseye.*

In this challenge, you are trying to explain to an alien what makes us human. You are trying to find out what makes humans, well, humans.

1.4 Research aim

Look at the list of questions below and choose which ones *do not* focus on the aim of your research.

→ Why do humans have hair?
→ Are humans the only creatures able to think?
→ Do all humans like football?

Collaboration
Working as a team

In Global Perspectives you will be working in teams to research local, national, and global issues, to think about possible solutions for these issues, and to present your arguments and evidence in a logical and interesting way.

Here are some areas you want to think about when working in groups:

→ You will need to think about how to divide your work to ensure that everyone is involved and feels appreciated.

→ You will need to ensure you can communicate within your group. It is important to be able to give each other honest feedback, but feedback can always be given in a kind and thoughtful way.

→ Conflict can happen! Find ways to decrease tensions. Perhaps take some time to calm down, and try to discuss the disagreements without taking personal offence. Sometimes, it can be helpful to get an outsider's perspective. You can ask your teacher to mediate if you cannot find a solution.

1.5 Working as a team

Cooking together

One way to think about what you need to work as a group successfully is to think of your team as if you were making a recipe together. Imagine your challenge is to make a cake together. What would you need to do to successfully make a cake as a team? Look at the list below and discuss with your team what you need to do and in what order.

→ Discuss what your favourite food is
→ Get upset if someone does not like the same flavour as you do
→ Find a recipe for the cake
→ Notice the steps in the recipe and assign each different step to a team member

Year 7 Challenge 1

- Make sure each team member knows what to do in the kitchen
- Taste the cake
- Look at how much time you have and how long you need to bake the cake
- Find the ingredients and an oven
- Take a nap
- Create a checklist
- Check that you did not miss any steps
- Make sure none of the ingredients are spoiled
- Make the cake look nice on a plate
- Anything else?

Note: making a cake with your team is a lot like working on a Global Perspectives Challenge together. You need to:

Find a recipe → Find a research question

Find ingredients → Find good resources

Break the recipe into parts → Break your research project into parts

Assign different parts of the of the recipe to different team members → Assign parts of the project to different team members

Make sure all parts of the recipe are completed → Make sure all parts of your project are completed

Can you think of other parts of making a cake which are like working on a Global Perspectives Challenge?

Working as a team is a skill we can all learn and improve on. When you start to work with a new team it can be a good idea to try to make something together, just for fun, to understand a bit about how each person works. Once your team understands how each member works, you can find a way to collaborate effectively. Ideally, teams should be stronger than the sum of their parts!

To build your dynamics as a team, try one of the following:

1. Build some origami. Take turns to be the person who folds the paper, the person who reads the instructions, and the person who checks diagrams.

2. Make a sandwich! Take the cake example to real life and try to make a simple plate of food. Notice how different people work and then share something tasty together.

Analysis 1
Recognizing arguments

A possible research question to follow is:

How are humans different from other animals?

Note how this is a clear, focused, non-leading question. The question is easy to understand and it has a specific focus (humans and other animals). It is not a leading question: it does not tell us that humans are better or worse, different from or the same as, other animals. The question is also not too narrow: we cannot answer it with a simple yes or no.

Now we need to find sources to help us answer this question. When we find a source, we need to recognize what it is arguing, and what evidence it is using to make its argument.

1.6 Finding arguments

Read the excerpt below. With a group of peers discuss: what is it arguing? List the reasons it uses to support its argument.

"Humans and animals both eat, sleep, think, and communicate. We are also similar in a lot of the ways our bodies work. But we also have a lot of differences.

Some people think that the main differences between humans [and] other animal species is our ability of complex reasoning, our use of complex language, our ability to solve difficult problems, and introspection (this means describing your own thoughts and feelings). Others also feel that the ability for creativity or the feeling of joy or sorrow is uniquely human. Humans have a highly developed brain that allows us to do many of these things. But are these things uniquely human?

A baboon is given a mirror test.

Gunnison's prairie dogs seem to have a fairly complex language – rather than just sounding a basic alarm call, researchers have found that their alarm calls can describe specific predator speed, colour, shape, and size.

Caledonian crows can solve problems and build tools and can solve multiple-step puzzles that require a plan.

Gorillas and chimpanzees have painted pictures of birds, describing (through sign language) that that is what they were trying to create. If they had a goal in mind and then made it, is that a sign that they had introspection? ... And that they are doing it by using their own creativity?

And animals do appear to feel joy and sorrow. There are videos out there showing a raven using a piece of plastic to sled down part of a snowy roof. They are enjoying sledding and having fun, perhaps feeling joy. And we continue to learn of more and more species that show sorrow, especially at the loss of members of their family or other loved ones.

So maybe there isn't that much that makes us uniquely human. Maybe we need to pay more attention to what animals are doing and try to view the world through their eyes. And, perhaps our ability to consider animals' feelings and hope for the well-being of these other amazing creatures is our best, and most uniquely human ability.

Adapted from: https://askabiologist.asu.edu/questions/human-animal-differences

1.7 Reading comprehension

Are humans the only animals able to problem solve?

Are humans the only creative animals?

Are humans the only introspective animals?

Discuss with your peers.

 Group activity

With a team create a collage that shows what makes us humans. Be as creative as you can!

Analysis 2
Checking the evidence

Evidence is facts or data that support an answer.

As you answer a question, you will need to provide evidence to prove that your answer is valid.

Evidence detectives

When thinking about evidence, you can think of yourself as a detective. When trying to solve a case, detectives need to look carefully and analyse what they find. What you find is evidence. You analyse this evidence to reach a conclusion.

 **Warning**

Detectives can be thrown off the right path by false evidence. A smart thief, for example, could leave someone else's shoes at the scene of the crime to throw police off! Be a smart evidence detective: make sure to check everything carefully and don't fall for false evidence!

1.8 Detective of the future

Imagine yourself as a detective in the year 3020. You are sent to another planet to look for evidence of life. What might be evidence of:

- simple life forms
- creative life forms
- life forms that lived in communities?

Year 7 Challenge 1

 1.9 Evidence from articles

Go back to the article on animals and humans used in the previous section.

Try to complete the table below using evidence provided in the article. Read the article to find facts that *prove* the author's argument. One has been done as an example.

Question: Are humans different from other animals?

Argument: Humans and other animals are not so different.

Reason	Evidence
Other animals are also creative.	
Other animals also experience emotions.	
Other animals also use complex language.	Gunnison's prairie dogs can describe a predator's speed, colour, shape, and size
(fill in other arguments here)	
(fill in other arguments here)	
(fill in other arguments here)	

 1.10 Analysing a text

Read the blog below and try to answer the questions with a partner.

1. What is the blog's main argument?

2. What evidence does the blog use to support its argument?

HUMANS ARE SMARTER THAN COMPUTERS.

Although computers have beaten humans at complex strategy games like chess, we cannot forget that humans came up with the games in the first place.

Computers can process information much faster than humans. Try asking a human to solve a really complicated maths problem and see how long it takes them. Then ask your computer. However, it is humans who developed maths.

We could also mention emotional intelligence, this is the intelligence to understand how you and others feel, and to respond appropriately. Computers do not have emotional intelligence because machines cannot feel.

Ultimately the greatest argument for humans being smarter than computers is that humans made computers.

27

Communication
Debating the answer

Remember the alien we started this challenge with? He is not convinced that there are many differences between humans and other animals on this planet. You invite him to a debate on the topic.

Divide your class into two groups. One side is going to represent the view of the alien: that there is nothing that makes humans unique from other animals on Earth. The other side will argue that humans are different from any other animal on Earth.

You can either take some time to look for evidence or you can do a speed debate, where each group only gets 30 minutes in the library to prepare their position.

Whichever option you decide, think of a strategy to ensure everyone's time is used effectively. How can you split the work to make sure you get as much useful information as possible? Perhaps you can send different people in your group to look at different sources. Perhaps one of you can take notes and another check the information gathered. Perhaps one of you will be the presenter putting together what others found.

To prepare for the debate remember to:

→ create a list of reasons or points that support your side

→ try to find evidence that supports your reasons

→ try to present your position in a persuasive manner. Use evidence to convince others of your position. Remember: the fate of humanity is in your hands!

> To present a strong case you need to make your argument clear, support it with clear reasons, and support your reasons with evidence. Argument ⟶ Reasons ⟶ Evidence is a winning combination.

1.11 Conducting the debate

Each side gets 20 minutes to present their position.

After both sides have presented, each side gets another 10 minutes to answer any questions. The winner of the debate will be chosen by judges.

It is important that debates are respectful. Each group should listen politely while the other speaks. Even if you disagree with what is being said, it is important to give others the opportunity to state their argument uninterrupted. Points could be deducted from groups that interrupt.

Try to convince others with good evidence, not with rude words or shocking statements. If you hurt other people's feelings, they are less likely to want to listen to you!

1.12 Judging the debate

Select who will judge your debate: your teacher, a group of students, or someone else. Judges will give points based on the following criteria:

→ 1 point per reason supporting an argument

→ 2 points per piece of evidence

1.13 Reflection

After all challenges have been completed, it is important to take some time to think about what you have learnt, what you have done, what went well, and what could have gone better. To help you reflect, take some time to write out your answers to these questions.

1. When the debate is finished, write a quick note about which side *you* think won and why. Was there particularly good evidence presented? Did you find one side easier to understand?

2. How do you think you could help your team improve in future debates?

3. What was the hardest thing about working in a group? Can you think of ways to make it easier next time?

Taking it further

What makes us human, and how humans are different from other animals, are fun areas to think about and research. Here are some suggestions to take your learning further:

Law

- Look at animal rights.
- If humans and animals are not that different, then why don't animals have the same rights as humans?
- Do different countries grant different rights to animals?
- Should all animals have equal rights? Should slugs and lions, for example, be given the same rights? What should rights be based on?

Philosophy

- Some people have argued that animals feel as much as humans do, and therefore should be respected like humans. Do you think the capacity to feel pain is a good basis on which to give rights?

Computers

- What makes humans different from computers, other than the fact that humans die?
- Research Sophia, a humanoid robot who was granted citizenship by Saudi Arabia. Do you think giving Sophia citizenship blurs the line between humans and robots?

Coding

- Imagine you were coding a robot. Your challenge is to make it as human as possible so that no one can tell it is a robot. What *behaviours* would you code into the robot to make it as human as possible? Once you write this out, find out what the Turing test is. Do you think your robot would pass the test?

Year 7 Challenge 1

Biology

- What makes our bodies human?
- Who are our nearest ancestors?
- Which animals are most similar to us?

Religion

- What are some religious arguments that separate humans from other beings?
- Consider interviewing one or more religious leaders to ask them for their views on what makes humans unique.

Literature

- Imagine you are in the year 35000. Humans have long since ceased to exist and have evolved into a new species. Describe the new species and why it evolved as it did. Does it have eyes? Is it more or less intelligent than humans?

What did you learn?

When you complete this challenge, take a moment to reflect over what you have learnt with the table below:

Skill	I get it!	I am starting to get it!	I need to review this.
Research: I understand how to and why we use 'free thinking'.			
Research: I know what makes a good research question.			
Analysis: I can recognize a source's main argument.			
Analysis: I can recognize evidence used to support an argument.			
Collaboration: I can work with others to present an argument.			
Collaboration: I understand that working with a team includes sharing tasks and planning.			
Analysis: I understand what evidence is.			

Year 7

Challenge 2
Diplomacy and national traditions

2.1 Traditions

1. Do you think all cultural traditions are good?
2. What is the most extraordinary cultural tradition you have heard about?
3. What should we do if two cultural traditions clash?
4. Do you think traditions unite us, or separate us?

32

Challenge overview

Imagine you are sent as Ambassador for your country to a distant land called Dragunste. You are the first Ambassador ever to be invited into this country. It is in your hands to create a positive relationship between the two countries. You want to create understanding and appreciation. Your job might prevent future wars.

People in Dragunste have only heard of your country through some biased and limited media. They have been told your country has some 'strange' customs. Your first job it to create a presentation to address this misconception.

As you work through this challenge you will need to think about where to find information about your national traditions. You will need to think about how to present your information. You will also need to think about how to understand traditions that might be very different from yours and how others might perceive your traditions. Using multiple perspectives will be key.

What skills will you develop?

Reflection: Curious customs
- You will start by thinking critically about traditions, practising using multiple perspectives to understand your world.

Research 1: Asking questions
- You will continue to work on developing good research questions.

Research 2: Finding information
- You will think about what sources you can use and why you need to keep track of these sources.

Analysis: Organizing your notes
- You will learn strategies to take useful notes.

Communication: Sharing your findings
- You will create a presentation of your research.

Taking it further
- This section will give you ideas to take your learning further, connecting it with other subjects and expanding your understanding.

Reflection
Curious customs

We will start this challenge by trying to see traditions from different perspectives. It is always a good idea to start your exploration of new topics by trying to understand these from different perspectives. Different perspectives let you might reveal challenges and also opportunities for improvement!

2.2 Thinking about traditions

1. Get together with some friends and discuss some national traditions you think are curious. You might need to do some research to find out what traditions are practiced in your country.

   For an extra challenge can you try to find information about your local traditions in: a blog, a podcast, a government website, and a newspaper?

   ###  Warning

   Some traditions you might see as curious might seem normal or beautiful and important to other students. As you start this discussion it is important to be respectful. Avoid mocking, criticizing, or putting down any tradition. Try to think about how your peers who practise these traditions might feel.

2. Make a list of traditions to research further.

3. Try to think about the traditions on your list from the **perspective** of those who practise them. Do they think these traditions are curious? Are there any traditions on the list that you practise? Why do you think others might find your traditions unusual? How does that make you feel?

   Look at the comic on the right to try and understand that what seems 'obvious' to you might seem different to somebody else. It takes effort to try to see things from the perspective of others. Think back to Exercise 1 on page 13 to help you.

The world is full of different cultures, each with their own unique traditions. Being aware of this diversity is a critical part of developing an informed and thoughtful global perspective. Here are some interesting traditions you might not have heard about.

2.3 Finding information

Research one of these traditions and present your findings to a class partner.

1. **'Milk teeth'** – What did your family do when your deciduous (also known as baby teeth or first teeth) fell out? In some cultures, people put baby teeth under a pillow and tell the children a magical creature will give them money for each tooth once they fall asleep on top of it. In other cultures, milk teeth are thrown on the roof of a house to bring wellbeing to the whole household. Elsewhere people wear their children's teeth as jewellery.

2. **New Year** – How does your country celebrate a new year? In some countries people throw fireworks into the sky to mark the beginning of a new year. In some cultures, people wear fancy dresses or a particular colour of clothes (often yellow or red). These are thought to bring wealth, love, or wellbeing into the new year. In Ecuador, a glass of water is thrown out of the front door, to symbolize throwing out tears and sadness from the past year.

3. **Local heroes** – Most cultures have days when they remember and celebrate a local hero or artist. They might retell the story of their life. They might put up pictures. They might recite poetry. Who does your country celebrate and why?

Research 1
Asking questions

Once you have created a list of traditions you are interested in, it is time to **research**!

Go back through the list of customs you have created. It is now time to choose one or two to look into.

Now you need to think about **what** you want to learn about these traditions. What information do you need? What questions do you need to answer? This takes you back to what you learnt in Challenge 1 about asking questions. *We need good questions to answer.*

2.4 Starting with questions

Write down some of the questions you want to answer about the traditions you will be researching.

Why do we need good questions?

Good questions should lead you to interesting, useful information. Bad questions will lead you to limited or biased information. Take the following example: Imagine you go to your country's Ministry of Culture to learn how your country celebrates the New Year. What might happen if you turn up at the Ministry like the cartoon on the right:

2.5 Better questions

Discuss with a partner what kind of information this student might get. Are there other questions the student could ask to get more, and better, information?

Good questions check list

When you create questions to find out about any issue, you want to make sure these questions are clear, focused, and unbiased. Use the following notes to assess whether your questions are good research questions:

➔ **CLEAR:** Can your question be easily understood? Is it confusing? Is your question actually multiple questions at once? Note the difference between:

✓ Could you tell me how our country celebrates New Year?

✗ Is there new year in our country?

➔ **FOCUSED:** If your question is vague, you will find vague information. The more precise your question is, the more relevant information you will find. Note the difference between:

✓ What New Year traditions are unique to our country?

✗ Our country celebrates New Year like others?

➔ **UNBIASED:** Avoid questions that force a particular answer or allow you to consider only one side of an argument. A question that tells you that something is good or bad before you carry out research is a biased or leading question. Note the difference between:

✓ How do country A and country B celebrate New Year?

✗ How does country A celebrate New Year better than silly Country B?

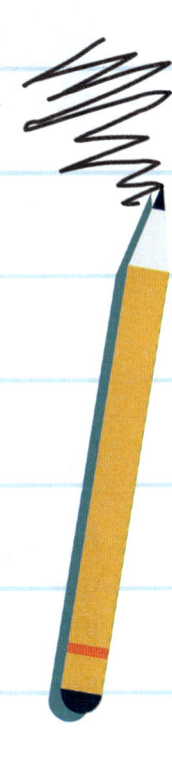

2.6 More questions!

Learning to ask good questions takes practice! Try to come up with good questions that use each of the five Ws and the H:

WHAT   WHO
WHERE   WHY
WHEN   HOW

Example:

Have you heard of Adamu dancing? This is a dance practiced by the Maasai in Kenya and Tanzania. To find out about it, you might want to ask questions such as:

WHAT is Adamu dancing?
WHERE does Adamu dancing take place?
WHERE did Adamu dancing originate?
WHEN was Adamu dancing created?
WHEN does Adamu dancing take place?
WHO participates in Adamu dancing?
WHY do people participate in Adamu dancing?
HOW does someone become an Adamu dancer?

Main question and smaller questions

When you research a topic you are likely to have one *main question*. To answer this question, however, you might need to ask, and answer, other smaller questions.

Your main question might be:

Is it appropriate that Adamu dancing be funded by a national government?

To answer this question, however, you will need smaller questions such as the W and H questions listed above.

Research 2
Finding information

Finding and tracking information

Where can you look for information on cultural traditions?

Once you have research questions, you will need to find sources with the information you need to answer these questions. It is time to start thinking about where to look for information and how to keep track of the information you find.

For advice on citing sources, please see page 118.

2.7 Sources of information

With a group of friends, write down all the sources you can think of to find information about a country's traditions. Create your own list before looking at the suggestions below. Note that you can come up with other sources not listed here.

Possible sources:

- Books
- Newspaper and magazine articles
- Encyclopedias
- Tourism and culture blogs
- People who participate in the traditions
- A country's embassy
- Government websites

2.8 Discussion: using sources

Different sources contain different information and need to be used differently. How would you present questions to different sources?

Would you ask a person in the same way you would ask a search engine?

Would you change the phrasing of your question if you are interviewing people from different cultures?

Would you ask a question in the same way to your classmate as to a government official?

Taking notes

What is the goal of taking notes? To help you store and easily retrieve relevant information to support your argument. To help you keep track of your ideas. To help you find sources you need to review again. Taking good notes is all about making your work easier!

2.9 Taking notes

Try your hand at note taking with the article below. In your notebook write down what you find most important about the article.

The word Nowruz means 'new day' and is the Persian, or Iranian, spring celebration of the beginning of a new year. The spring equinox (when night and day are equal length) marks the beginning of Nowruz, usually around 20th March. It has been celebrated for over 3,000 years in Iran, Kazakhstan, Azerbaijan, Afghanistan, Albania and other countries in South and Central Asia. It is a public holiday with up to 13 days' holiday from school.

Whole families prepare for Nowruz by cleaning the whole house and garden and by wearing new clothes. This symbolizes a fresh start and the washing away of the bad things from the previous year.

On the last Wednesday before Nowruz, bonfires are lit, and people jump over the flames. The flames burn away sickness and bad luck and give warmth and energy for the coming year.

Just before Nowruz, the whole family comes together around a specially-decorated table on which are arranged seven special items starting with the 's' sound in the Farsi language (e.g. *sir* (garlic) and *seeb* (apple). This is the *haft*-seen, which means 'seven Ss'.

2.10 Taking notes as part of a team

Taking good notes is particularly important when you are working as a team. Try the following:

Work as a team of three. Start with three or four articles your teacher has chosen. One of you reads one of the articles and takes notes.

The second person reads the notes and then tells the third person what the article was about, who wrote it, and what evidence the article gives.

The third person tries to find the original article.

The success of this exercise depends on the clarity of the notes taken. When you work as a team others will need to use your notes. Make sure your notes can help your team succeed!

Analysis
Organizing your notes

When looking through a lot of information one can feel a bit lost. What do you write down? Where? A good organization strategy can help you break down what you need to write down and where. The four-column system is one strategy. Divide your paper into four columns. On the left, write down the question you are trying to answer. In the second column, write down information that answers the question. In the third column, write the source the information came from. In the last column write your reflections: what do you think of this information? Do you have new questions? Are there areas you need to double-check?

2.11 Practicing taking notes

Use the four-column method to take notes on some of the sources you have found about your country's traditions.

Other strategies to help your note taking:

→ Write the **source** you are using at the top of each page – this will make it easy to reference sources later, or to go back to a source if you need to. If you are using an online source, make sure to write down the URL address and when you used it.

→ Back up your notes. There is nothing worse than losing all the work you have done. Make sure to keep your notes in a safe place, and if you are using a computer back up all your information at least once a day. You can, for example, email it to yourself every night.

→ Write the questions you are trying to answer at the top of your notes. This will help keep your notes focused on your research topic. Alternatively, write your questions on a sticky note and have it in front of you at all times so you remember what you are looking for.

→ Use colour! Colour can help you differentiate various topics, new sources, ideas to follow up, or new questions that you come up with. Colour can be a great tool to help you organize your notes.

→ Come up with your own shorthand – this will make note taking faster. Rather than writing traditions, for example, use 'TD'. Rather than example, use 'ex.'

→ Use diagrams! You can use arrows to note how ideas relate to each other; circles to note ideas that answer the same question, etc.

→ Come up with an organization system for your notes. This can be your own unique system, or you could use the one suggested above. The most important thing is that the system you use works for *you*.

Warning

There are some things you **do not** want to do when taking notes.

→ Do not write down everything you read. This is transcribing, not taking notes! Look for *main ideas* and for the facts that help answer your questions.

→ Do not worry about complete sentences. Notes are just for you to remember ideas and facts, not complete pieces of writing.

→ Do not lose track of where you found information. You do not want to end up having to find a source again to check facts or to be able to cite it in your research. Keep careful notes of what you find, where you found it, and when you found it.

→ Do not be messy! Your notes should help you find information quickly, not cause confusion.

2.12 Notes for your other classes

Use the suggestions (and warnings!) given in this section to take notes for one of your other classes.

41

Communication
Sharing your findings

By this point you should have chosen an interesting tradition to research, created some clear questions you want to answer about this tradition, found some useful sources, and taken good notes from these.

Now we need to return to **why** we are doing this. What is the **aim** of your research? What was the challenge? It is always important to remember why you are researching something, as that will affect what and how you research.

Remember, you are an ambassador for your country. You want to explain your tradition to others who have never heard about it. You want to help others understand your tradition – where and when it happens, and why and how it takes place. In short, the aim of your research is to inform others, to communicate with them, to help them understand.

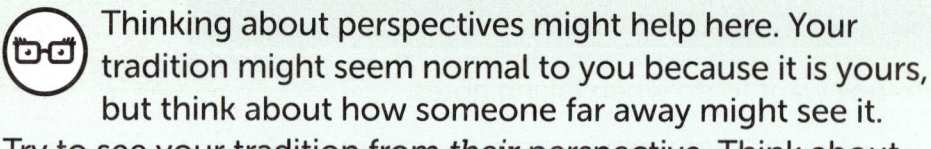

Thinking about perspectives might help here. Your tradition might seem normal to you because it is yours, but think about how someone far away might see it. Try to see your tradition from *their* perspective. Think about what someone from a distant country might find unusual or surprising about your tradition. If your tradition is one that is practised in multiple countries, such as Nowruz discussed in Exercise 2.9, you might want to take a **global** perspective showing how this tradition has links that go beyond the borders of one country.

2.13 Seeing from multiple perspectives

Think about, or discuss, how your tradition would be perceived from different perspectives. You could think about people from other countries, people who practise other religions, people who speak other languages.

2.14 Creating a presentation

With the information you have collected, create a PowerPoint presentation about your country's tradition.

To help prepare your presentation, complete the information below using the notes you have taken:

Tradition being researched (What is the tradition?)
Describe the tradition:
Where is this tradition practised?
When is this tradition practised?
Who practises this tradition?
Why is this tradition practised?

As you create your presentation think about:

→ how to introduce your tradition to get someone's attention

→ what information they will need to understand your tradition

→ in what order you should present the information so it makes sense to others

→ what kind of language you should use – formal, friendly, technical.

2.15 Peer review

When you have finished Exercise 2.14, consider trading presentations with a peer in your class. Watch, listen to, or read each other's presentation and then discuss these questions:

- Did your peer's presentation make the tradition clear to you?
- Was the presentation interesting?
- Was the presentation organized in a way that made it easy to follow?
- Did the presentation leave you with any questions?

Reflection

After reading your classmate's presentation, think again about yours. Take a few minutes to think through these questions.

- Is there anything you could have improved?
- Were your notes helpful in writing out your presentation? Could they have been more helpful if you had written things down differently?
- Has working on this challenge helped you to see traditions from different perspectives? Can you try to see your own traditions as someone from a different culture might see them?

Year 7 Challenge 2

Taking it further

Learning about traditions is a great way to learn about different societies, their history, their culture, their geography and more! Here are some suggestions to take your learning further:

ICT

- Convert your report into a video presentation. How can you use video to better explain the tradition you are discussing?

Anthropology

- Could you visit a place where the tradition you researched is practised and get some video footage or interviews? Please note the need to be safe while doing this – make sure you discuss with your teacher first and go with an adult. You also need to ask permission before you record or interview anyone.

History

- You could look at how traditions in your country have changed through history. Were some traditions introduced from other cultures? When? How?

Education

- Do you think you learn enough about traditions in your country? What traditions do you think you should learn about and why?

Marketing

- Imagine you were hired to run a publicity campaign to get more visitors to your country. You want to highlight local traditions as a reason to visit. Create a one-minute video or a poster promoting a tradition to possible tourists.

Art

- Art is often part of traditions – whether this is visual art (painting, sculpture, drawings) or performances (dancing, singing). Why not try to research more about particular art forms in tradition. Or you could try to replicate some art. Look at the decorations made for the Hana Matsuri festival in Japan or the Panagbenga festival in the Philippines.

Sociology and politics

- Some traditions are controversial. Why? Can you find any traditions that have been started as a way to give a particular group power over others?

Philosophy

- Ponder these questions: do traditions connect us to each other? Can traditions separate us?

Year 7 Challenge 2

Literature

- Read a novel that describes a local tradition (real or fictional). Does it describe it in a good light?
- Write a story based on a tradition you have recently learnt about.

Religious Studies

- Investigate and discuss whether and how local traditions are linked to religious beliefs. You might find that some traditions were originally religious but are no longer so – how did that change happen?

What did you learn?

When you complete this challenge, take a moment to reflect over what you have learnt with the table below:

Skill	I get it!	I am starting to get it!	I need to review this.
Perspectives: I can try to understand an issue, for example local traditions, from different points of view.			
Research: I know multiple sources I can turn to in search of information.			
Analysis: I have learnt some strategies for taking good notes and keeping track of my sources.			
Analysis: I can use my notes to create a presentation explaining what I researched.			
Communication: I can present an idea in a way others understand and enjoy.			

Year 7

Challenge 3
Globalization

3.1 Get thinking: Globalization

1. How important is it to have access to things that come from distant countries?
2. Could we survive if we permanently stopped all travel and all trade?
3. Can ideas that come from other countries change your country's culture and identity?

Imagine you are walking in your city when you suddenly come across a protest.

There are people with signs protesting about **globalization**. Someone stands next to you and screams, 'We need globalization; otherwise how will we get work?' One of the protesters answers, 'Globalization is taking our work away! It is taking all the jobs to poor countries with no labour laws!'

You are uncertain about what is going on. What is globalization? Is it good or bad? How can we find out?

Challenge overview

In this challenge, you will be learning about globalization. You will research arguments for and against globalization. You will analyse graphs and data on globalization and evaluate various claims.

You will complete the challenge by working with a team to create a poster where you express your own views on globalization.

What skills will you develop?

Analysis 1: What is globalization?
→ You will learn how to dissect complex concepts or problems, or how to break them into small pieces, to help you research and understand them.

Analysis 2: Opposite sides
→ You will learn to think about the two sides of an argument. You will also start to look at how a large topic can be narrowed into a smaller, and more researchable, issue.

Analysis 3: Analysing graphs
→ You will look at multiple graphs on globalization to enable you to work on interpreting, using, and making graphs.

Research: Surveys
→ In this section, you will learn about primary and secondary data and learn how to make a survey.

Perspectives and interviews
→ In this section, you will explore how perspectives are interconnected and learn about interviews and ethics.

Communication: Creating a poster
→ To complete this challenge, make a poster where you share your views on globalization.

Taking it further
→ This section will give you a lot of ideas to take your learning further, connecting it with other subjects and expanding your understanding.

Analysis 1
What is globalization?

3.2 Explain in your own words

Can you explain globalization in your own words? Try to explain globalization to a partner. With your partner, try to come up with a formal definition.

Don't worry about being perfect, we are working on clarifying our thoughts. Explaining things in your own words is a great exercise to help you check your understanding and clarify your ideas.

Now, compare your definition to the one below. How is it different? Which definition do you think is better, and why?

Definition: *Globalization refers to the many ways in which our world is increasingly interlinked. Globalization refers to how ideas, people, and things travel around the world more, and faster, than they did in the past.*

3.3 Use your knowledge

After thinking about and discussing the definition of globalization, try to explain how Christmas lights or McDonald's restaurants are examples of globalization. Can you think of other examples of globalization?

Whatever your topic, it is always a helpful exercise to try to explain what you are learning in your own words. It is a good way to make sure you understand new ideas and can communicate them clearly.

Understanding globalization

To understand globalization, you need to think about how distant goods, ideas, and people have affected you. You also need to think about how you can affect goods, ideas, and people that are far away. These links between you and the world at large can be difficult to imagine. Start by discussing the questions in Exercises 3.4 and 3.5.

3.4 Analysis: Global connections

- What ideas around you have originated from other parts of the world?
- What items that you use have come from other countries?
- Do you know anyone who has travelled around the world?
- Who in your class owns something that comes from farthest away?
- Who in your class owns something that was made in your neighbourhood?

3.5 Analysis: Local connections

To realize how connected we are it is sometimes useful to turn the questions discussed so far on their head! Rather than thinking about what things, ideas, or people are connected to distant lands, think of things, ideas, or people that are not.

- Can you or your classmates think of any idea or object that has no part or influence from another part of the world?

Group Activity

In teams, compete against the rest of the class to see which which team can find the most things that have come from other countries in 10 minutes. Can you find one object from every continent?

3.6 Speed discussion

Speed is part of the definition of globalization. The definition on the previous page notes that people, ideas, and things travel more **and faster** now.

→ What has allowed people, ideas, and things to travel faster?

→ Why does speed matter?

What you are doing in this section is **analysing** the definition of globalization by looking at and discussing its parts or components. You have thought about how things/people/ideas travel, and you have thought about why and how they travel faster. Looking at the parts of an idea or topic is a powerful strategy to help you understand complicated concepts or problems.

What does it mean 'to analyse' something? To analyse means to take something apart, look at its parts, and see how they fit together. To understand why something happens, and why it matters, we have to start by analysing it. We gather sources that explain parts of the issue to us. Then we use these sources to help us understand the different parts of the issue.

Analysing is like taking a machine apart, learning about its pieces, and putting it back together with a clear understanding of what each piece does. It is hard work, but it is very rewarding!

Once we analyse a problem (once we understand its causes and consequences), we can suggest ways to solve the problem. Realistic, good solutions can only be developed from a thorough understanding of an issue.

> *To analyse or to understand something complicated, start by taking apart its components and thinking about each part separately.*

Looking more closely at time

Time plays an interesting part in globalization. Some argue that the biggest marker of globalization is how much faster things happen!

Let's play fact search! Try to fill in the blank spaces in Exercise 3.7 with facts, and keep in mind how and where you found these facts.

3.7 Fact finding

1. During the Age of Exploration, it took _____ to get information between Europe and the Americas and to get goods between Europe and the Americas.

2. It now takes _____ to get information between Europe and the Americas and _____ to get goods between Europe and the Americas.

3. How have the costs of travel between continents changed over the last several decades?

4. Do diseases spread faster now than in the past? Why?

5. Challenge question: How has a faster flow of information affected diplomacy?

Where did you find the information you used to answer Exercise 3.7? Go back to your sources and copy a sentence from the pages where you found your data. If you are struggling, you might not have kept very good records of the sources you used. Remember, keeping track of your sources is a key research skill – and it will make your work much easier!

Analysis 2
Opposite sides

Why is globalization controversial?

Globalization is controversial. This means it has strong supporters and strong opponents. There are strong arguments in favour of, and against, globalization. To understand controversial topics like globalization, you need to research arguments on both sides.

To decide what you believe, you will need to research the consequences or effects of globalization, and evaluate if there are more positives or negatives. However, globalization is a large topic. Asking if 'globalization is good or bad', is too broad. We need to better focus our questions, as discussed in Challenge 1. To research globalization, we need to concentrate on a small part of it. We can look, for example, at how globalization affects the environment, or culture, or the economy.

Concentrating on specific areas can help us as we look for sources. It also makes the research process feel less overwhelming. A smaller focus can also help us come up with better research questions.

3.8 Narrowing your focus

Come up with some research questions about globalization looking at these four areas:

Environment   Shopping   Health   Education

Here are two possible research questions. Do you think these are good research questions? Why or why not?

- How does globalization affect water pollution?
- Can globalization help us improve education?

Arguments for and against

What arguments support the view that globalization is harmful? What arguments support the view that globalization is beneficial?

Let's spend some time thinking about the positives and negatives of globalization. This is a good exercise for any controversial topic. It is always productive to spend some time trying to think about why others hold the position they do.

3.9 Opposing arguments

With a team, come up with some arguments in favour of and against globalization. Make a list for each side.

Extra challenge:

Use the lists you have made to copy and complete a table like the one below, noting what perspective each argument is from.

Perspective	In favour of globalization	Against globalization
Personal/Local		
National		
Global		

Read the arguments below and add them to your lists (or to the table above).

* Globalization decreases poverty as people can move to find jobs.
* Globalization means job losses as jobs go to cheaper countries.
* Globalization allows us to access anything we want, improving our lifestyle.
* Globalization has increased endless consumption.
* Globalization is good for large businesses.

From topic to area to issue to question

All Global Perspective topics are large. To help us research them, we can look at a specific area within a topic (such as the political or economic area), and then research issues or problems in that area. Here are two examples:

* Transport → Environment → How can we make transport more environmentally friendly?
* Education → Economy → Should countries spend more money on education?

Analysis 3
Analysing graphs

Graphs are a powerful tool to summarize and show data. One graph can replace several hundred words! Learning to interpret and make graphs is, therefore, a powerful skill.

Graphs and numerical data

When using graphs remember these points:

→ Start by looking at the title of a graph: it should give you a clear guide as to what the graph is about.

→ Look at the overall graph – does it have a clear shape? A pattern? Get a sense of what it is trying to tell you before you look at its details.

→ Look carefully at the labels in the graph. These will give you important information about the scale of the graph. Are you looking at information over days, decades, millennia? Are you looking at information about a few people, or millions?

→ Check to see if the graph has a legend or key. This should give you more details about what you are looking at – does a particular colour represent something?

→ Check the source of the graph.

Learning to read graphs and infographics will help you to research any topic. Spend some time finding graphs in a newspaper and use the steps above to help you understand them.

3.10 Reading graphs

Below are a series of graphs with information related to globalization. With a partner, take turns explaining what the graphs show.

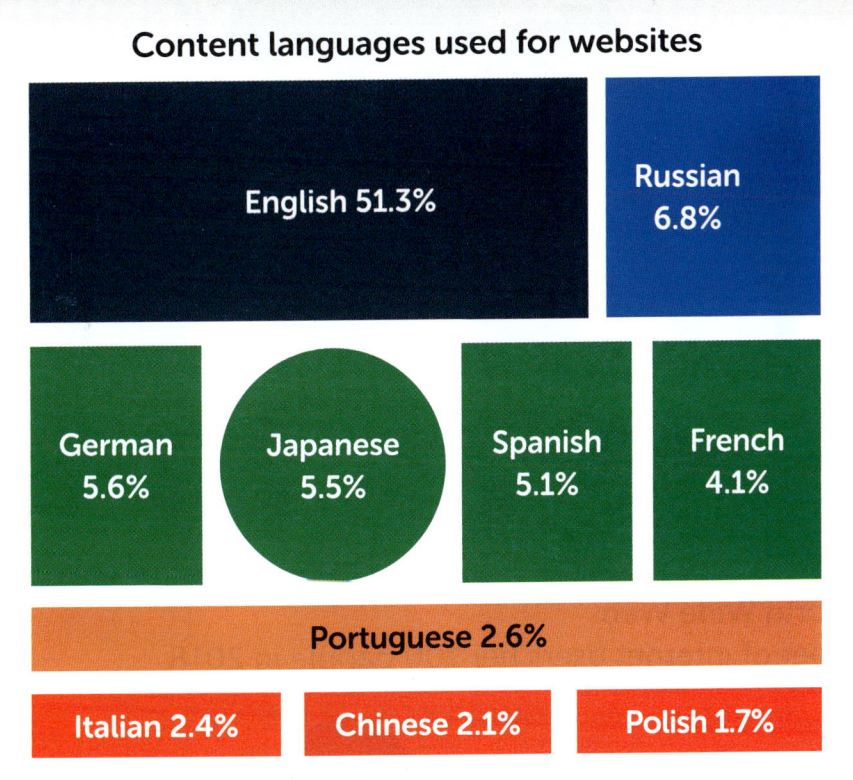

Content languages used for websites

- English 51.3%
- Russian 6.8%
- German 5.6%
- Japanese 5.5%
- Spanish 5.1%
- French 4.1%
- Portuguese 2.6%
- Italian 2.4%
- Chinese 2.1%
- Polish 1.7%

Source: http://blog.dynamiclanguage.com/language-in-numbers-the-most-captivating-statistics

Endangered languages
Overview of vitality of the world's languages

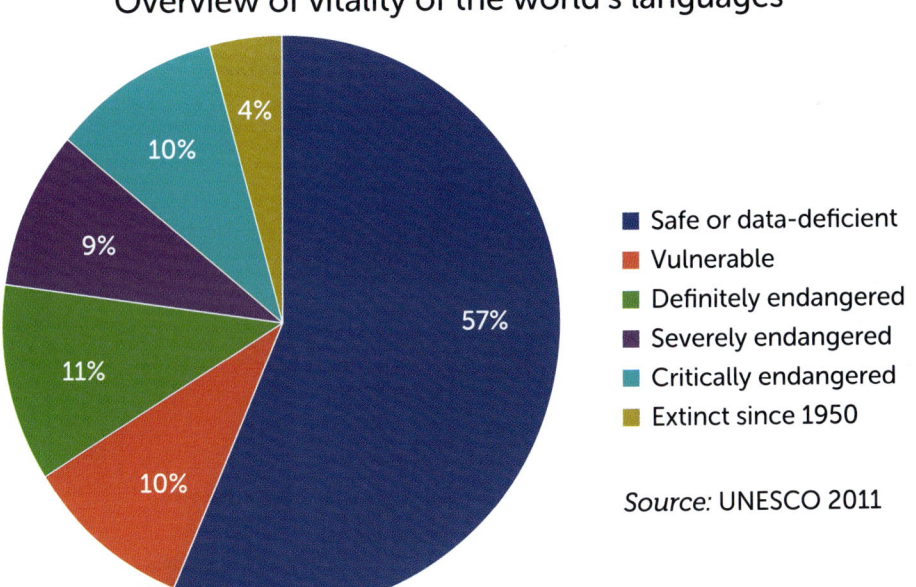

- Safe or data-deficient: 57%
- Vulnerable: 10%
- Definitely endangered: 11%
- Severely endangered: 9%
- Critically endangered: 10%
- Extinct since 1950: 4%

Source: UNESCO 2011

The most popular languages being learnt on Duolingo

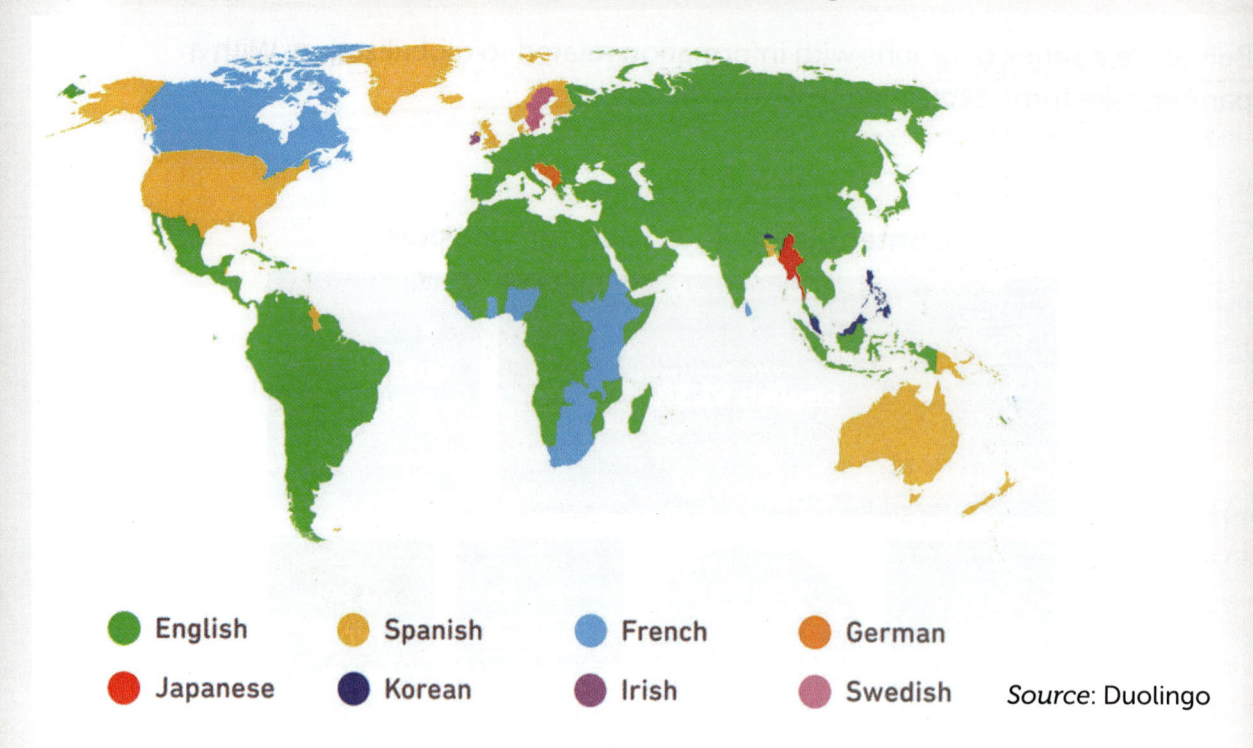

- English
- Spanish
- French
- German
- Japanese
- Korean
- Irish
- Swedish

Source: Duolingo

The (Not So) World Wide Web
Estimated number of internet users per 100 people in 2018

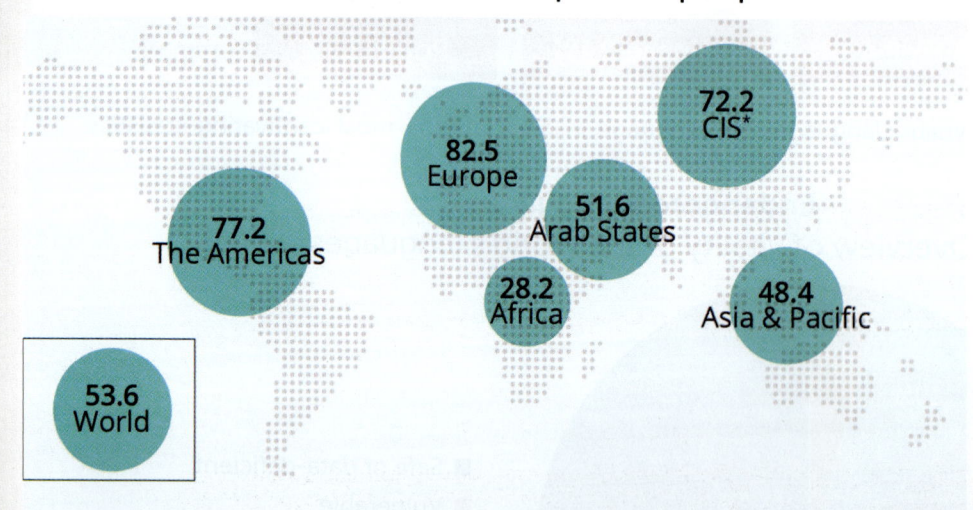

- 77.2 The Americas
- 82.5 Europe
- 72.2 CIS*
- 51.6 Arab States
- 28.2 Africa
- 48.4 Asia & Pacific
- 53.6 World

* Commonwealth of Independent States, a group of post-Soviet republics incl. Russia
Source: International Telecommunication Union

Source: www.statista.com/chart/3512/internet-adoption-in-2015/

Some of these graphs are more difficult to interpret than others. Do not worry if you don't understand them at first; you might need your teacher to help you.

Year 7 Challenge 3

3.11 Understanding graphs

To check your understanding, see if you can answer the questions below:

1. What is the most common language on the Internet?
2. What areas of the world have the most and the least access to the Internet?
3. What percentage of languages have become extinct since 1950?

3.12 Using graphs

The information provided in the graphs opposite can be used to argue in support of, or against, globalization. Find a graph that supports each of the claims below and explain how the graphs provide evidence.

1. Globalization is helping us all become connected through English as a common language.
2. Globalization is damaging local cultures and local languages.

3.13 Making graphs

Try your hand at creating graphs.

- Make a list of all your classmates' month of birth and make this into a graph.
- Find out where various things around your classroom come from (your pencils, your pens, your backpack, your desks, your computers). Make a graph to show this data.

Challenge:

Can graphs and numerical data be misrepresented? You can look at data on climate change and see how it is interpreted by those who disagree with the idea of humans causing climate change.

Research Surveys

A possible argument in favour of globalization is that globalization makes us better off by bringing us inspiring ideas from all over the world. How can you investigate whether international ideas have travelled to where you live?

Group Activity

Before reading further, discuss with your group how you would research this question. Where would you look for information? What information would you look for?

Choosing a question

To investigate whether foreign ideas have come to your community, you need a more focused research question. You could look at one of the following questions:

1. Do people in your community recognize art or music from other countries?
2. Do people in your community recognize international brands?
3. Do people in your community recognize politicians from other countries?

Choose your sources

Once you have chosen a question to research, you need to decide *what sources to use*.

If you want to look at *whether people in your area recognize art from other countries*, where can you find relevant information? Take a class vote on which of the following sources would be best.

1. Look for this information in a book.
2. Enquire in a government office.
3. Interview your neighbours.
4. Conduct a survey.

You have probably decided against options 1 and 2. These options will present you with secondary data, that is data someone else has collected. Options 3 and 4 require **you** to go out and collect the data – this is primary data. As you are trying to learn about what your neighbours recognize, it is unlikely that you will find this information in already existing sources. You will need to collect primary data.

Year 7 Challenge 3

Getting data: surveys

Surveys allow you to obtain information from a large number of people. In a survey, each person is asked the same questions. These questions are often used to collect quantitative data – that is, figures – such as 'how many of these pictures do you recognize?' or 'how often do you listen to music in a foreign language?'. Survey questions should be short, clear, and generally quick to answer.

⚠ Stop

Can you explain the difference between primary and secondary data?

Survey to understand the influence of foreign music:

Name (Optional): _____

Age ☐   Gender: ☐

1. Do you like music?
   - Yes
   - No

2. How often do you listen to music from other countries?

   a. Once a day ☐   c. Once a month ☐

   b. Once a week ☐   d. Never ☐

💡 Think carefully about the questions you put in a survey!

Make sure you are not using 'leading questions'. That is, make sure you are not telling people how they should answer! Leading questions try to persuade respondents to give a specific answer. You also shouldn't give them confusing questions or questions that have more than one possible answer.

3.14 Research: Bad questions

Read through this set of **bad** survey questions. Come up with a reason why each of them is poor.

1. Do you recognize the incredibly famous painting on the right?

2. When you look at the Mona Lisa, does she look familiar?

3. Do you recognize this piece of music and do you like it?

4. Can you see this famous piece of art from another country?

3.15 Research: Create a survey

Create a survey to collect information on whether your local community (family, friends, neighbours) recognizes international brands/arts/politicians, and how well they know these.

- Think carefully about your questions.
- You might want to discuss your questions with a group of friends to check for clarity and quality.
- Think about how you will get the survey out. Are you going to print it, email it, post it?
- Collect at least five responses to your survey.
- *Challenge question*: Do you think five responses are enough to draw conclusions about your local community? Why or why not?

3.16 From data to graphs

Can you present survey data in graphs? Try it with the data presented below.

Number of respondents: 27
Number of men: 12
Number of women: 15

Ages of respondents:

10–15: 10   20–25: 4
15–20: 8   25–35: 5

How often do you read books by foreign authors?

Once a year: 1   Often: 20
Twice a year: 3   Never: 3

Do you know who won the Nobel Prize for Literature last year?

Yes: 6
No: 20
Maybe: 1

Do you read books in other languages?

Yes: 6
No: 21

Challenge: Do you think the questions in this survey were good? Why, or why not?

3.17 Using surveys to predict the future

The information we gather from surveys might give us some insights into what could happen in the future. Think about what predictions these survey responses might help us make:

- A survey found that 90% of respondents understand that the use of plastic is a global problem.
- A survey found that four out of every five shoppers bought imported fruit.

Year 7 Challenge 3

3.18 Practise survey questions

Can you come up with two questions you could ask in a survey about each of these topics?

1. The impact of foreign fashion
2. Local businesses and globalization

Remember, the purpose of surveys is to help us understand the experiences and views of others. Our questions need to be clear, specific, and non-leading. A good survey can give us useful information. A poorly designed survey can confuse respondents and give us wrong information.

3.19 Poorly designed surveys

Why might these questions give us wrong information?

1. Do you not think that not changing global climate is wrong?
2. Does globalization concern you or affect you more than in the past?
3. Have you ever heard music that was not from another country?

3.20 Newspaper/magazine surveys

Newspapers and magazines often present surveys about what is happening in your country or what is popular in a certain community. Find a survey to bring to class and discuss what you found with your classmates.

61

Perspectives and interviews

Globalization demonstrates how the personal, the local, and the global are linked. For example, globalization includes the movement of people around the world. Most of us have family members or friends who have migrated. Have you ever thought about *why* they migrated? There might have been a personal reason – such as migrating to be with a loved one. But there can also be larger global forces, such as jobs opening up in a new country when oil was found. Perhaps your friends had to leave when a change in the global economy meant unemployment for their family. Perhaps a national reason, such as a civil war, led them to migrate. A combination of personal, national, and global reasons might have affected why your family or friends moved. In turn, their individual movement contributed to bringing ideas, traditions, and objects from one culture to another.

To find out why your friend or family moved, it is unlikely that you can use secondary data. You will have to use primary data. That is, you will have to collect the information yourself.

An **interview** would be a good tool to use in this instance. An interview is a *qualitative method* of research. This means it is not a method to gather numerical data, but rather a method to gather detailed information to understand a person's opinions, reasons, and motivations.

Ethics of research

When conducting any research, ethics should always be a primary concern. Before interviewing anyone, or collecting survey data, you must make sure to obtain the consent of those you are researching.

To consent, people have to understand what you are doing, why you are doing it, and how you will use any data you collect. They also need to feel free to refuse to answer any question, to stop at any time, and to request that you erase any information you have on them.

Interviewees can change their mind in the middle of an interview and ask you to stop. They can ask you to delete or give them any information you gathered on them. You must also seek not to hurt anyone you are interviewing. This means avoiding questions that might cause harm or pain. This also means being careful about collecting information that might be used against the interests of interviewees.

3.21 Consent

As a class, discuss:

1. why consent is necessary
2. how you can ensure you have the consent of all participants
3. cases where gaining consent might be particularly difficult.

3.22 Preparing an interview

Imagine you are going to interview a classmate about how global changes have affected their education.

How can you ensure you have their consent? What questions would you ask? Would you create questions that break the topic into smaller issues?

Write down some of your questions. As always, check the quality of your questions. Are they clear, focused and not leading?

3.23 Practising interviewing

In groups of three, practise conducting an interview on whether globalization is good or bad. (Careful: Is this topic too large? Should you ask about more focused issues?). One of you will be the interviewer, one of you will take notes, and one of you will answer the questions. Remember to practise gaining consent before any interview takes place. Work on taking good notes during the interview so you can go back and review the information you have been given. You could also choose to record the interview and listen to it later.

Communication
Creating a poster

Working through this challenge, you have learnt a lot about globalization. Now you need to share what you have learnt via a poster. In other words, your *aim* is to share your views on globalization, and you will be doing this through a poster (your *outcome*). To arrive at your outcome, you will have researched globalization, analysed what you found, and evaluated these findings to reach your conclusion.

3.24 Make a poster

Work with your team to create a poster that answers the question:

Is globalization good or bad?

A few things to keep in mind when you create a poster:

- Make sure you explain complex words to your audience. You may need to explain what globalization is, for example.
- Acknowledge arguments that disagree with your position – and answer them.
- Graphs are powerful ways to convey information. Try to use them.
- Think about your audience. Make sure they can read your poster easily. Try to make your poster clear and interesting.

Collaboration

When working with a partner you will need to decide how to divide the work. You will also need to decide on a system to review each other's work for completeness and quality.

As you do this, you want to make sure both you and your partner feel involved and appreciated. Think of ways to express kindness and gratitude to your partner as you work. Also think about kind ways to bring up any criticisms. If you are struggling, remember you can always seek the guidance of your teacher. Try to address any tensions quickly, rather than letting them become large obstacles to your work.

Year 7 Challenge 3

> Humour can be a powerful tool when working with others. Try to find things you can laugh about to decrease tensions. Take your work seriously, but don't take yourself too seriously!

3.25 Asking for feedback

Once you have completed your poster, hold a poster showcase, where people can walk around and read each other's posters. This is a good opportunity to learn from your friends' insights and to receive some useful feedback about your poster.

Create a short survey for people to fill out when they read your poster. You can include the questions below. What other questions would you like to ask?

Thanks for reading our poster! We would be grateful for feedback so we can make even better posters in the future. Could you please tell us:

- → How clear did you think our poster was: very clear, clear, unclear

- → How visually interesting did you think our poster was: interesting, could use some spark!

- → Did you find our arguments convincing?

- → Is there anything else you think we should have included in the poster?

Reflection

Think back to your opinion of globalization when we started this chapter. Has it changed?

What was the most surprising thing you learnt about globalization?

How inter-connected are you to international ideas, things, or people? Do you find this surprising?

Taking it further

Exploring globalization can help you see how the personal, the national, and the global are interconnected! Here are some suggestions to take your learning further:

Time

- Time is an important part of globalization – how quickly people, ideas, and things move. Time can be explored from multiple perspectives. Look at how our perception of time changes with movement – if you are really interested in physics, this could take you to the theory of relativity and how time and space are linked! Look at how time changes when astronauts travel. If you are interested in the social sciences, why not look at how politics has been moving faster and faster as technology advances. How have the Internet and communication platforms like Twitter affected how politics takes place around the world?

Communication

- Why not make this challenge part of the globalization of education? Try to get in touch with students from another part of the world to exchange perspectives on globalization, or to share an interesting part of your culture.

Literature

- Challenge yourself to read a book from a distant culture you have not read from before. You might be limited by language, or you might try to use an internet translator to read something in its original language!

Science

- Look further into the spread of epidemics. How has globalization affected the spread of disease?

Politics and science

- Did the coronavirus pandemic stop or derail globalization?

Economics

- Pick a consumer good (we suggest fireworks or computers) and trace its production process. See how many countries are involved in the process. If relevant, see how many languages its instructions are translated into.

Geography

- Look into how geographic features have aided, or stopped, the travel of goods, people, and ideas around the world. You could choose to concentrate on only one particular geographic feature – such as rivers. Alternatively, you could look at a particular area in the world – such as South Pacific Islands or the Mediterranean – and investigate how its geography shaped its history.

Year 7 Challenge 3

What did you learn?

When you complete this challenge, take a moment to reflect over what you have learnt with the table below.

Skill	I get it!	I am starting to get it!	I need to review this.
Analysis: I understand how to analyse a complex concept by looking at its parts.			
Analysis: I can interpret and use graphs to support arguments.			
Research: I understand the difference between primary and secondary data.			
Research: I am beginning to understand the ethics of research.			
Research: I am beginning to understand how to build a survey.			
Research: I am beginning to understand how to write an interview.			
Analysis: I understand that an issue can have arguments supporting both sides.			
Communication: I can create an interesting poster where my arguments are clearly presented.			

Challenge 4 Education

4.1 Education

- What would you change about your current education?
- Do you think education should be optional or mandatory?
- Should all education be free?

Imagine the Earth is sending a mission out into space. We are starting a new human colony on planet Kepler-452b.

You have been selected to design the education system in this new colony. You are in charge of designing the perfect education.

But what would a perfect education look like? Would you let each family choose what their children learn? Would you make sure everyone learnt maths? Would you make it mandatory to read certain books? You have all power. Choose wisely!

Stop

Spend some time jotting down what you think you need to know in order to design a perfect education system. Write down some quick notes of where you might find this information. You could also write some ideas you already have about what a perfect education would be like. Try to be creative and think outside the box.

- Do we need schools for education? Can't we just learn on the job? Do schools *cause* learning?
- Do we want education to benefit the individual, their country, or the world?
- Why is it that we need to study? Why do you go to school?
- Not everyone in the world has the same access to education. How is education different in different areas of the world?

Challenge overview

In this challenge, you have the opportunity to think about what education is – why you do it, what it should be like, and how it could be improved. You are welcome to research alternative models of education. As you explore education you will be practising your research and analytical skills. You will be finding information about educational differences. You will analyse arguments that support different educational models. To finish this challenge you will work with a team to create create promotional videos to support education for girls.

What skills will you develop?

Evaluation 1: Facts versus opinions

→ You will start by reviewing the difference between facts and opinions. You will explore your opinions on education and learn that, while it is fine to have opinions, you need to use facts to support your arguments.

Evaluation 2: Facts and arguments

→ You will practise analysing arguments to understand what evidence they are using. You will work on preparing an argument and practise working as a group.

Analysis 1: Understanding causes

→ You will learn to think about the causes of a problem. You can practise looking at causes from different perspectives.

Analysis 2: Thinking about consequences

→ You will practise thinking about the consequences of actions; in particular why we educate.

Analysis 3: Fixing the problem

→ You will use your understanding of causes and consequences to create videos to support more equitable education. You will practise creating a plan to achieve your goals.

Taking it further

→ This section will give you a lot of ideas to take your learning further, connecting it with other subjects and expanding your understanding.

Evaluation 1
Facts versus opinion

It is important to be able to separate facts from opinions. This is a valuable research skill, and a major citizenship and survival skill. You need to be able to spot campaigns or adverts that try to convince you with opinions that are not supported by facts.

It is fine to have an opinion – we all have opinions but opinions may change. Once you start researching you might find that you change your opinion. For example, in Challenge 3 you might have started with the opinion that globalization is always good or always bad, but after completing the chapter and looking at various facts, you might have changed your opinion.

Facts do not change. Facts can be tested. As you learn new facts you might change your opinion.

While you can start with an opinion on an issue, you need to find facts to use as evidence in support of your view. If the facts you find contradict your opinion, it may be time to change it. Poor arguments use opinions as if they were facts.

Remember

An opinion expresses a belief or a feeling. You can agree or disagree with an opinion. An opinion can change.

Ex. I would like to float around without gravity.

A fact is something that can be proven with evidence. You cannot disagree with facts. Facts cannot be changed.

Ex. There is gravity on Earth.

4.2 Facts versus opinions

Try the quiz below. Which are facts, and which are opinions?

1. Children should only be exposed to classic literature.
2. Girls are less likely to be in school than boys.
3. Some children have to walk several miles to get to school.
4. School is the best experience children can have.
5. Children should be asked if they want to learn maths.
6. Children's access to education can be limited by natural disasters.
7. All education should include weekly quizzes.
8. Girls like school more than boys.
9. All education should be free.
10. Learning to read is a key skill.

The perfect education

If you could create a perfect school what would be taught?

Would you make it mandatory for all students to learn maths? Would everyone have to participate in a sport? Would you allow students to choose at what time they came to class? What if some want to start their classes at 10 p.m.?

4.3 Opinions and evidence

Take some time to 'free think' what you would want in a perfect school. Discuss your ideas with your team. These are your opinions. Then try to fill out the table below, where you write what you would want the school to have, and why. As a next step try to find evidence that supports what you want. Will you change your views if you cannot find evidence or if evidence contradicts your views?

My perfect school

Opinion	Reason why	Facts to support my opinion	Facts that do not support my opinion
Schools should start later in the day.	Kids can get more rest.	Children, particularly teenagers, need to sleep more as they are growing fast. A study on a university's website says teenagers need more sleep than children.	Parents need to get to work!

Evaluation 2
Facts and arguments

The truth is the world is flat.

Anyone walking on the Earth can notice that it is flat. How can we deny the truth of what our senses tell us?

If the Earth was round, how is it that things at the bottom don't fall off? How can people in what they call the 'Southern Hemisphere', walk with no problem? If we could leave Earth we could see that Earth is a flat disc, surrounded by a wall of ice so we do not fall off.

Claims of rockets leaving the Earth and landings on the moon are all lies. NASA and similar organizations are traps to steal government money and confuse the naive. We cannot trust scientific organizations. We must spread the truth.

4.4 Discussion: evaluating a text

What do you think about the text above? Do you think it builds a valid argument? Why or why not? Think about:

- What evidence does the text use to build its argument?
- Does the text use facts or opinions as evidence?

4.5 Critical thinking: education

Break into small groups and discuss the following:

1. Should education be only about facts, or also about opinions?

2. Should people whose beliefs contradict science – for example, those who argue the Earth is flat – be allowed to teach this to their children, or in schools?

3. Who should determine what schools teach? The government? The school? The parents?

Year 7 Challenge 4

Imagine a group who believes the Earth is flat came to your school to present their case. You and a group of friends are put in charge of finding facts to demonstrate that the Earth is not flat. You are particularly asked to respond to the textbook article shown above. Prepare your case.

⚠ Stop

What steps would you take to prepare your case? There are suggested steps below, but you might want to try something different.

4.6 Preparing an argument

1. Start by looking at the text you are supposed to address. Make a list of points to refute (prove wrong).

2. Split the research among your group. Either one group member, or a pair, should look for evidence to disprove each point in the text.

3. Gather evidence. Remember to keep track of your sources. (Keep track of authors, title of books/articles/webistes, URLs, year of publication, and, if a website, date accessed.

4. Review your evidence. Make sure you have collected *facts* rather than opinions.

5. Prepare to present your case: write it out or create a presentation in which you show each argument made by the textbook and your evidence against it. Then add any other facts you have to prove that the Earth is not flat. Make sure you list arguments and data in a logical and clear way. Prepare a list of sources used. This list should be handed in with your presentation, so people can review your evidence if they want to.

4.7 Communicating effectively

While it might be clear to you that the Earth is not flat, as you work through this exercise it is important to consider how people who do believe the Earth is flat might feel when they are proven wrong. Understanding this will help you present your case more effectively and kindly. Think about it: would you listen to someone who spoke rudely to you or mocked your ideas?

Reviewing your teamwork – collaboration

Think over your teamwork. Did splitting your research work well? Is there anything you would have done differently?

Analysis 1
Understanding causes

The **Sustainable Development Goals** (SDGs) are a series of goals that member countries of the United Nations committed to in 2015. These are goals to end poverty, protect our planet, and support the wellbeing of all people.

Goal 4 of the SDGs is:

Ensure inclusive and equitable quality education. To achieve this goal, we need to look at how equitable, or equal, education is for children throughout the world. We need *facts* to understand how equal or unequal education is worldwide.

4.8 Finding facts: education inequalities

In groups or individually find facts to answer these questions:

- Is there a difference between how many girls and how many boys attend school in your country?
- Is there a worldwide difference in school attendance between girls and boys?
- How many years of education do most children in your country receive? What is the average worldwide?
- How much money is spent on the education of each child in your country? What about in other countries (choose three or four countries to look at)?

Stop

Education equality is a large topic. To research it we can look at various areas such as: gender (do girls and boys receive the same education?), religion (do children of different religions receive the same education?), age (do governments spend more money on the education of younger or older children?).

Causes

To be able to solve a problem, we need to understand what causes it. For example, to stop deforestation from happening, we need to understand why trees are being cut down. To help girls to stay in education, we need to know why girls are not attending or finishing school.

Analysis: causes

In the previous exercise, you will have found that girls lag behind boys in their access to education. Have you thought about *why*? What *causes* girls to go to school less or to drop out earlier?

4.9 Venn diagram

With your group discuss some possible reasons why girls might not attend school. Then fill in a Venn diagram like the one below.

Why girls don't attend school

- Personal reasons
- National reasons

Perspectives are inter-related

Spend some time thinking about the area where the circles intercept. This area shows you how different perspectives are inter-related and overlap. Think about how other perspectives overlap. How does the global affect the personal?

4.10 Analysing Malala's story

Have you heard about Malala Yousafzai? You can read about her here: https://malala.org. As you read Malala's story try again to find the personal, local, national, and global forces that tried to keep Malala from going to school, and the forces that helped her stay in school. Then answer the following questions:

1. How was Malala's life affected by national politics?
2. Would Malala's story be different without global support?
3. What would you have done in Malala's place?

Analysis 2
Thinking about consequences

What is education all about?

Have you ever thought about *why* we educate? This is again a **why** question, but while you were just looking at **causes** (why do girls drop out of, or don't attend, school?), in this section we are looking at **consequences**: what *effects* does education have?

4.11 Consequences of education

What do you and your classmates think education should do? What should the consequences of education be? In other words, why do we educate?

As a class, come up with a list of reasons why you think we should educate. Here are a few more reasons you can add to your list:

A. Education should prepare youth for their future jobs

B. Education should make people kind

C. Education should make people happy

D. Education should teach us to fit into our society.

Consequences

Consequences are the effects something has. To understand a problem we need to understand its consequences. Understanding the consequences of a problem helps us to understand why we need to solve it. For example, why does it matter if we cut down trees? Why does it matter if girls do not get an education? We need to understand the consequences of deforestation or girls not getting an education to understand why these problems need to be solved.

Reflection

Think about why you go to school. What do you want the consequences of your education to be?

4.12 Why does it matter?

With your peers, spend some time discussing why you think it matters if girls attend school. Then compare your predictions with information you find through research. Find what the World Bank and UNICEF write about this area.

4.13 Perspectives on consequences

To understand the many effects of girls not attending school we could look at this problem through different perspectives. Can you copy and complete a table listing possible personal, local, national, and global consequences of girls missing education?

Personal consequences	Local consequences	National consequences	Global consequences

4.14 Analysing a text 1

Read the article below. What is its main argument? What does Bladen believe education is for?

Should maths be compulsory?

Terry Bladen, leader of a teacher's union, has stated that secondary school pupils should be able to choose whether to study maths to GCSE level. He understands that all children should be taught basic maths to the age of 14, but suggests that more advanced maths should be for those who have the aptitude and enthusiasm to continue.

"Mathematics has always been a main subject, but why?"

"I would always argue that pupils should be numerate, with numeracy taught throughout all the key stages, but numeracy can be divorced from mathematics."

"How often do the majority of people need or use mathematical concepts once they have left school?"

"Maths classes would for the first time be made up of pupils who actually enjoyed and wanted to pursue the subject."

"This would also help schools to overcome the problem of recruiting specialist maths teachers. It would also allow more time in the curriculum for other subjects."

Remember

To understand a problem, we need to understand what causes it and what are its consequences.

The consequences game

With your group try to think about as many consequences for a problem as possible. Your goal here is to think outside the box. List as many consequences as you can of:

- making education mandatory
- closing all schools
- teaching all children English.

4.15 Analysing a text 2

Read the following article about uniforms in schools, and find:

- the main argument of the article
- the consequences listed in the article.

There is some debate as to whether school uniforms should be mandatory. Schools want to create a uniform policy that promotes learning and student happiness. Do uniforms help students to learn better, or do they distract them? I think uniforms, while having some negatives, help students to learn better.

Some argue that uniforms do not allow students' individuality to shine through. Uniforms impose conformity and sameness. But even with uniforms, students can show their creativity through hairstyles and accessories. On the other hand, school uniforms can help build a sense of community and belonging. Moreover, with everyone wearing uniforms, it is harder for students to waste their energy comparing clothes and styles. To create a sense of belonging and to avoid poor students feeling disadvantaged, I think uniforms should be worn in schools.

4.16 Causes and consequences

Look at the issues below. In a small group, think about possible causes and consequences for each problem.

Causes	Issue	Consequences
	Increased international travel	
	Greater number of students applying to university	
	Fewer students doing sports	
	Schools lack sufficient technology	

Analysis 3
Fixing the problem

In this challenge, we noted that not all children have access to high quality education. Now let's think about some possible solutions to this problem.

Mission: girl school attendance

As you have found, in many parts of the world fewer girls attend school, or attend school for a shorter time, than boys. Your challenge is to help resolve this inequality.

Aim: Improve girls' access to school.

4.17 Using analysis to find solutions

Go back over your research. Look at the reasons *why* girls don't attend school or stop going. List them. Then think about ideas for addressing each of these causes.

Warning

Notice that to propose a solution you need to understand the **cause** of the problem. Without this understanding, your proposal might solve nothing or even cause more problems!

When proposing possible solutions, you should also think about unintended **consequences**. For example, if you decide to pay girls who have dropped out of school to return to school, you might find that some shrewd parents choose to have their daughters drop out too … until they can get your payment.

Outcome: campaign for change

4.18 Drafting a solution

Imagine you and your team have been hired to create a video to help increase girls' school attendance. Using what you have learned in the previous sections, come up with a video you can share to promote the importance of education for girls. Use the form below to plan your video.

Title of video:
What problem is it addressing?
What is the solution it proposes?
What will the video show?
What facts will the video use as evidence?
Who is the intended audience for this video?

Note: filling in the form helps you to clarify what you are doing, why, and how. Having a clear purpose and plan makes work more effective and efficient!

Year 7 Challenge 4

4.19 Assigning the tasks

List the tasks involved in making a video and write down who in the group will do each task.

4.20 Making the video

Now it is time to produce your video.

Some ideas to create videos include:

→ Making motion animation with drawings, plasticine, or toys
→ Recording yourself or others on smartphones
→ Using free illustrating apps or websites
→ Conducting interviews of girls, parents and teachers (remember to ask for consent before any interviews).

Make sure your video is interesting and clear. Your main argument needs to be easy to understand.

Notes on collaboration

When working as a group, it is important to think about how to distribute work so that everyone is fairly involved.

You could:

→ assign jobs by lottery
→ have your teacher assign jobs
→ discuss among your group who will do what.

If you choose the last option, how will you ensure that quieter team members are listened to?

Reflection

Has your opinion on an ideal education changed? Think back to the beginning of this challenge. If you were about to be sent to an extra-terrestrial colony to be in charge of education, what educational policies would you put in place. Are your ideas different from what they were before you started this challenge? Are they more detailed? Do you have more evidence to support your ideas?

When you worked with your team, did you feel the quieter members of your group were listened to? Do you think you are a quiet member in the group? How do you make sure your voice is heard?

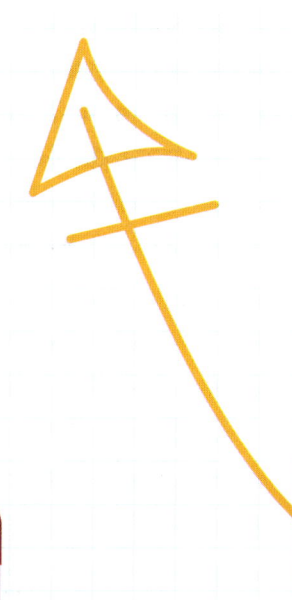

Taking it further

Want to think and research more about education? Here are some suggestions to take your learning further:

Surveys and education

- Use your research skills to improve your own education. Conduct a school-wide survey on how the students in your school think their education can be improved.
- Or survey teachers on what they need in order to improve their teaching.

  As always, think carefully about your questions. Make sure they are clear and focused, and make sure they are not leading questions. Present your findings to the leaders in your school. Think carefully about how to best present your findings – take care to write clearly and use evidence to support your arguments.

Religion

- Should religion be a part of education? If so how? Write an opinion piece which might be submitted for publication in a newspaper. This is a large and important question. To answer it you could consider local, national, and global perspectives.

Maths

- How should mathematics be taught? How is it taught in your school? Are there other methods? You could interview your maths teachers and/or email teachers in other schools to compare strategies.

History

- Some say, 'History is the story of the victors.' How is history taught in your school? Do you think it could be taught from different perspectives?

Sociology

- Home education is becoming increasingly common in many countries. Can you create a short podcast explaining to your audience **why** parents choose to home school? The answer might be different for different countries, or for different communities in a country.

Art

- Should art be a mandatory part of education? If so, how should art be taught? What do you think are the consequences of learning art?

Year 7 Challenge 4

Exams
- A regular criticism of education is that it is all about exams. Do you think we could get rid of exams? How would we ensure that children are learning?

Inclusiveness
- All students are different. Some really like maths. Others love writing. Some need extra help with writing. Some work best in quieter places. How can schools be designed to make sure all children are included?

Education
- Look into Howard Gardner's theory of multiple intelligences. Find a personal assessment you can do of your own learning capacities. Does this knowledge give you insights into how you work in school and what you want to do in the future?

What did you learn?

When you complete this challenge, take a moment to reflect over what you have learnt with the table below:

Skill	I get it!	I am starting to get it!	I need to review this.
Evaluation: I know the difference between facts and opinions.			
Evaluation: I understand the need to use facts to support my arguments.			
Analysis: I understand what causes are.			
Analysis I understand what consequences are.			
Evaluation: I can evaluate whether an argument is supported by evidence.			
Collaboration: I practiced how to share tasks in a team.			
Analysis: I am learning how to use my analysis of a problem, to come up with possible solutions.			

Year 7

Challenge 5
Seeking refuge

5.1 Refugees

How would you feel if you had to leave your house suddenly without warning?

Do you think countries have an obligation to take in people who are in trouble?

Should countries prioritize who gets help? Should children or the elderly be welcomed before adults of working age?

Hello my name is Amira and I am from Syria. I wish I was still in Syria. I miss my home. I miss my family. I miss my friends. I miss my normal life... getting up early, having breakfast with my mom rushing me to get to school. Playing with my neighbours in the road in front of my house after school. Going to bed warm and tired.

One day everything changed. My family had nothing to do with it. I am not even sure what happened. I just know suddenly there was fire raining from the sky and my dad grabbed our jackets, filled a backpack with phone chargers, food, and anything we had that could be sold and told us we had to go.

We cried and ran and got into a man's truck. I was hungry and cold and scared. Days went by when we had nothing to eat and I thought we were all going to die. Then we went on another car to the border of Lebanon. I saw my dad kneeling before an officer begging to be let in for help. My mother just cried.

I learnt that I am a refugee. I need asylum.

Challenge overview

In this challenge, you will be discussing refugees and asylum seeking. These are issues with global, national, and local implications. As you work through this challenge we will be discussing biases, reviewing numerical data, and working to develop complex arguments. To complete this challenge you will conduct a debate and write an article on refugees.

What skills will you develop?

Evaluation 1: Bias
→ You will learn what bias is and work on evaluating resources for biases.

Evaluation 2: The power of words
→ You will continue to work on your evaluation skills, looking closely at the language of sources you find to understand possible biases.

Analysis: Reading stories
→ You will work on analysing text (stories) to understand the many issues that overlap in migration stories.

Communication: Active listening
→ You will put your findings together to debate when asylum should be granted. You will work on creating and presenting clear arguments, and on listening actively to your peers.

Reflection: Refugees amongst us
→ You will use your research skills to learn more about refugees in, or from, your community. We encourage you to spend some time reflecting on what you have learnt, and your feelings about these issues.

Taking it further
→ This section will give you a lot of ideas to take your learning further, connecting it with other subjects and expanding your understanding.

Evaluation 1
Bias

5.2 What is bias?

What does the term 'bias' mean?

A bias is a prejudice against or in favour of an idea, a person, or a group. A biased source may give evidence for only one side of an argument, or present information in an unfair manner. A biased source might present information in a way that supports its own interests, rather than a search for truth.

5.3 Looking for bias

Each set of paragraphs below discusses the same thing: Set 1 discusses a visit by new neighbours; Set 2 discusses the characteristics of pet owners. Each paragraph, however, has a different bias. What are they biased for, or against?

Set 1

A
The new neighbours came by to introduce themselves. They were uncertain of social protocol but kindly, and bashfully, brought us some lilies. They didn't say much and then, embarrassed, they quickly left.

B
The foreigners who recently moved into our neighbourhood came to knock on our house uninvited. They brought a large bunch of lilies, which to me signify death. Then they turned around and left almost without even saying goodbye.

Set 2

A
Dog owners tend to be particularly friendly people. This is demonstrated by the fact that they can expand their love beyond humans to dogs. Their ability to take care of pets demonstrates greater responsibility and time management than that of non-pet owners. Cat owners are not quite so advanced in their development.

B
Pet owners take on a serious responsibility when adopting a pet. Having a pet is a commitment that lasts the entire lifetime of a pet. Taking care of any pet requires time, patience, and kindness. Some pets are more demanding than others, but all need love. Some people might not realize what they are taking on when choosing a pet.

Year 7 Challenge 5

📝 5.4 Impact of biases

To understand the impact of bias, think through these questions.

- If you only read paragraph 1B, what would you think of the people being described?
- As you read paragraph 1A, what do you think the new neighbours felt?
- As you read paragraph 1B, what do you think the new neighbours felt?
- What problems do you find with paragraph 2A?

📝 5.5 Why bias matters

As a class, discuss the following:

- Why does it matter if someone presents information in a biased way? Try to think of an example in your class or community where you felt an issue was not being presented fairly.
- Can you think of historical examples when groups of people have been presented in a biased way?

Propaganda

An extreme case of bias is propaganda. Propaganda is created to persuade people that only one particular point of view is correct. It does not present a balanced argument. Propaganda can exaggerate claims of what is good and what is evil or it can present falsehoods as truths. Propaganda can misuse facts to build its arguments and often appeals to people's emotions, particularly fear and anger, rather than to their reason.

📝 5.6 Researching propaganda

Find some propaganda posters from wars (WWII and the Cold War are particularly rich in examples). In small groups, discuss how these posters are biased. What misrepresentation are they spreading? How do you think they influenced how people thought and felt?

Evaluation 2
The power of words

What difference does it make if we call someone a refugee, a migrant, or a job seeker?

All of these words have been used to describe people moving from one country to another. But each word means something different. Each word implies different explanations for *why* the people moved. And the different reasons might result in different responses to the movers. *Words matter*. How stories are written or told will lead people to think about the stories differently and to respond to them in a different way. Word choice can make a source biased.

⊘ Stop

Find out what each of these words means: refugee, migrant, asylum seeker, job seeker. The UK Refugee Council has clear definitions on its website you can use.

5.7 The power of words

You have been hired as a newspaper editor to check articles for bias. Review the sentences below. Think about how the different phrasings might be interpreted by readers.

	Why might readers assume the people moved?	What might the readers think the government of your country should do about these people?
Many refugees are asking our country for help.		
Thousands of migrants want to live in our country.		
Illegal immigrants arrive at our borders daily.		
Should we help the needy?		
Should we support illegal migrants?		
Should we let in people seeking jobs?		

Newspaper analysis

How refugees are described in newspapers has been the subject of much research. As you can see from the exercise above, how things are presented will have serious implications for how a country's population, and their government, react.

5.8 Evaluating newspaper headlines

Look at these newspaper headlines about refugees. Can you describe if/how they are biased?

Asylum: You're Right to Worry
Daily Mail, UK

Send in Army to Halt Migrant Invasion
Daily Express, UK

EU Migrants to get British Pensions
Daily Express, UK

Please Save Us
Daily Mirror, UK

It's Life & Death
The Sun, UK

Migrants, the never ending massacre: 800 deaths in five days
La Repubblica, Italy

Abuse of the terrorists: How IS fighters want to mix with refugees so as to make their way to Europe
Die Welt, Germany

Whatever topic you are working on, you must always check your sources for bias. Make sure any sources you use present information accurately. Be careful of sources that present a version that benefits their interests.

Media collage

With your team, find articles from different media sources looking at the same topic. You can look at refugees, or at other topics such as climate change, criminal laws, etc. Compare the articles you find. Are they biased? How are they biased?

Data and graphs

5.9 Reading graphs

Look at and discuss the graphs and information below. Think about the implications of representation – how a person or group is portrayed in public. Then discuss the questions that follow.

How refugees are labelled in European media

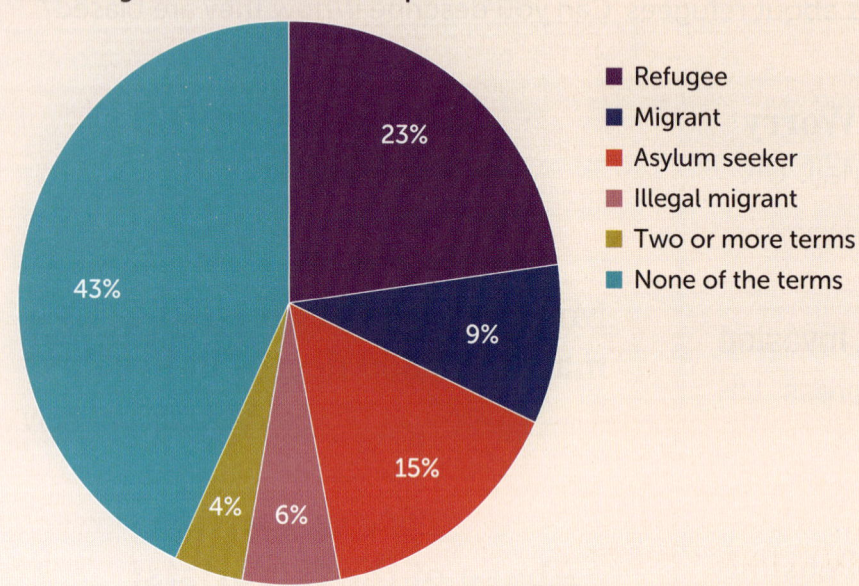

- Refugee: 23%
- Migrant: 9%
- Asylum seeker: 15%
- Illegal migrant: 6%
- Two or more terms: 4%
- None of the terms: 43%

Top four stated occupations of people identified as refugees/migrants in European media

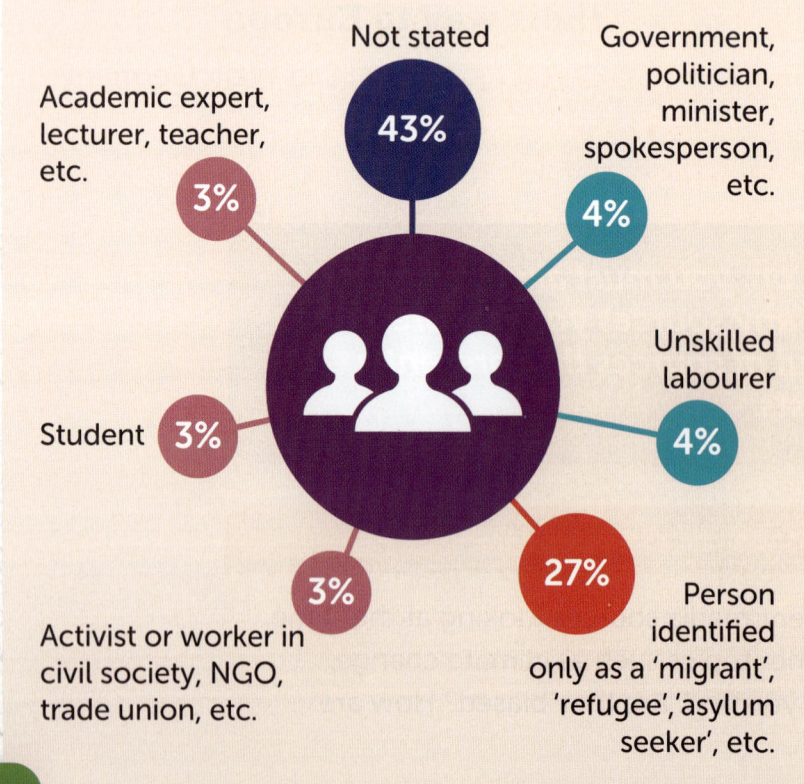

- Not stated: 43%
- Government, politician, minister, spokesperson, etc.: 4%
- Unskilled labourer: 4%
- Person identified only as a 'migrant', 'refugee', 'asylum seeker', etc.: 27%
- Activist or worker in civil society, NGO, trade union, etc.: 3%
- Student: 3%
- Academic expert, lecturer, teacher, etc.: 3%

Refugees represented as perpetrators of crimes in media: 33%

Refugees represented as victims in media: 26%

Gender of refugees according to European media

■ Women ■ Men

Country	Women	Men
Greece	17%	83%
Italy	48%	52%
Norway	50%	50%
Serbia	0%	100%
Spain	7%	93%
Sweden	36%	64%
United Kingdom	16%	84%
Total	27%	73%

Source: www.refugeesreporting.eu

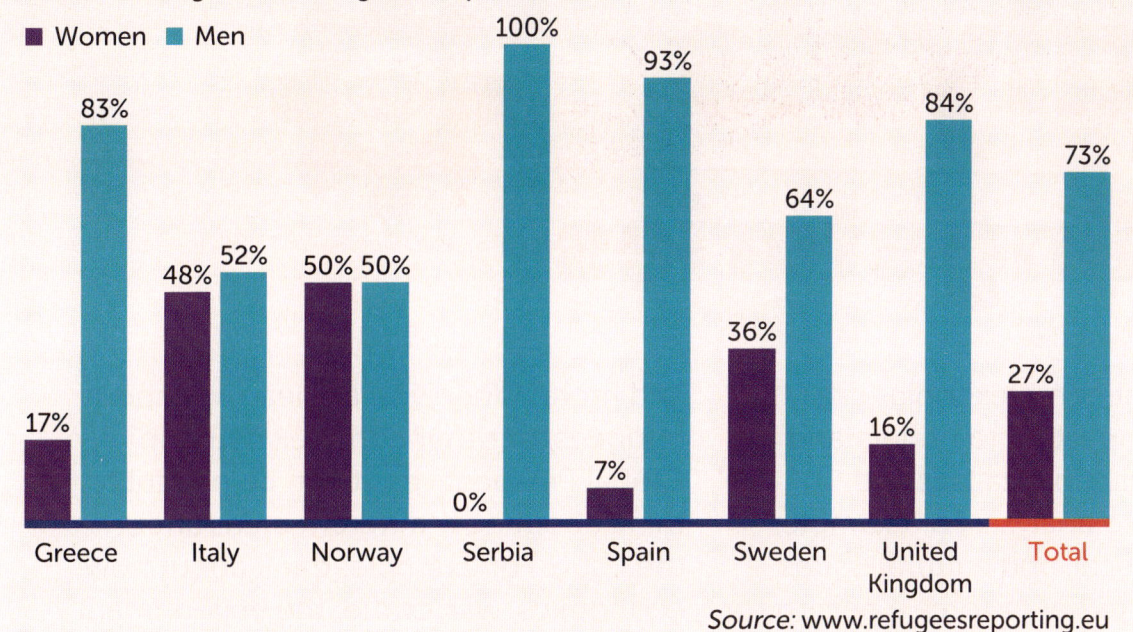

1. Do you think how refugees are labelled by media has an impact on what policies voters support?

2. Why does it matter if refugees are presented as men or women, or as a mixture of both?

3. Do you think differently about a refugee if you are told about their profession?

5.10 Local newspapers

Find newspaper articles from your country discussing refugees/immigrants/asylum seekers. It might be the case that your country is currently sending refugees or migrants to other countries rather than receiving them. Look at the words used to describe refugees. Look at the newspaper headlines and the pictures used. What bias, if any, do they have? You can also choose to look at newspapers from other countries.

Media bias

Spend some time researching media bias in your country to enable you to read the news with a critical perspective. You could look into who owns different media, or try to find a ranking of different media by their political bias. Remember: just because you read it in the news, does not mean it is necessarily true. Media can be biased or inaccurate. You need to carefully evaluate your sources in any topic you research.

Analysis
Reading stories

When looking at complex topics like refugees, it is important to understand that there are multiple causes and consequences to analyse. For example, economic, political, and cultural issues might come together to force a person to flee their country. Refugees, on the other hand, will affect their new home in many ways. Their effects might be felt in the economics, in the culture, in the language, and more. When you are learning about refugees, or other complex issues in Global Perspectives, it can be helpful to think about how different areas affect the issue. For example, think about how economics, war, crime, the environment, and culture affect who seeks refugee and why. You can do this while you take notes, for example, by highlighting each area in a different colour.

5.11 Refugee stories

Read the following stories and, with a partner, discuss how each story was affected by politics, economics, culture, and family.

Doaa's story

Doaa is a 19-year-old whose family fled Syria due to the war. In Egypt, without a work permit, Doaa was only able to work for low wages and live in fear.

She fell in love with another refugee, Baseem, who promised to take her to Europe where they would marry and start a new life. Doaa knew the risks but felt she had no choice. Baseem paid his life savings to smugglers, $2,500 each, to get them onto an old fishing boat. On the fourth day at sea, an old and rusty boat approached the fishing boat and told them to get on. When they fearfully refused, the smugglers rammed a hole on the fishing boat and left laughing: 'Let the fish eat your flesh'. Within minutes, the boat capsized and sank, with 300 people trapped below deck.

Baseem found a water ring, held Doaa's hand and treaded water. 100 survivors prayed for rescue, but as time went on, they started to lose hope. A Palestinian approached with his nine-month-old granddaughter, Malek.

'Please take the baby,' he said, 'I am very tired.' Later that day, a mother struggled towards Doaa with Masa, an 18-month-old girl. 'Save her,' she said, 'I will not survive.' Baseem could not keep going and died. Doaa was now in charge of two babies.

On the fourth day at sea, Doaa saw a merchant boat. For two hours she shouted until she was saved.

Adapted from: https://www.weforum.org/agenda/2015/12/3-real-stories-from-refugees/

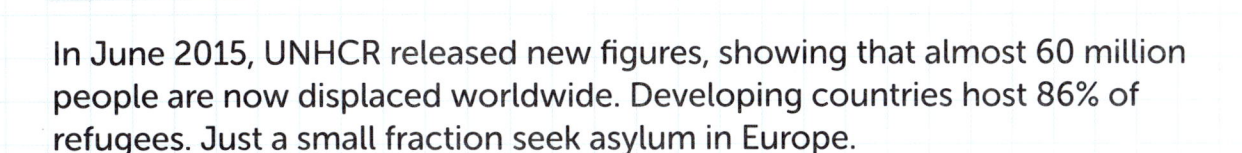

In June 2015, UNHCR released new figures, showing that almost 60 million people are now displaced worldwide. Developing countries host 86% of refugees. Just a small fraction seek asylum in Europe.

Emmanuel's story

My mother died when I was very young, and our father abandoned us. I felt I had no choice but to leave Ghana and try my luck in Europe.

After months of travelling through West Africa by whatever means, I eventually made it to Libya, where I paid €800 to men who promised they would put me on a big boat that would finally take me to Europe. It is difficult to explain and I have bad memories about this, but I had a terrible time in Libya. Those of us from certain African countries were treated very badly by men who kept us in dirty houses without much clean water and with very little edible food. They were very abusive and they seemed to enjoy the way they treated us. It did not matter to them that we had paid them all this money.

Finally, one day I was shoved onto a small rubber boat in the early morning when it was still dark. We spent five days aimlessly floating around and basically lost at sea. When the boat started losing air, we thought we were all going to die.

As our food and water ran out, we eventually drifted towards the Tunisian coast where we were rescued and sent to a detention centre in Tunis. I was in this centre for a month before I was freed and returned to Ghana.

One thing is certain, if I had opportunities here, I would not have been so desperate to try and go to Europe the way I did. If young people like me had jobs and a way to earn a living, we would not set off on these dangerous journeys.

Adapted from: https://www.weforum.org/agenda/2015/12/3-real-stories-from-refugees/

Communication
Active listening

Active listening is a key communication skill that can help you better understand controversial topics and communicate more effectively with your peers.

Active listening means listening not just to be ready to speak when it is your turn, but listening to understand what the other person is trying to explain and how they are explaining it. Active listening requires you to be active. To look at the speaker, to to makes notes on what you are hearing, to be ready with questions to clarify any points you missed.

5.12 Debating refugees

Use active listening to debate asylum.

Split your class into three groups. Two groups will debate whether all refugees should be granted asylum, or whether asylum should be limited.

*Make sure both sides prepare for **both** arguments. You will be assigned a side to debate for at random, so you must be ready to argue for either side.*

The third group will be the 'audience', whose job it is to judge the debate.

To help you prepare your argument, you could look into different areas that affect this issue, and prepare information on each area. For example, you could try to research:

→ How do asylum seekers affect unemployment?

→ How do asylum seekers affect cultural diversity in the countries that receive them?

→ Do states have a moral choice to receive asylum seekers?

Rules for debaters
When debating, it is important to remember some basic rules.

1. *Listen to the other side politely and **actively**.*
2. Put in place time limits for each speaker and each side. This prevents any side, or any person, from taking over the debate.

3. After each side presents, the opposition has a set time to raise criticisms and queries.

4. Put in place rules of engagement. Does the speaker need to take questions while they are presenting? Should all the questions be raised at the end of each group's presentation? Should questions be written down or raised verbally?

5. Do not interrupt other speakers.

6. Decide how the audience will vote. Will it be by show of hands, or by secret ballot?

Notes for the audience: judging a debate

These notes are good advice for all of us when we watch politicians or experts debating, when we read the news, or when we get information from social media. Judging or evaluating information is about understanding arguments, deciding if they are logical and supported by evidence. It is also about being aware of any prejudices, or assumptions, you already have before you hear any new information. Finally, it is about being aware of how information is affecting your emotions as much as your reason.

As an audience member your job is to listen thoughtfully. It might be useful to ask questions to the debaters. Think about insightful questions that help you understand why a position is strong or weak.

Audience members should keep the following in mind as they decide which side to vote for:

1. Did you already have a favourite side before the debate began? How will you ensure you give both sides a fair hearing?

2. Are speakers giving you facts that they can back up, or are they simply listing their opinions?

3. Are speakers trying to convince you with facts? Or are speakers trying to get your support by appealing to your emotions: making you feel angry, sad, scared, guilty?

4. Are speakers using humour, good looks, or florid language rather than good arguments to try and convince you?

5. Are speakers trying to intimidate or interrupt the opposing side?

6. Have speakers considered counterarguments or are they simply repeating their own arguments over and over?

Reflection
Refugees among us

Are there refugees in your country? Where did they come from? What were they escaping?

5.13 Refugees in your community

Take some time to research the refugee communities in your area.

Think about these questions:

- Where could you find information about refugees in your country? Could you contact government offices? Could you check newspapers?

- How can you find out when and why these refugees came to your country?

As you start this research you might find that there have been several waves of refugees. Recent ones due to current conflicts, and older ones from previous wars such as WWII or the Gulf War. It might also be the case that your country has sent out refugees to other countries. Consider making a timeline to help you understand what has happened and when.

Interviews

If there is an organization that represents refugee communities where you are, you could consider contacting them to see if an interview is possible. They can probably give you much greater insight into the condition of refugees and also teach you more about where they came from and why.

Ethics

Whenever we interview another person we must ensure that we have their full informed consent. This means making clear to the person what information you are seeking and how you will use it. You must also ensure that none of the information you gather hurts the people you interview in any way.

It might be prudent, for example, to avoid enquiring about the legal status of refugees who might be waiting for government documents. You must also consider how answering certain questions might emotionally and psychologically affect a person. Refugees who have gone through great suffering might not want to, or be able to, recount what they have experienced.

You should also be prepared to go off-script during interviews. While you prepare for an interview with a set of questions, once in the interview you might find other areas the person being interviewed wants to discuss. These might be rich areas of information, and it is ok to go off-script in such cases.

5.14 Interviews

Use the information you have gathered to write a short, 300–500 word, magazine article about refugees in, or from, your country. The aim of this article is to help others understand the situation of refugees in your country. You can add images to your article. Your class could collect all the articles together to create a special magazine edition on refugees.

5.15 Reflection: your feelings

Learning about people who have been forced to leave their country can be emotionally difficult. Within this topic are also stories of great kindness, of people going out of their way to help refugees and to welcome them into their new home. See if you can find some uplifting stories.

As you think about refugee situations around the world, and as you process your views and feelings about these, you might find it helpful to translate some of these feelings and views into creative forces. Try writing a poem about refugees. Paint a scene from what you have read or thought about. Make a cartoon retelling a story that moved you.

Finally, take some time to think about your team's work during the debate. How successful was your preparation for the debate? Did everyone research? Did everyone speak? Did everyone contribute?

Taking it further

Learning about refugees can help us see how our world is interconnected, and how our history affects our present. Take some time to expand your learning with the activities below.

Geography

Try to create a physical representation of refugee flows. You could use a map and arrows, a map with threads of different colours, or something else. Be creative in trying to make the information come alive for others.

Literature

There is a growing number of fantastic novels about refugees and their experiences. The UK BookTrust has an excellent list. Try one of the books in their list. You could start by reading *Refugee* by Alan Gratz.

Politics

How do you feel about the situation of refugees in your country? Do you think your government is doing the right thing? Why not write to your government about what you have learnt and what you think needs to be done? Remember to use facts to support your arguments.

Art

How would you represent the experience of refugees? What would you like your art to say to the world about refugees?

Civics and writing: new perspective on your country

Imagine you have just arrived in your country as a refugee. Everything might seem confusing and strange. What sort of guide would you be grateful for? Create a guide for new arrivals. Try to give them information about things they need to understand to feel safe and welcomed – things that may appear obvious to you but might be confusing to them.

Languages

Look into the languages of various refugee groups in your community. Could you learn a few welcoming sentences in each language to use if you meet a refugee?

Media

Look again at how media portrays refugees in your country. Do you think their portrayal is accurate? Do you think they are missing an angle or particular information? Write a letter to the editor of a newspaper to either congratulate the paper for its accurate portrayal or to let the paper know how you think it can do better.

What did you learn?

When you complete this challenge, take a moment to reflect over what you have learnt with the table below:

Skill	I get it!	I am starting to get it!	I need to review this.
Evaluation: I understand what bias is.			
Evaluation: I understand why checking sources for bias is important.			
Evaluation: I understand how word choice can affect audiences.			
Evaluation and analysis: I can read actively and critically to identify different issues in an article.			
Research: I can research and understand opposing arguments.			
Research: I know where to find information about a topic.			
Communication: I know how to prepare for a debate.			
Communication and collaboration: I know how to actively listen to information.			

Year 7

Challenge 6 Employment

6.1 Get thinking

Should children be allowed to work?

Do you get paid for doing your homework?

Is taking care of children work? Should mothers be paid for taking care of their children?

Should all work have mandatory vacations?

In this challenge we will be looking at what work is, what people get paid, and discuss whether these payments are fair or not.

My name is Carla. I have to work to help my family. I wish my work was just going to school. When I do go to school I am tired and it is hard to pay attention. I think children's work should be to study. And I think the government should pay us to study. What do you think?

My government has set up programmes to help people access work. We think everyone should work for pay outside the home as soon as they are 18. Not working should be a crime and our society will not support it.

Challenge overview

As you work through this challenge you will need to think about what work is, who works, why they work, and how much they are paid. You will also have time to think and reflect about what work you want to do. There will be many ideas to explore and you will need to think carefully about the best way to research and learn about work.

What skills will you develop?

Collaboration: Teamwork challenges
→ You will spend some time thinking about the strengths and weaknesses you bring to group work and how you might encourage your teammates in their strengths.

Research 1: Work and wages
→ You will work on finding sources of information and look at what makes *bad* questions.

Analysis: Unpaid work
→ You will expand your understanding of research methods and learn about a new method: fieldwork.

Research 2: Forced labour
→ You will use graphs to understand the topic. You will also spend some more time thinking about the power of good questions.

Analysis and evaluation: Your personal goals
→ In this section you will spend some time thinking about what you want to do with your life. You will reflect on what you value and why, and think about what steps you need to take to prepare for your future.

Taking it further
→ This section will give you a lot of ideas to take your learning further, connecting it with other subjects and expanding your understanding.

Collaboration
Teamwork challenges

Hard work: working as a team

Collaborating with peers is fun, but it can also be hard! There will be moments when you find something funny and share a good laugh, and there will be times when you disagree on where your project should go and feel a bit frustrated.

As you work with others, remember:

→ there will be hard moments when tensions are high

→ there might be times when your group makes choices you disagree with and you have to compromise

→ there will be times when you have to do things you don't like; for instance, you might be assigned to do library research when you would rather be interviewing experts

→ there will be times of fun and laughter. Enjoy these!

In difficult moments, remember:

→ your aim. Having to read a difficult text, or compromising on an idea might not appeal, but if you keep in mind that you are doing it to help your team solve a challenge, you will have the energy to keep going.

→ that working as a team is a good opportunity to help others. Some of your team members might be feeling insecure or scared. Your kind words and support might help them not just finish the project, but be happier and healthier as people!

→ that there will be more projects. There will be opportunities for you to stand in the limelight and opportunities for others to shine. Try to help your classmates shine!

6.2 Skill survey

Knowing your strengths and weaknesses can be helpful when working in a team. It means you know what you can support others with, and what areas you might need help with.

Look at the list below and think about where you are strongest and where you would like to develop.

	Very good	OK	Could get better
I am good at listening to people.			
I am good at pointing out what others do well.			
I am good at using positive language.			
I am good at noticing flaws.			
I am good at coming up with solutions.			
I am creative.			
I am good at speaking in public.			
I am good at research.			
I am good at taking notes.			
I am good at keeping things organized.			
I am good at doing things on time.			
I am good at working under pressure.			
I am good at finding humour in various situations.			
I am good at keeping on track.			
I am good at following instructions.			
I am good at making things look cool.			
I am good at writing clearly.			

Remember: no one is great at everything without some work. We can all improve. If there are areas you are particularly struggling with, try to spend some time practising these in your next project: for example, do a little more research, try to speak in front of the group. If you feel the need for more support you can always ask your teacher for tips and guidance.

6.3 Supporting your team

Sometimes we are not aware of what we can do well, and a kind word can be powerful. Try the following:

Write each team member's name on a piece of paper. Write two things that each of your teammates is particularly good at on their piece of paper – the more specific the better. It can be anything from 'The way you say hello to everyone makes us all feel welcomed!' to 'Your writing is clear and powerful!', or 'Thanks for helping us resolve conflicts with humour and kindness'. Make sure everyone gets a note, and make their day!

Research
Work and wages

6.4 Critical thinking: minimum wage

Do you think there should be a minimum payment for work, regardless of what the work is? What about a maximum payment?

Divide your class into groups to debate these questions. As you discuss, try to think about the questions from different perspectives, including an individual, a national, and a global perspective.

As you conduct your discussion you might come to an agreement that there should, or that there should not, be a **minimum wage**. A minimum wage is the minimum payment a government decides people should be paid. It may be set per hour, and it may be set by a local or by a national government.

6.5 Wage facts

Find whether your city (or country) has a minimum wage.

If you are going to use the Internet to find this information, what steps will you follow?

1. Will you use a particular search engine? Why? (Can you ensure this engine will not lead you to dangerous or inaccurate websites?)

2. What search terms will you use? Of the list below, which do you think would work best and why?

   → Minimum wage

   → What is the minimum wage in my country please?

   → Minimum wage [name of your country] [current year]

   → Should people be paid at least some money?

Now let's take a *comparative perspective* — that is, we will compare what we found in your city/country with other cities/countries.

6.6 Comparing data

Get back in research mode and find out:

→ the minimum wage, if it exists, in neighbouring cities/countries

→ the five highest minimum wages in the world

→ the five lowest minimum wages in the world.

Critical thinking: do you think there should be global minimum and maximum wages? Why or why not?

6.7 Research methods: interview

Imagine you are a newspaper reporter and have been granted an interview with the Minister for Work and Employment in your country.

You want to find information about work and minimum wage in your country. What questions would you ask the Minister?

Write five to ten questions you would ask. Exchange your list with a classmate to see where you overlap and to get inspiration for areas you might not have thought about.

Would it make sense to write a survey and use it to get information from the Minister? Why or why not?

6.8 Feedback on questions

Look through your classmate's questions and give them some quick feedback. Note if any questions are too broad, too vague, biased, unclear, or irrelevant. Remember to give feedback kindly and in a positive way.

6.9 Writing bad questions

The editor of the newspaper was so impressed by the work you did with the Ministry of Work and Employment that they have hired you to run a tutorial for new reporters. The editor wants you to show the reporters some examples of **bad** questions.

Choose one of the issues below and write a series of questions that are: too broad, too vague, biased, unclear, irrelevant.

→ Child labour

→ Work in dangerous situations

→ Women in the labour force

→ Working for foreign companies

Analysis
Unpaid work

Should all work be paid?

This question takes us back to consider what work is. While this might seem easy at first, it is actually a challenging concept.

6.10 Critical thinking: work

Try labelling each of these statements as True or False:

Work is only what one does not enjoy doing.

Work is only what is done with the body.

Work is only what is done with strangers.

Work is only what one is trained for.

Work is only done for the benefit of others.

Work is only done for payment.

If you think about each statement, you will find that there are always exceptions. Figuring out what work is, is surprisingly tricky. This is part of the reason why there is some debate about unpaid work. Unpaid work refers to work people are not paid for. This includes parents caring for children and volunteer work such as helping to clean a community park. Some argue that some of these activities are not work. What do you think?

6.11 Critical thinking: unpaid work

Do you think stay-at-home parents should be paid? Is taking care of one's house and family work?

Find sources that argue that YES, stay-at-home parents do work and should be paid and sources that argue NO, they are not working and should not be paid.

Take notes from one or two of these sources, including:

→ what evidence do they use to support their point

→ whether you find that they are biased and what evidence you have of their bias.

Quantifying work

In discussions of unpaid work, it is necessary to measure how much work is being done, so we can understand how many hours of paid work this might be equal to. What research methods could we use to measure unpaid work?

6.12 Research methods: uses

Work with a partner to discuss whether and how you could use the following research methods to research how much unpaid work is being done:

→ Interviews (Whom would you interview? What would you ask?)

→ Surveys (Whom would you survey? What questions would you ask?)

6.13 Research: fieldwork

One way to measure unpaid work might be to undertake some fieldwork – this means going to the place where people are doing what you want to understand, observing, and taking notes. As always, you need to think of safety: make sure you have permission, don't go on your own, and let another adult know where you are.

Try it out! Ask a person who does unpaid work for permission to observe them during the day. As you do, take notes on what they do. Your notes might look a bit like this:

→ 8 a.m. – made breakfast – 30 mins

→ 8.45 a.m. – cleaned up after breakfast – 30 mins

→ 10–11 a.m. – cleaned house – 1 hour

→ 11 a.m.–12.30 p.m. – made lunch, answered postman, and watered garden – 1 hour, 30 minutes

Challenge:

Think about some of the challenges of undertaking fieldwork. Do you think your presence might affect the people you are observing?

Reflection

As you accompany someone through their unpaid work you might be surprised at how much work they do: how many acts that require energy, some skill, and that benefit others are done without you ever noticing. This is why some people refer to unpaid work as invisible work. It is not that it is not important; it is extremely important, but, because it happens so often before us, we grow used to seeing it to the point where it becomes invisible to us. Can you find any 'invisible' work happening around you?

Research
Forced labour

Not all people choose their work freely; some are forced to work against their will. For example, some might accept a job and then find that their employer has lied to them, forcing them to work for little or no pay. In some cases workers find themselves in a foreign country, unable to leave and forced to work incredibly long hours in unhealthy and dangerous jobs.

Forced labour is big business. In 2014, the ILO (International Labour Organization) estimated that forced labour generates about US$ 150 billion in profit each year.

6.14 Data on forced labour

- As a class, discuss why it might be difficult to research forced labour.

- If you wanted to research forced labour, what research methods would you use?

- Look at the graphs that follow. Do you think they support or contradict the following statements?

    - Forced labour is not an important international concern.
    - Forced labour is mostly a concern for the Americas.
    - Forced labour takes places in gold mining.
    - Forced labour doesn't include children.

Year 7 Challenge 6

Forced labour generates annual profits of US$150 billion

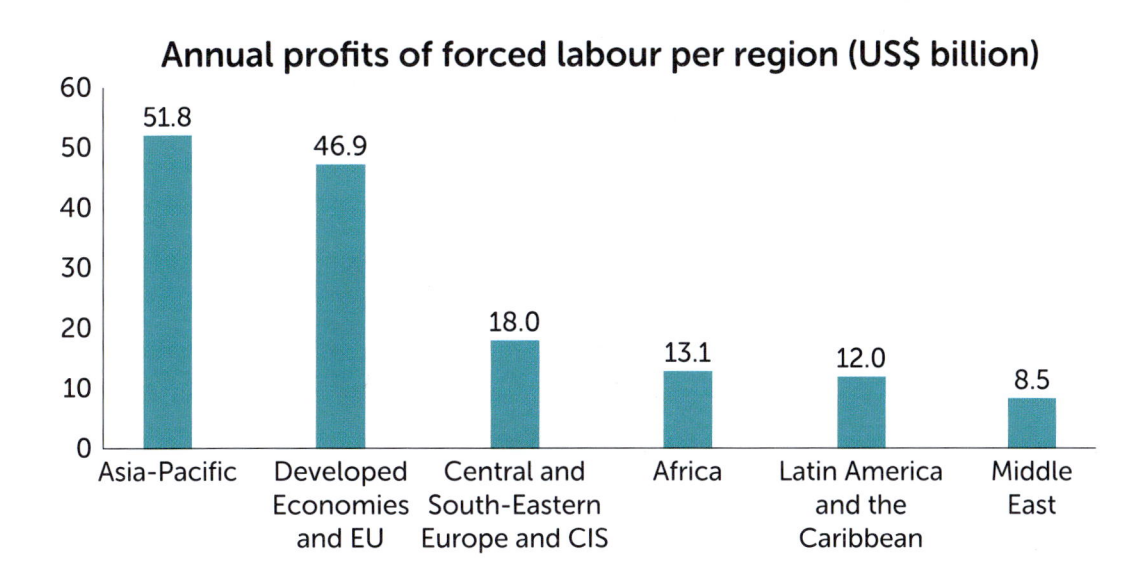

Annual profits of forced labour per region (US$ billion)

Region	Profits
Asia-Pacific	51.8
Developed Economies and EU	46.9
Central and South-Eastern Europe and CIS	18.0
Africa	13.1
Latin America and the Caribbean	12.0
Middle East	8.5

21 million people victims of forced labour

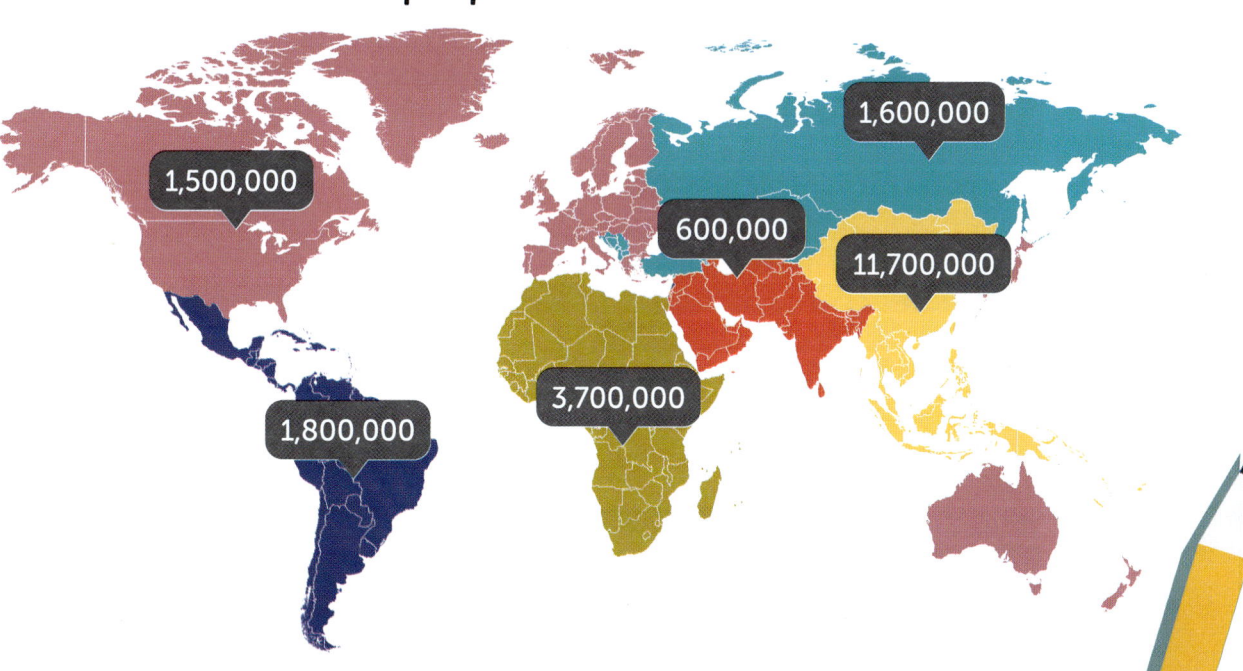

- North America: 1,500,000
- Latin America: 1,800,000
- Europe: 1,600,000
- Africa: 3,700,000
- Middle East/North Africa: 600,000
- South Asia: 11,700,000 (Asia-Pacific region)
- Central Asia: shown on map

Source: https://www.ilo.org/global/topics/forced-labour/policy-areas/statistics/lang--en/index.htm

Number of goods produced by child labour or forced labour: 148 goods from 76 countries

Percentage of goods produced globally by child labour or forced labour, by production sector

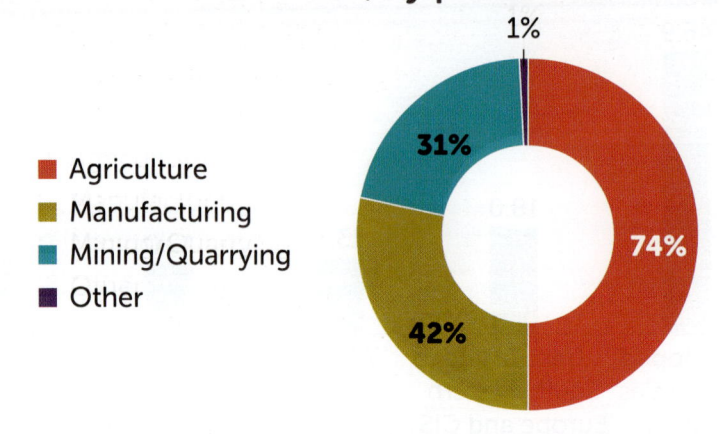

- Agriculture: 74%
- Manufacturing: 42%
- Mining/Quarrying: 31%
- Other: 1%

Goods with most child labour and forced labour listings by number of countries

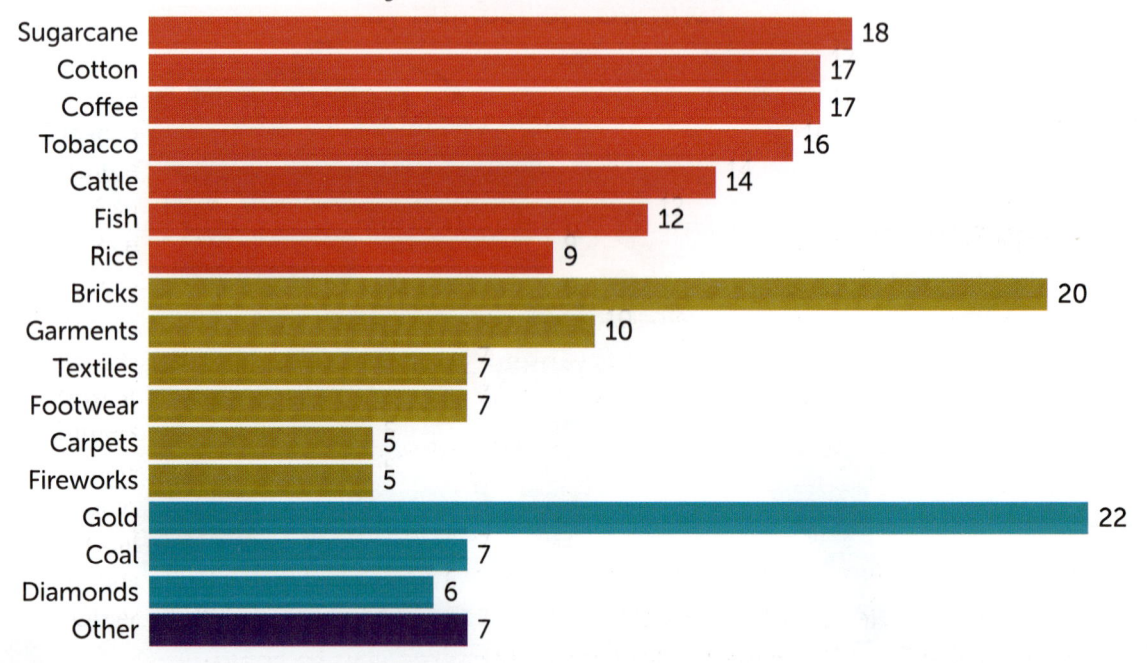

Good	Number of countries
Sugarcane	18
Cotton	17
Coffee	17
Tobacco	16
Cattle	14
Fish	12
Rice	9
Bricks	20
Garments	10
Textiles	7
Footwear	7
Carpets	5
Fireworks	5
Gold	22
Coal	7
Diamonds	6
Other	7

Source: Based on research by the U.S. Department of Labor's Bureau of International Labor Affairs https://www.dol.gov/agencies/ilab/reports/child-labor/list-of-goods

Child labour

What do the graphs on these pages tell you about child labour? If you wanted to learn more about child labour what research questions could you use?

As you know, good questions are important. Good questions guide productive research. A good question will help you to find information that you can evaluate to decide on a possible solution to a problem.

6.15 Assessing questions

Look at the following questions on child labour. Which do you think is the best question for a challenge and why?

- Is child labour bad?
- Should all child labour be banned?
- Does child labour exist?

After discussing the questions, match the questions with the descriptions:

→ **Question quality:** This question is too narrow. It requires a yes or no answer.
→ **Evidence:** To support your answer you can provide evidence such as the number of children working and where they work.
→ **Question quality:** This question requires you to make a choice, thus it requires some evaluation. However, the question is broad. Bad can mean so many things.
→ **Evidence:** To support your answer in this question you would need to decide what bad is and then find examples of how child labour is bad ... I think this needs more focus.
→ **Question quality:** This is a good question. It requires you to make a choice to answer it – yes or no to all child labour being banned; therefore it requires evaluation.
→ **Evidence:** To support your answer you would need to show why child labour should or should not be banned: show why it is positive or negative.

Analysis and evaluation
Your personal goals

Where do you want to work in the future?

Having a vision of where you would like to work might help you plan your studies and motivate you to keep going when you encounter difficult times. In this section, we will be thinking critically about the multiple aspects a job can have.

Dreaming and thinking: start by thinking about types of jobs you are interested in. Let your heart and mind fly and think about all the options you can imagine. Are you interested in a particular area, such as IT, medicine, fashion? Are you interested in more than one area? Is there something that links all the areas you are interested in?

Now let's analyse the many criteria that make a job desirable or not. Can you make a list of what makes a job good?

6.16 Why you want to work?

Let's analyse the jobs you are interested in. How do they rank in relation to the list you made? Fill out a table like the one below or create a similar table to analyse your job options.

Criteria	Job 1 Ranking 1–10	Job 2 Ranking 1–10	Job 3 Ranking 1–10
Money			
Prestige			
Stress			
Working environment			
Need to travel			
Opportunities to work with others			
Family time			
Adventures			
Health			

6.17 Your values

Once you complete this table for the various jobs you are interested in, consider how you will decide what is most important to you. You might find that a job offers less money (gets a 3 in this area) but offers you the opportunity to interact with many interesting people (gets a 9 in this area), and you find it more important to socialize with interesting people than to make money. How do you make this decision?

This is a process of evaluation – here you are making a **judgement**. You have to decide what you think are the most important criteria for you. Is it to travel? To have prestige? To be able to spend time with your family? Take some time to look over your table and think about what matters to you and why. You can highlight the areas that are most important to you.

6.18 Comparing values

Work with a friend to discuss your job options and your evaluation criteria. They might have other evaluation criteria for you to consider. Do you and your friend agree on what is most important in a job? If you don't, have a gentle conversation about what is most important to each of you and why.

6.19 Future jobs

Do you think some of the jobs you are interested in now might not exist in the future? Could there be jobs in the future that have not yet been created? What could these be?

6.20 Research: preparing for the future

How could you find out more about the jobs you are interested in? Make a list of places you could go to for information. Try to find data that can help you make predictions, such as how AI is advancing.

Challenge:
Find someone who is doing a job you would like to do in the future. Learn about them and write them a letter asking for advice.

Taking it further

We encourage you to research options for your future. Spend some time thinking about the work you want to do and how work can be made better for everyone.

Economics

Should countries help unemployed people? If so, what shape should that support take? If not, why not?

Journalism

Find the best and worst jobs in the world and write a magazine article about them.

Philosophy

Could you argue that individuals should be able to choose not to work? What about arguing that everyone should work? Think about whether working should be a right or an obligation.

Art

Create a piece of art about work; either something you want to do or something you have seen others do. An option is to write a song about it. Alternatively, find music that has been written about work.

Maths

How much do people get paid? Find information about different salaries and then figure out what their salary is per day, per hour. Does looking at salaries this way make sense? Why or why not?

Sociology

What do you think the jobs of the future will require? Do you think that in order to work in 2050 you will need some skills that are not currently taught?

Literature

Creative writing: write a description of some of the jobs of the future.

Year 7 Challenge 6

What did you learn?

When you complete this challenge, take a moment to reflect over what you have learnt with the table below:

Skill	I get it!	I am starting to get it!	I need to review this.
Collaboration: I understand some of the challenges, and benefits, of working in a group.			
Collaboration: I have thought about some of the strengths I can bring to a group, and areas I need to work on.			
Research: I can find facts about new topics, such as minimum wage, in multiple sources.			
Evaluation: I understand that I need to think about whether sources are relevant and accurate.			
Research: I understand why different research methods, such as interviews or surveys, make more sense in some instances than others.			
Analysis: I can read graphs and use them to discuss complex issues.			
Reflection: I have spent some time thinking about what I want to do in the future.			

End of Year 7
Bringing it all together

You have now completed a year of work in Global Perspectives. Congratulations! You have learnt about many interesting topics, expanded your research skills, worked with friends, and learnt a lot about yourself. Take some time to reflect on what you have learnt.

1. What is the most interesting topic you discussed this year?
2. Have you changed your views on any of the topics discussed this year? What led you to change your opinions?
3. What was the hardest part about teamwork?
4. What was the best part about teamwork?
5. What was the most helpful thing you did in your group?
6. What skill do you feel you particularly improved on this year? Some of the ones you could choose include:
    a. finding sources
    b. finding useful information in sources
    c. judging whether sources are biased
    d. building a clear argument
    e. using evidence well
    f. making interesting presentations
    g. seeing problems from multiple perspectives.
7. What other topics would you like to learn about?
8. If you could solve any local, national or global problem, what problem would you solve?

Skills learnt

Below is a quick review of the skills you have learnt and particular goals you want to reach. Check what you have done and what you still need to work on.

Research

Through the year you have worked on writing questions that are clear, focused, realistic, and not-leading. You have thought about the many different resources you can use for research, from books, to websites, blogs, podcasts, magazines, and more. You have learned that sometimes you need primary data, which is data you need to collect yourself. To collect primary data, you have learned about surveys, interviews, and fieldwork. You have learned that all primary research should consider ethics and obtain informed consent. You have learned the importance of keeping track of your sources, and citing all sources you use. You have practiced taking notes, and understand the importance of taking clear, concise notes.

Analysis

This year you have learned to analyse complex issues by exploring their causes and consequences. You have understood that causes are the reason something happens, and consequences are the effects something has. You have worked on analysing a variety of materials: from articles, to biographies, to information presented in graphs and charts. You have learned to read, interpret and use graphs. You understand what evidence is and understand that arguments need to be supported with factual evidence.

Evaluation

This year you have spent time thinking about whether sources present information in a fair way, or whether they are biased. You have learned that you need to evaluate all sources to make sure they are valid, relevant, current, and unbiased. You understand the difference between facts and opinions and know that valid sources do not present opinions as facts. You have learned that good arguments are clear and logical, and are working to present your own arguments in a clear, focused, logical, and well-supported manner.

Collaboration

You have worked with peers in a variety of projects which require discussion, planning, time-keeping, compromise, and sharing tasks. You have talked about your strengths in a team, and areas you need to strengthen. You have worked to discuss ideas with peers without taking offense. You have practiced sharing tasks and noticing your peers' actions with gratitude and kindness. You have practiced active listening to learn from, and support, your peers.

Communication

You have practiced expressing yourself clearly in a variety of media: from presentations and speeches, to debates, videos, articles, and posters. You have learned to always keep your audience in mind, to try to be clear, and to be organized with your arguments.

You have spent time this year thinking about how group projects have worked, and what you find challenging about working with others. You have discovered new skills, and developed new ideas. You have thought deeply about a variety of topics and might have changed how you see this topic and yourself.

Citing sources

Citing sources

As you find sources, it is important to keep track of these. When you use a source in your work, you need to ensure you cite the source properly.

What is citing a source?

- Citing a source means telling your reader where they can find the original source for the information you are using.

Why is it important to cite sources?

- To give the authors credit for their work.
- So your audience can verify that you have used existing information, and that you have used it well.
- So that your audience can verify the quality of your sources.
- So your audience can learn more about your topic, if they are interested.

Keeping a careful list of your sources will also help you! If you need to go back and review some of your information, make sure you wrote facts down correctly; you don't want to have to start your research all over again! Keeping a list of your sources, and noting where you got each piece of information, will make your life much easier!

1 Thinking about citations

What information do your readers need to find the sources you used? With a partner, discuss which of the following is likely to help you and your readers go back and find the original sources if needed.

- Author of the source
- Date of publication
- Type of paper used in publication
- Size of book
- Pages information is found in
- URL if the source is a website.

Warning! Using information from a source without giving credit to the original author can be considered **plagiarism**. Plagiarism is stealing someone else's intellectual work, and you can get in serious trouble for doing it.

2 Starting your reference list

As you find sources on your research topic, start making your reference list. Your teacher will need to tell you what citation style you need to use. It is best to make your reference list, or bibliography as you find each source, rather than waiting until the end when it can be overwhelming.

Year 8

Welcome to Year 8 of Global Perspectives. Are you ready for all the exciting things this year holds?

For those of you who are new to Global Perspectives: this is not your ordinary course. In this course you will be exploring a number of interesting topics - from water, to crime. However, our focus is not on teaching you facts about these topics. Rather, our focus in on giving you the skills you need to become an independent explorer. We want you to be able to lead your own research journeys into any of the Global Perspectives curriculum topics and beyond! We want you to learn to ask incisive questions, to know where to find sources, to know the importance of checking the quality of sources, and to share your ideas clearly and powerfully. We want you to know how to work effectively and efficiently with your peers. And we want you to develop a global perspective, while also understanding the perspectives of different countries, and your own personal perspectives.

As you explore new topics in Year 8, you will be guided through various exercises to develop your research, analysis, evaluation, communication, collaboration, and reflection skills.

- All skills take practice to develop. If you found evaluation tricky last year, you might just find that this year you love discussing whether a source is biased or not!

- Finding the causes and effects of local, national, and global problems also takes practice. This year we will work at looking closely at what others argue to see if their arguments are logical and based on solid data.

- Becoming a great team member is a powerful skill! This year you will reflect on how to collaborate and communicate to make you a key player in all teamwork.

- And this year you will continue to expand your thinking by exploring topics from different perspectives. Learning to see a problem from different perspectives is a powerful tool that will make you a sharper thinker and will prepare you to succeed in the future – whatever your career choice might be.

Working through Year 8 material

As with Year 7, Year 8 is split into distinct challenges. In each challenge, you have the opportunity to complete exercises to help improve your Global Perspectives skills. Each section will tell you what skill you are working on. Some sections cover more than one skill.

New in Year 8

This year we wanted to highlight the process of completing challenges. In each challenge we have suggested an outcome and provided steps in each section to achieve this outcome. Do remember that this is just one suggested outcome. You and your class can decide on a different aim and outcome for each challenge. The exercises we provide will still be useful to help you sharpen your thinking and skills, and to introduce you to the topic.

Whatever topic and outcome you choose, the exercises we provide will still sharpen your Global Perspective skills. For example, while we look at 'water crisis' you could choose to look at 'aging populations' or 'soil erosion'. The key is to develop your Global Perspective skills as you work on your topic. Make this course yours!

We have made the last challenge in Year 8, 'Improve your community', slightly different. Rather than guiding you to a particular outcome, we have used it to remind you of everything you have learnt in Years 7 and 8. Use this information as a guide as you tackle any challenge in any topic.

As in year 7, there are numerous activities that can be carried out in pairs/groups, which provide opportunities to practice collaboration.

As you work through Year 8 material, you might want to review some of the skills you are using. You can always return to Year 7 material to review and practice. To help you find relevant exercises you can refer to the exercise list by Learning Objective provided at the end of the book.

Year 8

Challenge 1 Water crisis

1.1 Water

Think about the following questions. You can try to answer them on your own or discuss them with others in your class.

- Should people be allowed to own rivers and lakes?
- Should people be fined for using too much water?
- What would you do if you had no water?

Challenge overview

Would you ever fight with someone over a glass of water? The idea of fighting over water might seem silly if water has always been easily available to you. But what if you had to walk several miles every day for just enough water to drink? What if you saw the water in your country slowly disappear as glaciers shrunk before your eyes? What if your harvest shrivelled and dried out for lack of water, causing you to fear a year of hunger or starvation? Or what if all the water you had access to was polluted, causing high levels of cancer and death in your community?

Some sources have predicted water as a major source of conflict during this century. Yet the Earth is 71% water. How is it possible that we might end up fighting for what seems so abundant?

Some water facts, taken from WaterAid:

- 3 billion people don't have handwashing facilities at home.
- Diarrhoea caused by dirty water and poor toilets kills a child under 5 every 2 minutes.
- 785 million people don't have clean water close to home.

The water crisis is complicated! Different parts of the world have different access to water and use water differently. We can think of a large topic like the 'water crisis' as made up of smaller issues. Each issue can be researched separately, but they all interact to create a complex problem.

Water crisis

Key questions:
- Who owns the water?
- Why is there water pollution?
- Can science help us use salt water?
- How does water access differ between men and women?
- How can we use less water?
- Who is polluting the water?
- Can we use water more sustainably?
- Which countries have most/least water?

Your challenge: You have been hired as a reporter to write a special magazine issue on the water crisis. You will be working with a group of reporters to collaborate on this magazine. This means you have to work together. The editor would like each of you to write about a different aspect of the water crisis and then put these pieces together.

To complete this challenge you can follow this path:

1. Come up with a research question.
2. Conduct research.
3. Summarize your findings.
4. Share your work with peers.
5. Write and edit your final piece.

What skills will you develop?

In this challenge, you will work on developing the following skills:

Research 1: Choosing your agenda
➜ You will review how to come up with an interesting, clear, research question.

Research 2: Choosing your sources
➜ You will think about different types of sources and sharpen your internet research skills.

Research 3: Summarizing your findings
➜ You will improve your summarizing skills.

Collaboration: Working as a team
➜ You will reflect on how to improve your teamwork.

Communication: Sharing your work powerfully
➜ You will edit your writing and your citations.

Taking it further
➜ Here you will find suggestions to explore this topic further, linking it to other subjects like maths, science, arts, and more.

Research 1
Choosing your agenda

In this challenge, the topic has been chosen for you: the **water crisis**. However, you need to come up with your own research agenda. In other words, you need to focus your research into a clear, manageable, question that requires analysis. This analysis will help you come up with a solution to the problem you are researching.

1.2a Drafting questions

Start by free thinking a list of questions that you might want to research. This is an opportunity to write down anything that comes to your mind, without worrying about whether these ideas are good or bad. This will help get your creativity going and might just help you find an unexpected interest!

1.2b Reviewing possible research questions

Now that you have some questions, use a table like the one below to evaluate them. As always, your questions should be:

- **clear** – if you ask your question to a friend, will they understand what you are asking?
- **relevant** – is the question about the topic you are interested in?
- **focused** – is the question precise enough to help you find information? Or is the question so broad that you end up looking at a whole library of books?
- **not too narrow** – your question shouldn't be so narrow that there is nothing left to research.
- **realistic** – your question needs to be something you can actually find out.
- **unbiased** – your question should not tell you what to think before you look at information.

Question	Is it relevant?	Is it clear?	Is it focused?	Is it too narrow?	Is it realistic? Is it something I can research?	Is it biased?
Question 1						

Struggling for a question?

If you are struggling to find a question, you might consider different areas of a topic. You might find one area particularly interesting and thinking about this area might inspire a question. Think of areas like different parts of reality: politics, economics, science, culture, history, and so forth. Looking at the **water crisis**, for example, you could look at:

Economics Who pays for water?

How much will it cost to fix water pollution?

Politics Should governments provide water to all their citizens?

Should there be laws about how much water you can use?

Science How is environmental change affecting water?

Can we use science to clean polluted water?

Remember: all of these questions need to be evaluated for quality. Some questions might not be focused enough, or they might be unclear. What do you think?

1.3 Peer reviewing questions

Share your questions with the other reporters in your team and discuss them for five minutes. What is the best question each of your classmates came up with? Can you make your questions better with your classmates' feedback? Make sure each of you researches a different aspect of the water crisis.

When you give feedback on other people's questions, remember to keep feedback *kind* and *honest*. Try to think about how a question could be made better, rather than only pointing out what is wrong with it. This is **constructive feedback**. It helps others to build on what they have, rather than simply destroying what they have attempted.

When you listen to feedback, remember that errors in your questions do not mean that *you* are wrong. They simply mean that the questions need more work.

When you have chosen a question to research, consider how to research it from different perspectives.

To complete this section: choose a question to research. Present this question to your teacher for feedback.

Research 2
Choosing your sources

As you look for information to answer your question, you need to consider what kind of information you will find in different sources. If you are looking for a brief overview, you might want to use a different source than if you are looking for statistics or for a detailed account. A personal diary, for example, is unlikely to contain statistics, but it is likely to have details on how an issue affects a person in their daily life.

Remember: Where you look will affect what you find.

1.4 Different sources

Can you match the type of information you want with the type of source where you might find it?

1. A short summary of the change in water levels in the world
2. Recent research on how water needs are changing in Country A
3. Personal accounts of needing water
4. Statistics on water levels in various countries

a. Academic article
b. Government document from Country A
c. Blog
d. Encyclopaedia
e. A personal diary
f. Water NGO website

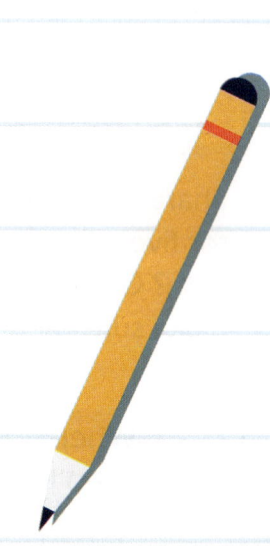

Using the Internet

The Internet is quickly becoming the main research tool for most students. When undertaking internet research there are a few things to consider.

Search engines

Which search engine will you use? Is it safe? Is it likely to give you information biased by your previous research?

Some internet search engines support good causes when you use them (Ecosia, Ekoru, for example). Some search engines are set up to be particularly safe for young users (KidzSearch, for example).

1.5 Search engines

Search for 'Water crisis' in different search engines (Google, Yahoo, KidzSearch, DuckDuckGo, Ecosia). How are they different? Which is your favourite and why?

Search terms

What you find online will only be as good as the search terms you use. If your search terms are vague, you will find lots of resources, but these are unlikely to be focused enough to be useful. If you are very clear about what you are looking for, you are more likely to find it.

Search techniques

There are some techniques you can use to make your online search more powerful. These are known as Boolean modifiers.

- "quotes" – if you put a phrase within quotation marks, your search engine will only show you documents that contain that *exact phrase*, such as: "Where is water most expensive?"
- (parentheses) – if you put a phrase in parentheses, your search engine will search for the phrase, rather than for the words separately.
- AND – if you put AND in your search, the search engine will make sure both things are included. For example, if you search for: water AND pesticides – you will get results that include water AND pesticides.
- OR – this asks your search engine to show you results that have two or more options: (water AND pesticides) OR (water AND plastic), will show you resources that discuss water and pesticides OR water and plastics.
- NOT – use this term if you want your search to *exclude* a particular word or phrase: (water pollution) NOT (pesticide) will show you documents that have the phrase water pollution but exclude any that also have the word pesticide. Some search engines use a minus sign – rather than the word NOT.

1.6 Boolean modifiers

Which search terms would you use online to find information about:

- pesticides used in Europe, not in Asia
- countries with a lack of clean water
- companies that sell water in Latin America.

For more guidance look up 'Google Advanced Search'.

To complete this section: research your question online.

Research 3
Summarizing your findings

As you research a topic, you will need to be able to summarize the information you find. Summarizing information will help you to limit the amount of material you need to review as you look through your research notes to analyse data and evaluate your position on any issue. If you do not summarize, you can easily find yourself overwhelmed by large quantities of material – too much to put into a useful project or presentation.

Summarizing means looking for the main ideas and relevant information, and getting rid of anything that is superfluous.

Summarizing lunch!

To understand what summarizing entails, you can think of this example: when you have a very fancy meal there are all sorts of additions that you do not *need* for the meal – they are there to make the meal more pleasant, more exciting, more delicious. But they are not necessary for you to eat and survive. Summarizing is like getting rid of all the fancy extras at dinner!

Thus, we could say: roasted and creamed peanuts, paired with a compote of seasonal berries, served on a bed of fresh, toasted, crusted bread, sliced into fourths, and served on a plate made of baked clay decorated with flowers … or you could summarize and say: a peanut butter and jelly sandwich!

When we summarize, we want only the main ideas and the relevant facts.

1.7 Summarizing

Let's give it a try. What are the main points in the following text?

In the 1980s, the government of Malawi began providing piped water to low-income households in 50 districts, establishing community-run tap committees to collect bills and manage systems. Men made up 90 percent of committee memberships – and problems quickly became apparent.

The men were often away from home, while women were the ones actually using and managing water day-to-day. The tap committees failed to collect payments, manage their money or retain membership. To salvage the project, the government recruited women into the tap committees and trained them. Once women made up the majority of members, they paid water bills more reliably, held regular meetings with high attendance rates, and redesigned communal taps to be more user-friendly. The result was that nearly 24,000 low-income families across Malawi gained access to reliable water supplies.

This story is hardly unique: A growing body of evidence shows that water projects can become more effective when women participate. Yet women's representation in the overall water, sanitation and hygiene (WASH) sector is dismal. In 2014, women made up less than 17 percent of the WASH labor force in developing countries. They were particularly underrepresented in technical jobs such as engineers and hydro-geologists, and in leadership roles such as policymakers, regulators and managers.

Source: https://www.wri.org/blog/2018/10/women-are-secret-weapon-better-water-management

Telegrams

Another way to think about summarizing is to imagine you have to send the main points of an article in a telegram. Telegrams were a form of communication popular before telephones, where messages were transmitted as electrical signals across telegraph lines. Senders were charged per word. To avoid spending all your money, you need to be able to summarize your message into as few words as possible! Try to use the telegram challenge to summarize the information you found in one of your sources.

1.8 Telegram game

Compete with a peer to see who can summarize an article more succinctly. Or set up a make-believe telegraph office and try to send summaries with a limited amount of money!

To complete this section: use your new, or improved, summarizing skills to summarize what you have found for your team members to read.

Collaboration
Working as a team

1.9 Reflecting on yourself as a team member

Spend some time thinking about what you will contribute to the group. What have you been researching and what can it bring to the overall project? What other skills can you contribute to the team? Are you good at making other people feel good? Are you good at helping others get along? Are you good at leading others to the goal? Are you good at finding areas of agreement?

1.10 Reflection on teamwork

Spend some time making a list of two to five things that contribute to effective teamwork. Spend another few minutes making a list of two to five things you find tricky in group work. Can you come up with ways to address these? You do not have to share these lists, they are private spaces for you to think and reflect.

1.11 Discussing teamwork

With your team, discuss or role play some common team problems and talk about how you would solve them:

- Two of the team members have done research and written great reports. The third person keeps taking naps and doing no work. What would you do?

- One of the team members writes a piece without any research, making up information or listing what they heard their friends say. What would you do?

- One of the team members is bossy and wants to tell the others what they should do. What would you do?

- Your reports are due tomorrow and your third team member has not shown up. What would you do?

Year 8 Challenge 1

1.12 Planning teamwork

To work effectively as a team, you have to have a **plan of action**. When you come together you have to decide what you will do, who will do it, how, and when.

1. As you begin your teamwork, which of the following should you do? Which should you avoid?

   - Discuss your plans for the weekend.
   - Review what each of you have been researching.
   - Write the conclusion for your joint magazine issue.
   - Write the introduction for your joint magazine issue.
   - Discuss holes in your individual research that need to be filled in.
   - Discuss themes that tie your individual research together.
   - Split up the writing of the introduction and conclusion.
   - Discuss who has been the best and worst team member.
   - Decide on a plan to check all articles for quality.

2. In what order should these be done?

Improving as a team

1.13 Group games

It might be good to release some tension with games and, in the process, build up your team's communication and friendship. Here are a couple of games you can try.

Crazy and serious solutions

In this game, you will take turns to to come up with solutions for the global water crisis. The tricky and fun part is that for every serious solution someone proposes, the next person needs to come up with a creative, even wacky, idea. Don't be afraid to have fun. As you do this, you might find that some of your crazy ideas inspire reasonable solutions.

Stellar retelling

Try to retell one of your teammates' research reports as though it is set in a different galaxy. Change water for something more exotic – like molten diamond lava. Change other characters and ideas as you wish. Be creative.

To complete this section: write out the first draft of your report, share it, and discuss it with your team members.

Communication
Sharing your work powerfully

1.14 Editing your work

You are now writing the final draft of your article. The editor gives you a checklist to ensure you have communicated your argument as powerfully as possible. The checklist is below. Use this checklist to review your article. Note things that could use improvement and then spend some time improving your writing. For example, if you don't have an interesting first sentence, try to add one to capture your reader's attention.

	Done	Could use improvement	Missing
Clear research question			
Interesting first sentence			
Provides a good summary of the issue			
Clearly explains the current situation			
Clearly explains the cause(s) for problem			
Clear presentation of possible solutions for problem			
Uses factual evidence to explain the causes of the problem, and to support the proposed solution.			
Interesting conclusion			
All sources are cited properly			

Note: Reviewing your work is a key part of improving as a researcher and as a writer. Good writing requires hard work and lots of revisions. Don't worry if you are not 100% sure about all the items in the checklist – you will learn more about them as you work through this book.

Year 8 Challenge 1

1.15 Pieces of an argument

Another writer accidently dropped some of his papers on the floor. Can you help him figure out which of the areas in the table opposite each of the paragraphs below fits in?

> It has been noted that attempting to solve the lack of drinking water by converting sea water is expensive. Moreover, it does not help areas that do not have access to sea water. It might not, therefore, make sense to spend time and resources developing this technology.

> Accessing clean water is not easy for many people in our world. Some have to walk many miles to access water. Some only have access to water that is highly polluted. Some are finding that previous sources of water are drying out. In this article we will look at why water is becoming increasingly less available to rural populations in South Africa, and what can be done about it.

Citing your sources

Why do you think it is important to cite your sources?

We cite sources to ensure authors receive credit for their work. We also cite sources to ensure our readers can find our original sources.

Your teacher will guide you to the system you need to use to cite your sources. It is important to follow it closely and to be consistent. You cannot underline a book title in one source and make it bold in another! Make sure you carefully add all necessary periods and commas.

1.16 Citing sources

The same writer who misplaced part of his article is struggling with his list of sources. Look through the references below and note what might be missing in each case. The writer needs to use MLA style. The first one has been done for you.

- Good, author's name
- We need the title of the article
- We need the name of the newspaper
- We need the URL. We also need what date the article was accessed online.

Johnson, Michael. Article about water or something. In a newspaper. Get URL

Jones, Susan. 'Why Water is Getting More Expensive.' *The New Times of Oxford*. www.oxfordnewspaperwemadeup.com. (Accessed March 1, 2020).

Nancy Cain. Article in *Issues in Science and Technology*. Title "The global water crisis". Pages 79–81.

Blue, Stefan. The Global Water Crisis... Oxford University Press. *2007*.

Igor Shiklomanov. 'World fresh water resources.' In Peter H. Gleick (Ed.) (1993) *Water in Crisis: A Guide to the World's Fresh Water Resources*.

To complete this section: edit your work and bring it together with your peers' work to complete your magazine!

133

Taking it further

Do you want to take your thinking further? Use the following ideas to expand on what you have learnt.

Economics

- What is precious? Adam Smith, one of the most famous economists who ever lived, noted that humans value something based on how scarce it is. Look further into what Adam Smith argued in regard to value and see if you can explain the diamond/water paradox.

Art

- Lots of art explores the mystery and importance of water. Research some artists who have worked with water. Try to create a piece that reflects your views and feelings about water, or that represents the importance of water. Can you create a piece that uses water itself as an art medium?

Engineering and art

- Water fountains can be found all over the world. Look at how they are constructed. Explore fountains that are particularly impressive and tell your audience about their engineering.

Science

- Water is a unique material. Research how it is different to other liquids. Do its properties change depending on what part of the world you are in?
- What are some of the many uses of water? How can water be used to create power?

Philosophy

- Some ancient philosophers thought that water was one of the fundamental forces of life. Why do you think they held this idea?

Geography

- Learning about and tracking the life of rivers can be a fascinating way to learn about water. Look into the life of the Nile, for example. What great cultures evolved around it? How has the Nile changed over the last few centuries?

Maths

- Have you ever thought about how much water goes through a river? How would you calculate this? We need to know this in order to decide how much water can be channelled off for various uses, or whether we have enough water to run a power plant.

Year 8 Challenge 1

What did you learn?

Skill	I get it!	I am starting to get it!	I need to review this.
Research: I know how to explore large topics by looking at smaller areas and issues.			
Research: I understand there are different types of sources for different information.			
Research: I know about different internet search engines.			
Research: I can use Boolean modifiers to sharpen my online research.			
Research: I understand what summarizing is.			
Collaboration: I know what I can contribute to a group.			
Collaboration: I can work with team members to resolve problems.			
Communication: I understand I need to review my work for clarity and quality.			

Challenge 2 Migration

2.1 Migration

- If you were the president of your country, what rules would you put in place for migration?
- Do you think former colonial powers should be required to receive migrants from the countries they colonized?
- Do you think people should be able to buy citizenships?

Hola, my name is Manuel. I was born in the USA, but my parents are from Guatemala. Before I was born they walked more than 4000 miles, and crossed the desert, almost dying in the heat, so they could work in the USA. They could not afford to apply for immigration and wanted me to grow up in a safe place.

Some people think my family should have never come here. But now that we are here we work hard, my dad does two jobs and I am the best student in my class. I have friends who came to the USA with a Green Card, legally. I just don't think that was an option for my family.

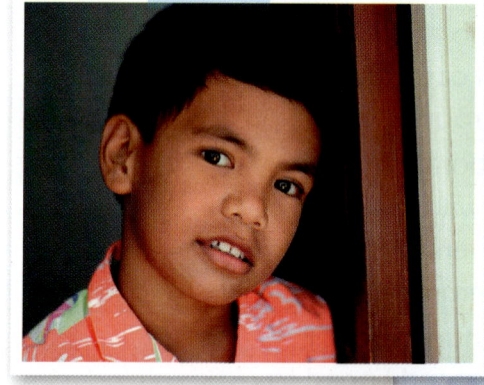

"No human is illegal" – this is the message that activists on the Mexico-United States border want to spread. They argue that movement is a human right and that people should be able to cross borders whenever they wish. President Trump, on the other hand, argues that uncontrolled migration is dangerous and has promised to build a wall to control migration into the United States from Mexico and the rest of Latin America.

Challenge overview

Please note that not all migration is international. You can also think about people who move from their place of birth to other parts of their country (often from rural to urban areas).

In this challenge, you are going to be thinking about borders and migration. Can you imagine a world that is borderless? Where people can move freely between countries? Or do you think migration controls are necessary? What do you think is the best migration policy and why? As we think and discuss this topic, we will be considering the causes and consequences of migration and focusing on becoming better analysts.

To complete this challenge, you will write or record a short presentation to a government of your choice, advising the government on how it should improve its immigration policy. The challenge will follow this path:

1. Research the causes for migration to your country of choice.
2. Research the consequences of migration to your country of choice.
3. Evaluate the consequences of migration and migration policies.
4. Expand your thinking by considering different perspectives.
5. Work with a team to write a letter or make a video advising the government how to improve its migration policy.

What skills will you develop?

Analysis 1: Causes of migration
→ You will practise finding the causes of problems and events. You will learn to avoid falling for the *post hoc, ergo propter hoc* logical fallacy.

Analysis 2: Consequences—thinking about impact
→ You will practise thinking about the consequences of problems and actions.

Evaluation: Judging sources and policies
→ You will sharpen how you evaluate sources and possible solutions.

Perspectives: Migration—from the global to the personal
→ You will practise critical thinking by looking at migration from multiple perspectives.

Communication: Giving advice
→ You will work on communicating your message clearly.

Taking it further
→ Here you will have suggestions to explore this topic further, linking it to other subjects like maths, science, arts, and more.

Analysis 1
Causes of migration

One of the big questions surrounding migration is **why** it happens.

Asking *why* something happens means looking for its *causes*. You are trying to understand the **causes or reasons** for migration. When you research and write about **causes**, you might want to look for and use words that signal causation.

⚙️ Can you think of some words that signal causation?

It is rarely the case that there is only one cause for something. More often, human actions and human problems have multiple causes. It is likely that several reasons lead a person to choose to migrate, not just one.

2.2 Finding causes

The article below notes that there are 'push' and 'pull' factors that lead to migration. Read the article to understand what these two types of factors are and also try to highlight words or phrases that signal causation.

Why do people migrate?

There are multiple reasons that might lead a person to choose migration. We often speak of these as 'push' and 'pull' factors. 'Push factors' are conditions in the country of origin, or the migrant's home country, that 'push' migrants to leave the country. For example, a person might feel unsafe in their country and, therefore, choose to leave. People might also leave because of a civil war or violent conflict, which makes daily life dangerous. The poor economic situation of a country might make it difficult to survive, resulting in people deciding to leave. Political corruption might also make life in a country dangerous and unfair. People might also migrate as a result of environmental change destroying areas where they live, leaving them destitute and homeless. People can also be pushed to migrate due to lack of access to necessary healthcare and education.

'Pull factors', on the other hand, are what attract or 'pull' a migrant to another country. Common pull factors can include economic and work opportunities and the promise of a better quality of life. People can choose to migrate due to the educational and cultural opportunities promised in other countries. The possibility of being united with family members is also a powerful pull factor.

Choosing to migrate is a big choice. It means leaving behind everything you know and much of what you hold dear. It is likely that each person who chooses to migrate does so based on a complicated mixture of 'pull' and 'push' factors.

Critical thinking: a bit of Latin!

Have you ever come across the Latin phrase, *post hoc, ergo propter hoc*?

This phrase means 'after this, therefore resulting from it'.

This phrase highlights a common logical error: just because something (B) happened after something (A), *it does not mean that A caused B.*

Warning!

When trying to understand what *caused* something, you have to be careful not to assume that something was caused by what came before it, or that because something happened alongside another event, the first caused the second. Causality is complicated. Don't fall into this trap! Looking at migration, for example, just because someone lost their job and then migrated does not mean that they migrated *because* they lost their job.

2.3 The post hoc game

To think about how complicated causation can be, and to have some fun, we're going to play a game!

First, think of a sequence of events. Then, try to argue that earlier events caused later ones. Be truthful, but also try to be funny!

Here are some examples:

'Everybody who has died has drunk water. Therefore, water kills people.'

'Most crime happens at night. Therefore, the night causes crime.'

'When you look up at the sun, you hurt your eyes. Therefore, looking up hurts your eyes'.

To complete this section: use your growing understanding of causes, and their complexities, to research why people migrate to your country.

Analysis 2
Consequences – thinking about impact

Causes are *why* something happens.
Consequences are what *effect* or impact something has when it happens.

Think of this short story: you bend down to smell a beautiful rose. A bee in the rose thinks your nose is going to hurt it, so it stings you. You yell in pain and your nose quickly swells up.

Cause of the sting: the bee *felt threatened by your nose*
Consequences of the sting: *your nose swells up and you are in pain because* the bee stung you.

Just like causes, consequences are complicated.

Most actions have more than one consequence.
Not all consequences are immediately apparent; some appear only after some delay.
Some consequences are unintended.
Moreover, like with causes, just because something happened after an action, it does not mean that it is the consequence of that action.

2.4 Critical thinking: migration

Think about what consequences migration can have. Then copy and complete the table below after discussing it with peers.

Some possible immediate consequences of migration:
Some possible delayed consequences of migration:
Some possible unintended consequences of migration:
Some possible intended consequences of migration

Year 8 Challenge 2

2.5 Policy consequences

With a group of peers discuss the consequences of one or more of the policies listed here. You can use the Table in Exercise 2.4 to guide your discussion.

Policy 1: Forbidding all immigration

Policy 2: Allowing only rich immigrants

Policy 3: Allowing free entry to all immigrants

2.6 Researching consequences

Borders have been used to stop, limit or control migration. Borders however, can have unintended consequences. Research one of the following borders and list some of its consequences. Think about the impact of the border not just for people but also for nature. Consider unintended and delayed consequences.

- U.S.–Mexico wall
- Berlin Wall (East Berlin–West Berlin, pictured)
- North Korea–South Korea Demilitarized Zone
- West Bank barrier

2.7 Responding to an argument

Read the short argument below. Do you agree with the consequences it attributes to national borders? Why or why not?

> *Could national borders cause wars? Many national borders were established not by the will of the people but by external powers during the process of colonization. The result of this has been endless strife. Borders were not put in place to reflect cultural, religious, or linguistic differences, but rather to serve the interests of the colonizing powers. These borders divided families and communities, while bringing people together who did not share the same culture, values, or beliefs. We can attribute a great part of the wars of the twentieth century to the borders imposed by colonial powers.*

To complete this section: analyse the consequences of your country's migration policies.

Evaluation
Judging sources and policies

'Evaluating' means judging or assessing to what extent something fulfils its goal. You must evaluate if the information you are receiving is giving you accurate, relevant, and valid knowledge. It is important to judge or evaluate all the information that you come across – everything from vlogs, to the news, to what your friends suggest.

Let's look more closely at what we do when we *evaluate* different things:

If we are *evaluating a source of information*, we are assessing the following:

- Whether it provides *accurate and reliable* information
    - Is it biased? Does it lie? Does it provide references for the facts that it uses so you can check them?
- Whether it provides *clear* information
    - Can we understand it? Does it cause confusion?
- Whether it is logical
    - Does it draw logical conclusions about causes and consequences?
    - Does it draw its conclusion from verifiable evidence?

If we are *evaluating an idea or proposal to solve a problem*, we can assess whether the idea:

- addresses the problem it is supposed to be looking at – or does it actually address something else?
- addresses the causes of the problem – or does it only solve the symptoms of the problem?
- provides a realistic and clear answer – or does it provide a solution that is unachievable?
- has considered all its possible consequences – be careful of unintended consequences!

2.8 Evaluating blogs

Evaluate the blogs below. Are they: clear, accurate, logical, unbiased? Do you think blogs are a good sources of factual, unbiased information about migration?

BLOG 1

Posted by TruePatriot@newworld.com

There is a truth that most people don't want to face. The truth is that immigration is a serious problem. Immigrants bring ideas that are not compatible with the countries they go to. Sources claim that 95% of immigrants don't speak the language of the country they move to or don't believe in democracy. Countries who have had no immigrants tend to be richer and more peaceful. It is worth considering whether our country would not be much better if immigration here was stopped.

BLOG 2

Posted by drjackarrow@connectstate.edu

Immigration is complicated. Research suggests that immigration leads to innovation, as migrants make the labour force more competitive, increase occupational specialisation, and increase economic productivity (see research by the University of Pennsylvania in 2016 'the effects of immigration on the US economy'). However, not everything is wonderful. Less educated populations might lose their jobs to immigrants willing to work for lower wages, and some public services can feel the strain of supporting more people. But the world would not exist without migration. So perhaps we have to be willing the take the good with the bad?

2.9 Thinking about the authors

Questions for thinking or discussion:

Does the name of the blog's author tell you anything about their viewpoint?

Do the authors provide facts or opinions?

Why do you think it is important to review who the author of a source is?

2.10 Evaluating policies

With a small group, try to evaluate a policy on immigration. Is it relevant, clear, realistic, thorough and evidence-based? You could look at President Trump's proposal for a border wall, or you could look at the EU's migration policies.

To complete this section: evaluate your country's immigration policies.

Perspectives
Migration: from the global to the personal

The impact of migration is complex. Migration can have economic, social, political, environmental, psychological, and other impacts. Migration has global, national, and personal consequences. This is often the case with topics in Global Perspectives — they are likely to impact most areas of life and they impact these at the personal, the local, the national, and the global level. You need to practise looking at these multiple effects or consequences and trying to understand how they are connected. Don't worry if you can't do it perfectly now! This is a tricky skill and takes practice. Keep practising!

2.11 Effects of migration

What are the consequences of migration? Try to think creatively and critically to create a mind map like the one below. A mind map is a 'map' where you write down different ideas and use lines, arrows, and circles to show how these ideas are connected. It is a great tool to explore your thinking and data.

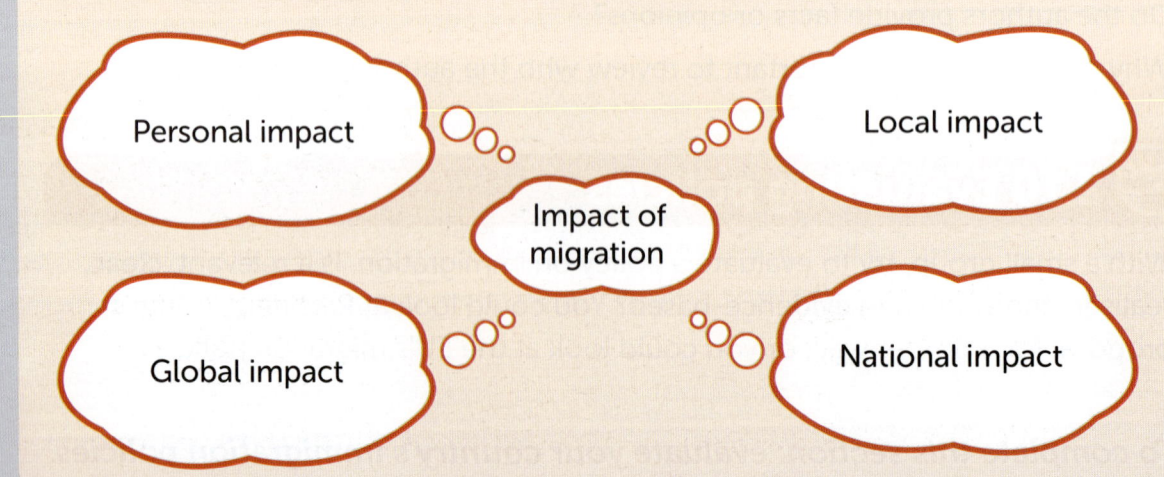

- Personal impact
- Local impact
- Global impact
- National impact

Impact of migration

2.12 Freedom and migration

Have you ever come across a border you could not cross? Examples might range from one of your siblings forbidding you from entering their room, to countries you are not allowed to enter because of your nationality.

How does facing such restrictions make you feel?

Look into migration restrictions placed on people, now or in the past, for characteristics they could not easily change, such as their nationality, religion, or ethnic group. How do you think these restrictions made people feel? What do you think migration restrictions should be based on?

2.13 Discussing migration

Discuss: what would the world be like if migration had never taken place? What if we forbid all future migration? How would that change our future?

2.14 Choosing to immigrate

What would you consider when deciding whether to emigrate to a new country? Research to find the stories of migrants who explain why they migrated. Then create a list of reasons that might lead you to emigrate.

As you think about why you would, or would not, emigrate from your country, try to think about personal, national, and global issues that might affect your choices.

Note: it is possible that you or your classmates have experienced migration. You could share your experiences with your class to help them understand what you found challenging and why. Do you think all migrants experience migration in the same way? Why or why not?

To complete this section: discuss how you think your country's migration policy should change. Write down your ideas.

Communication
Giving advice

2.15 Your advice

To complete this challenge, bring together everything you have learnt to write a letter or make a video advising the country you have been researching on how it should alter, or why it should maintain, its current immigration policies.

Try to organize your video or letter in a way that makes sense to your audience and keeps them interested. Remember to use what you learnt about the causes and consequences of immigration to support your argument.

2.16 Plan your writing

It is always a good idea to start a piece of writing by outlining, or making a quick guide, of how you will organize your argument.

What will you say first? What will you say last? To help you think about the order in which you will write your piece, you can use the suggested structure below:

Introduction: How will you catch your audience's attention? _____
Main argument: What are you arguing for? _____
(Example: Borders should be open to immigrants.)
Point 1: Make a point to support your argument. _____
(Example: Migrants can bring new ideas and talents.)
Evidence: Albert Einstein was an immigrant.
Evidence: What evidence can you provide to support your point? _____
Point 2: Make a second point to support your argument. _____
Evidence: What evidence can you provide to support your point? _____
Conclusion: Use your conclusion to remind your audience of your main argument. _____

Remember to cite your sources.

2.17 Effective communication

As you create your advice piece, remember that how you phrase your views will have an impact on who listens to you and how they listen to you. Read the following excerpts, or small parts, from other students' vlogs about immigration.

"Let me start by listing why everything our country does about immigration is bad."

"To decide what to do about immigration, one needs to start by understanding why people immigrate. So, I will start by explaining some of the reasons immigrants list for coming to this country."

"At the end, a country must choose its immigration policy thinking not only about its citizens but about the world at large."

"I want to finish by thanking the government for its attempts to create a just immigration policy. I hope to have shown how it can be improved for the benefit of our citizens and for the world at large."

"Keeping the immigration system we have is just bad."

2.18 Communication games

As you create your advice piece, always keep your audience in mind. Will they be clear about what you are trying to do? Will they be able to understand everything you have written? Will they find it engaging?

Communication is a skill that requires practice. Try the following game to expand your communication skills.

Partner drawing

Work with a partner. Take turns to describe an animal or a scene while the other person draws what you describe. Don't tell them the name of the animal. Describe the components of the scene. You will have to think about how to describe things, what words to use, what order to describe things in. Your partner will need to listen carefully, to think about what you are trying to describe.

2.19 Collaboration: constructive feedback

Listen to/read your peers' advice on immigration. Point out three things they did well and one thing they could have improved on. Make sure you tell them how they could have made it better. Does their work give you any ideas for how to improve your own piece of advice?

Taking it further

There is so much more to learn and investigate about migration. Use the suggestions below to expand your learning.

History

- Take some time to learn about the biggest migration waves in history. What caused them? What were their consequences?

Art and photography

- There is some fantastic art on the topic of immigration. Try to create your own art exploring the idea of immigration and/or borders. Remember art can take many forms. It could be a poem. It could be a song. It could be a dance. It could be a photograph. Explore an art medium that you have not tried before and think about what you want to express about migration and borders through it.

Languages

- Research how languages have been affected by migration. Would English exist without migration? Do you speak another language? Has it been affected by migration?

Politics

- Try to attend a political discussion on immigration. Listen to how people present their arguments. Do you think they are well constructed? If you feel able and prepared, contribute to the discussion.

Science

- Did you know that Einstein was an immigrant to the USA? Research to find out about other scientists who have also migrated. Why did they leave their country of birth?

Sociology

- Do you think the outbreak of Covid-19 will change immigration trends? How so?

Law

- What are the laws about immigration in your country? What is the penalty if you enter your country illegally? When were these laws established?

Philosophy

- Do you agree with the view that movement is a human right? Should humans have the right to move whenever and wherever they want?

Year 8 Challenge 2

What did you learn?

When you complete this challenge, take a moment to reflect over what you have learnt with the table below.

Skill	I get it!	I am starting to get it!	I need to review this.
Analysis: I understand what a cause is.			
Analysis: I understand what a consequence is.			
Analysis: I understand what *post hoc ergo propter hoc* means.			
Evaluation: I know how to evaluate a source.			
Perspectives: I can think about the effects of migration at the personal, national, and global level.			
Evaluation: I know how to evaluate possible solutions to a problem.			
Communication: I understand the importance of planning my argument.			
Communication: I understand that an effective communicator always thinks about their audience.			

Year 8

Challenge 3
Beliefs about food

3.1 Food

- Should some foods be made illegal?
- Should people be allowed to eat very unhealthy food?
- Should the government (local or national) be responsible for feeding its citizens?

Challenge overview

Bear Grylls is a survival expert. In his TV show he jumps off a plane into remote locations, where he must survive in extreme weather conditions and among dangerous animals, eating only what he can find in the wild. In some episodes the only things he can find are unpleasant looking insects, some of which are poisonous. Bear Grylls demonstrates how to survive eating these unappealing meals, often looking rather nauseated in the process.

However, some of what Bear Grylls eats might not be unpalatable to some of us. In some of our cultures we eat insects. Some of us eat no animal products and would struggle to eat any, even to survive. Some of us are allergic to certain foods, so eating them is not a choice.

Our food choices are affected by personal preferences, cultural values, health concerns, and local availability. Thinking about our food choices, why we eat what we eat, what we believe about food, is a fun way to learn about ourselves, our cultures, and our present and future needs as individuals, as countries, and as humans.

In this challenge, you will be thinking about food. You and a partner will be working to launch a new restaurant and need to create the perfect menu. In order to make this restaurant successful, you want to make sure you understand what people want to eat and what they should eat.

To complete your challenge, you will follow this path:

1. Research what people eat
2. Research why people eat what they do
3. Decide whom you want to research, and send out your questionnaire
4. Review the information you collect and decide on your menu
5. Create a menu that looks fantastic

Some statistics about food from https://www.one.org/us/blog/14-surprising-stats-about-global-food-consumption/:

- Poor people in developing countries often spend 60–80% of their income on food.
- 75% of the world's food is generated from only 12 plants and 5 animal species.
- 80% of a cricket can be eaten, while only 55% of a pig and 40% of a cow are edible.

What skills will you develop?

Research 1: Finding numbers
→ You will learn about quantitative and qualitative research methods. You will practice writing a survey with quantitative and qualitative questions.

Research 2: Asking why
→ You will learn about and write open questions.

Research 3: Thinking about whom to ask
→ You will learn about sampling, and choosing your research population.

Analysis: Making connections
→ You will think about the national and global impact of personal food choices.

Collaboration: Sharing tasks
→ You will learn how to break projects into steps; the challenges of sharing tasks; visual communication of ideas.

Taking it further
→ Here you will have suggestions to explore this topic further, linking it to other subjects like maths, science, arts, and more.

Research 1
Finding numbers

To start your restaurant planning, you want to find out a bit more about what the people around you like to eat and why.

"How can we find out what your friends and family like to eat?"

3.2 Types of data and methods

1. Where can you find information about what people around you eat and why?

2. Would you need primary or secondary data? (Go back to Challenge 3 in Year 7, if you need to remind yourself what these are.)

3. What research methods could you use to collect primary data?

Quantitative and qualitative data

Quantitative research focuses on things that can be *measured* – that is, information that can be put in numbers. Quantitative research collects numerical data through quantitative research methods, such as questionnaires, in which people are given rating options. These answers can then be counted.

Qualitative research is useful to help us understand people's behaviours and beliefs. Qualitative data can be collected through qualitative research methods such as interviews, focus groups, and participant observation. Qualitative data tends to be more detailed; it cannot be easily quantified or made into numbers.

To simplify, we could say that quantitative data tell you what, how much, how often, and when. Qualitative data help you to understand why or how.

Year 8 Challenge 3

Note: This is a simplification as statistical models seek to understand why by investigating relations between quantitative data. This is an area you could research further if you are interested.

To understand *what* people eat, therefore, you need quantitative data. To understand *why* people eat what they do, you need qualitative data.

A questionnaire is a set of questions used to collect quantitative data from a group of people. Every person receives the same set of questions, and questions usually have yes/no, choose and option, an ranking and option answers.

3.3 Thinking about questions

Discuss with a partner how you can ensure you ask good questions when writing a questionnaire. (If you need a reminder look at Research 2 on page 20.)

3.4 Writing a questionnaire

Create a questionnaire to find out what people in your community eat. Exchange your questions with your partner and give each other thoughtful feedback. Combine the two questionnaires to come up with your final version.

Remember: Good research questions need to be relevant, clear, focused, and not leading.

To complete this section: finish your questionnaire.

153

Research 2
Asking why

As you prepare your questionnaire, you might also want to understand **why** people eat as they do. For example, if people have a severe allergy to a certain food, you will need to make sure that they are not exposed to that food at all. If they simply don't like how an ingredient looks, then you can avoid it in their food but don't need to worry about health concerns. Therefore, why people eat as they do will affect how you create your menu.

To collect qualitative data that looks at people's reason for eating particular foods, you will need to create **open-ended questions**. These are questions that cannot be answered with a simple 'yes' or 'no'. They give respondents space to explain *why* or *how* they behave or believe as they do.

At the same time, you do not want your open-ended questions to be so vague that they confuse or overwhelm your respondents. A vague question such as, 'Why do you eat the food you do?' might give you only a vague response back, such as, 'Because I like it'. To avoid unhelpful, vague answers, your question needs to be focused and clear. You might choose to focus on some of the following areas.

→ **Health**
- People with allergies or with chronic illnesses such as diabetes need to modify their diet to ensure good health.
- People might also choose to eat a particular food to stay healthy.

→ **Environmental concerns**
- All food has a carbon footprint or environmental costs. Some people might want to eat food that creates a smaller footprint, for example, food that is local and not transported by plane.

→ **Cultural traditions**
- Some foods have a long tradition of being eaten, or avoided, in particular cultures.

Year 8 Challenge 3

→ **Personal beliefs**
- Personal beliefs, such as religion, also affect what people choose to eat, how they choose to eat it, or when they choose to eat.

3.5 Discussing perspectives on food

Discuss your food choices. What affects your food choices? Are there cultural, family, personal, health, or environmental reasons why you eat what you do?

3.6 Open-ended questions

Write some open-ended questions you could add to your questionnaire to understand why your community chooses the food they do. Share your questions with your partner and discuss which questions work, and why or why not. Then combine the questions as you think best to complete your survey.

Thinking outside the box: access to food

Do you think access to food plays a role in what people eat?

According to the Food Aid Foundation, "795 million people in the world do not have enough food to lead a healthy active life. That's about one in nine people on earth. The vast majority of the world's hungry people live in developing countries, where 12.9 percent of the population is undernourished." Yet 1.3 billion tonnes of food are wasted globally each year, one third of all food produced for human consumption, according to the Food and Agriculture Organization (FAO) of the United Nations.

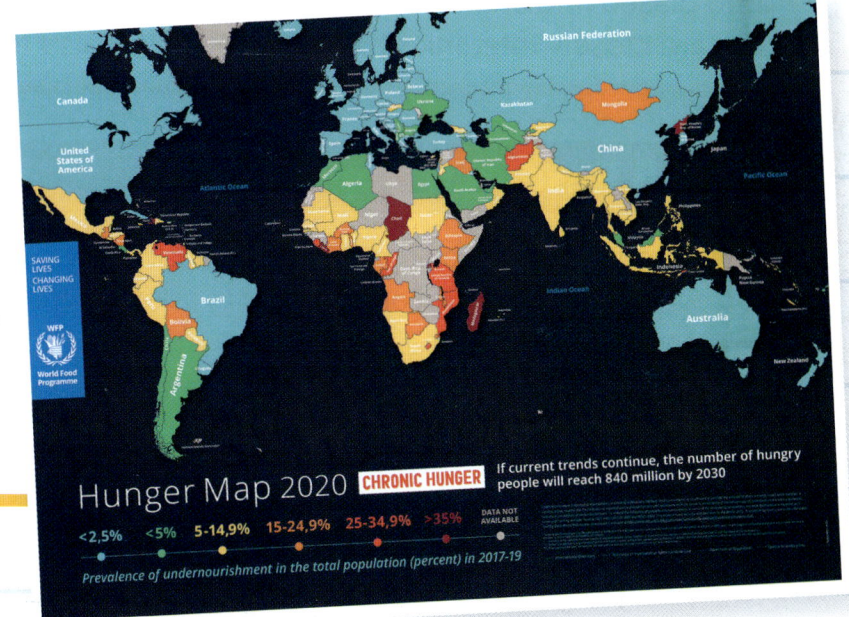

Hunger Map 2020 — CHRONIC HUNGER
If current trends continue, the number of hungry people will reach 840 million by 2030
<2.5% <5% 5-14.9% 15-24.9% 25-34.9% >35% DATA NOT AVAILABLE
Prevalence of undernourishment in the total population (percent) in 2017-19

3.7 Critical thinking: food waste

Why do you think people lack food if so much food goes to waste every year?

To complete this section: complete your questionnaire with the open-ended questions.

Research 3
Thinking about whom to ask

Whom to ask

As important as **what** you ask, is **whom** you ask.

Imagine you attend a vegan festival to try to understand why people choose to eat no meat. Or imagine you attend a medical congress on peanut allergies to discuss how to make peanut butter sandwiches. Or a hunting convention to ask about vegetarianism. At these events, it is quite likely that you will find information from only one perspective, find no information, or find biased information. What you want to find out and whom you should ask are closely interlinked. Whom you ask is also linked to where you ask.

3.8 Research population

Think about **whom** it would make sense to ask about each topic, and where you could find the population you want to ask, by matching phrases in the two columns below.

Column A	Column B
If you want to find the most popular food in your city …	… ask random people at a swimming pool.
If you want to find out how easy it is to find allergy-friendly food …	… ask people exiting a Synagogue.
If you want to understand how food choices are affected by environmental concerns …	… ask students in a Quran class.
If you want to understand how Islamic beliefs affect diet …	… ask every household in your city.
If you want to understand how Jewish beliefs affect diet …	… ask every student in your school.
	… ask members of the Allergy Sufferers Association.
	… ask random people on social media.

Year 8 Challenge 3

Samples – understanding how they work

What should you do if you want to understand what a large population likes or wants – for example, if you want to understand what everyone in your country likes to eat?

In such cases **samples** are used. These are smaller groups of people that represent the larger population.

While the mathematics of sampling is beyond the scope of this book, it is useful for you to understand the logic of sampling so you can evaluate sources that claim to present the opinion of large numbers of people. Check to see what sample they used – was it large enough to make it representative? For example, do you think you can draw conclusions about 10 million people by having your two best friends fill in a questionnaire? Is the sample likely to give you a biased perspective? For example, can a survey tell you what men and women think if only women are surveyed?

Inter-cultural communication

When conducting research, it is important to keep cultural differences in mind. You need to think about how your respondents will interpret your questions based on their culture. For example, don't assume the foods you eat are familiar to everyone in the world. This is another opportunity to use perspectives to get a better understanding of an issue.

3.9 Challenge: intercultural research

One of the challenges of intercultural research is having to translate questions. Translating is not just about exchanging one word for another, but also keeping an idea or meaning intact. Try to translate your questionnaires into another language and see how challenging this can be.

To complete this section: decide on your research population, and send your survey to them.

Analysis
Making connections

What is your favourite food? What if you were told that your choice is suddenly illegal? Would you risk a fine, or even prison, to keep eating your favourite meal?

3.10 Critical thinking: food impact

As a class, discuss these questions:

1. Do you think people should be allowed to eat whatever they want?
2. What reasons, if any, do you think are good reasons to make some foods illegal?
3. Do you think people should be forced to eat something they do not want?

Individual choices can have effects well beyond the individual. Let's try to make some connections between our food choices and their consequences at different levels.

3.11 Personal choices, global impact

Think about how your food choices can affect your body, your city, your country, and the world.

3.12 Case study: shark fin soup

Let's look at a particular case: shark fin soup.

Read the following excerpt and note the:

→ personal reasons for eating shark
→ cultural reasons for eating shark
→ personal **consequences** of eating shark
→ national **consequences** of eating shark
→ global **consequences** of eating shark.

When you think about consequences, go further and think about consequences in different areas: environmental consequences, political consequences, economic consequences, health consequences.

Shark fin soup originated in the Song dynasty in China between 960 and 1279 AD. It is believed to have considerable health benefits, although there is no scientific basis for these beliefs. In fact, because of the increase in contamination by mercury and other heavy metals through pollution, it is now thought that shark fins may actually be detrimental to health. But shark fin soup is still viewed as a luxury delicacy that is still commonly served in Asia, particularly at special occasions such as weddings.

The fins are boiled and the skin and meat are separated from the softened protein fibre. It is this fibre that is used to make the soup. The fins themselves do not actually have a great deal of taste but are used to add texture. Fins are sold dried, cooked, wet and frozen. The soup can also be bought ready-made. Demand is greatest in Asia, but there is also significant demand in the USA.

12 states in the USA have made the sale of shark fins illegal, yet you can still order shark fin soup in these states even though it is against the law. 'Finning' – removal of the fin from live sharks – was made illegal in US waters in 2000 to try to stop the decline in shark numbers.

Finning involves slicing fins off live sharks, often returning the butchered live shark to the sea. The either die of blood loss, get eaten by other predators or, because they are unable to swim without their fins and pass water over their gills, they suffocate.

Many countries don't regulate shark finning, reducing the already dangerously low global populations. So it is from these countries that countries, such as the USA, can import fins,

More than a quarter of the world's sharks, rays, and chimaeras (ghost sharks) are considered to be threatened. This is because of overfishing, partly to meet the demand for shark fin soup. In 2012, a study in the USA found DNA from eight different species of shark in soup samples. These included endangered or vulnerable species such as the scalloped hammerhead, shortfin mako and the spiny dogfish.

To complete this section: review your survey findings. Spend some time thinking about the impact the food you put on your menu might have for your country and the world. Start drafting your menu.

Collaboration
Sharing tasks

Before you finish your menu, take a moment to reflect. Look at what you have done and notice the different steps in this challenge. Recognizing and listing the steps you need to accomplish a project is an important skill. Breaking down a project into steps will help you successfully accomplish all sorts of activities: from your homework, to playing a game, to completing a fundraiser. Looking at a project as a sum of small steps makes it feel doable, less overwhelming, and helps you carefully plan what you need to do, when, and how.

3.13 Listing a project's steps

With your partner, list the steps you have taken to decide what to serve in your restaurant. Think back to how you found information, what you did with this information, what you used to make your decisions. Once you have listed your steps, try to divide these steps into research, analysis, evaluation, collaboration and communication.

3.14 Non-Global Perspective projects

Think of another project (or two) you are working on. This might be studying for exams, creating a piece of art, or working with friends to build a band. Try to break down the project into parts. Look at each of the parts and see if there are steps where you are gathering information (research), steps where you are trying to understand a problem (analysis), steps where you decide how you want to proceed (evaluation), steps where you share your ideas with others (communication), and steps where you work with your peers (collaboration).

3.15 Design your menu

Now that you have all your information, work with your partner and decide what you want to put in your menu. Will you offer exotic dishes? Fancy dishes? Simple and healthy meals? List your food and design your menu.

As you decide on what your menu will look like, think about:

- what graphics can you add to make your menu more interesting and appealing – remember you want people to eat your food!
- what text size you should use so that it can be read clearly
- whether you should use different sizes of text
- how much information can a menu have before it becomes confusing
- whether you should include facts that are interesting or relevant.

Sharing tasks

When you come together to work on a project with peers, sharing tasks is important. You need to think of ways to ensure that tasks are shared so that everyone feels involved and valued. If all group members feel respected and valued, they are more likely to put in the time and energy that the project needs. Not all tasks in a project take the same amount of time or energy, and some parts are probably more fun or more prestigious than others ... but all tasks need to be completed.

3.16 Challenge: writing about impact

Write a short paragraph for your menu discussing the impact your food might have on the environment, people's health, and the local culture.

To complete this section: complete your menu!

Taking it further

Food is such a fun area to explore! Humans are so creative with their meals, there are endless opportunities to learn with food!

Science

- You could look further into food allergies. What causes them?
- You could look further into why some foods are healthier than others. What does your body need in order to stay healthy?
- Look into the science of cooking. Why do some foods need different temperatures to cook? Does it matter if a food changes temperature quickly, or if its temperature is raised slowly?

History

- Look into the history of a specific food. For example, how did chocolate become such a popular food throughout the world? Where did chocolate originate? What about salt? What about saffron?

Literature

- Food often plays an important role in literature. Look over some of your favourite books and find scenes that discuss food. Find a book where food is central. Try to write a story where food is a key part of the plot. Or even a story that is just about food!'

Maths

- Try to figure out the carbon footprint of your diet.

Sociology

- Look into table manners. How did they develop?

Art

- There is a saying in Spanish *'La comida entra por los ojos'*, which can be translated as 'Food enters through the eyes'. It refers to how important the appearance of our food is to make us want to eat and enjoy our meals. Making beautiful food is an art. Research 'food art' and try to make your own meals into pieces of art.

Year 8 Challenge 3

What did you learn?

When you complete this challenge, take a moment to reflect over what you have learnt with the table below.

Skill	I get it!	I am starting to get it!	I need to review this.
Research: I know the difference between quantitative and qualitative research methods.			
Research: I can list some quantitative and qualitative research methods.			
Research: I understand how to write a questionnaire.			
Research: I understand what open-ended questions are for.			
Research: I understand what sampling is.			
Research: I understand why it matters to *whom* I ask questions.			
Perspectives: I understand that I need to think about cultural and language differences when looking for information.			
Perspectives and analysis: I understand how personal food choices can affect others.			
Collaboration: I can break a project into small parts; and I am beginning to understand what skills are needed to complete each part.			

Year 8

Challenge 4
Looking at the future

Imagine coming home from school one day. A robot opens your house door and greets you "Welcome home, small human. I have made you food and will now watch to ensure you practice your learning". It is your nanny robot who takes care of you instead of parents. This is the future. In this future, we have changed our diet. We now eat mostly fungus and insects. We live underground as a response to global warming, but everyone gets to go to the surface for 15 minutes a day, and 30 minutes on your birthday. What do you think of this future? Do you think it is realistic?

4.1 The future

1. When do you think this picture of life as imagined in 2000 was drawn?

2. What do you think life will be like in the 22nd century?

3. If someone who lived in 1800 came to visit our world, what do you think they would be most surprised by?

4. If you could change one thing about the future and one thing about the past, what would these be?

Electric Scrubbing

Challenge overview

In 1983 Isaac Asimov, a well-known science fiction writer, predicted that by 2019 our "... first space settlement should be on the drawing boards; and may perhaps be under actual construction ... It would be the first of many in which human beings could live by the tens of thousands, and in which they could build small societies of all kinds, lending humanity a further twist of variety."

Despite what Asimov predicted, we are not living outside planet Earth ... yet. But technology has advanced dramatically since Asimov's prediction. Perhaps we will be able to live in space in the future ... or perhaps we will be able to travel around our planet with personal propulsion jets, fuelled by ... water? What do you think our lives will be like in a century, or two?

In this challenge, you will think about where we have come from, as a human species, and where we might go. Your challenge is to work with a group of peers to create a time capsule!

To complete this challenge, you can follow this path:

1. You will think about what the aim or purpose of your time capsule should be.
2. You will spend some time thinking about what the future might be like and choose items to share with the future.
3. You will write some warnings to add to your time capsule.
4. You will write some advice to add to your time capsule.
5. You will work with your team to finish and put away your time capsule.

What skills will you develop?

Evaluation
→ You will learn what the aim of an outcome is.

Reflection
→ You will expand your critical thinking discussing what the future might be like. You will use data to make predictions and to inspire creative thinking.

Research
→ You will learn how to synthesize information.

Communication
→ You will practice being an active listener and a powerful communicator.

Communication and synthesizing
→ You will learn how to organize your arguments effectively.

Taking it further
→ Here you will have suggestions to explore this topic further, linking it to other subjects like maths, science, arts, and more.

Evaluation
Proposing a solution

In all your Global Perspectives Challenges you have created something: a report, a poster, a booklet, a video, and more. These are your *outcomes*. They are your creations at the end of your challenges. Each outcome demonstrates some of the skills you have learnt and uses some of the information you have gathered during a challenge. Importantly, in Global Perspectives, each outcome should be designed to help improve the issue you are researching. How will it improve the issue? This depends on the purpose or *aim* you choose. Your outcome needs to have an aim. There are many possible aims for your outcomes including:

- To share information with others (to educate)
- To help a cause through fundraising
- To help a cause by recruiting volunteers
- To create a community event such as a park clean up
- To help change people's minds in a particular way (to campaign)
- To create plans for future improvements
- To help stop a particular activity
- To encourage others

In this challenge, your outcome will be a time capsule. This capsule will contain information for people in the future. The future can be next year, or 50–1000 years from now. You now need to decide what the purpose of your time capsule will be. Do you want to educate people in the future about how our present might create problems for them? Do you want to let them know what we thought the future would be like and why? Do you want to offer a solution for a problem they might have? Do you want to encourage them to stop doing something? Do you want to encourage them to do something – such as getting together to tell stories or clean up their community?

Year 8 Challenge 4

4.2 Discussing your aim

Take some time to discuss the aim of your time capsule. You might find this quite challenging. It requires creativity to come up with new ideas. It also requires courage to try something new! Are some aims more urgent than others? Do you need to start by educating others about a problem, for example? Are some aims simply too ambitious to be realistic?

Think about:

- how you will communicate your purpose clearly to your audience
- how you will physically build a capsule. Where will you leave it for future people to find? (One option is to leave it in your school, for future students of this class to read!).

To complete this section: decide on an aim for your time capsule.

Reflection
Get creative

4.3 Changing the future

To get your creativity flowing, start by discussing with a group of friends what you would most like to change in the future. Be creative. Consider different aspects of our life that might change in the future: what will our houses look like in the future? How might we communicate in the future? What will happen to travel? Will our diets change? Will fashion change? Will there still be countries in the future?

- Try to think of as many different areas that might change – from politics, to economics, to culture.

- Practise active listening. Listen to what your classmates say and try to build on their ideas. Try to inspire each other. Actively listening means carefully listening to your peers so you can react to what they share, ask thoughtful questions, learn from them, and make them feel heard. It does not mean just listening carefully so you know when it is your turn to speak.

Thinking about the future is fun. It is also essential for the future of all humanity. Our actions and behaviour now will decide the type of world our children and grandchildren will be living in and the challenges they will face.

To think creatively about the future, literature can provide fantastic inspiration.

Year 8 Challenge 4

4.4 Flash fiction

Read the pieces of flash fiction below. Flash fiction stories are stories that are extremely short: as short as five words! See if you agree with the predictions that these stories make. Do they have any grains of truth?

> It was 2440. Another year, a new allocation of water. To make it last the year, I gently pour it into my water-recycler machine. Make sure not a drop is lost. The machine cost me *everything* my family left me, but it was worth it. Bargaining or gambling for water was one thing I did not have to do. If only the machine did not break down. If only I could ensure electricity would not stop. Maybe I will survive to be as old as 30!

> It was 2440. My life was pretty much like yours in 2020, from what I have read. The difference is that we are now all connected to the computer. Not just through the Internet like in your time. Now our thoughts are all joined in the cloud. We are all one. No worries about misunderstandings. And now the robots do the messy work. Think well or the robots get you.

4.5 Writing about the future

Try your hand at writing a flash fiction story about the future. Concentrate on what you think will be the most striking aspect – whether positive or negative – of the future. Try to get your readers to think about that aspect by showing them what you think will happen, rather than by telling them.

4.6 Predicting the future

Try a different approach to thinking about the future. Read some recent science news. Try to think about how recent scientific discoveries, advances, or debates might affect the future. For example, do you think our advances in science might allow humans to choose to have extra organs in the future? What if athletes in the future could have three lungs to make them more competitive?

To complete this section: with your group choose a some objects that you do not think will exist in the future, and which are important to your present. Add them to the time capsule.

169

Research: Synthesizing information

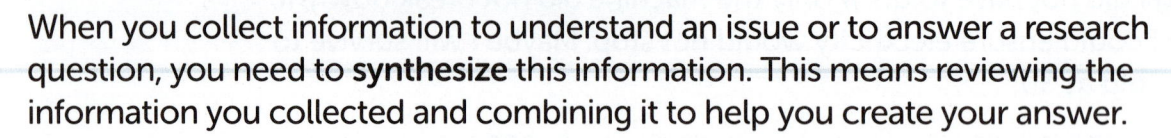

When you collect information to understand an issue or to answer a research question, you need to **synthesize** this information. This means reviewing the information you collected and combining it to help you create your answer.

Collecting information is like going out to an apple orchard and collecting apples. You will get some that are riper than others (more relevant), some that are rotten (false information, unreliable sources), and some excellent ones (relevant, useful information). Synthesizing information is going through the apples, getting rid of the bad ones, or parts that are rotten, and then making something with these apples – perhaps a delicious apple pie! Synthesizing goes beyond collecting: it includes reviewing, selecting, and using the material to build something new.

Synthesizing treasure hunt

Think of synthesizing as a treasure hunt. Your goal is to put together a magnificent piece of jewellery. To create this piece, you need to search for precious jewels and metals in various areas – this is your researching and collecting of information. However, it is not enough to find these treasures, you also need to put them together to create something magnificent. Otherwise you will just have a pile of things – not a piece of jewellery.

4.7 Synthesize information

Opposite is a collection of predictions of what 2030 will be like. Use these predictions to answer the question: what might be the most serious problem of 2030? Go through the predictions and collect anything that you think will help you to answer the question – this is you collecting gold nuggets. Once you have collected the nuggets, put them together to answer the question – this is you synthesizing the information you have collected.

Prediction 1

It is predicted that the world's population could reach an amazing 9 billion people by 2030 – almost triple the population of 1960 and double the population of 1980. The greatest increases will be in the poorest regions of India, South America and Africa. Africa's population is expected to double to 2.4 billion people by 2050. India is expected to overtake China as the country with the highest population by 2027.

Prediction 2

More than 70 billion animals are killed each year for food. China alone consumed 88 million tons of meat in 2017. According to the United Nations, meat and dairy consumption is responsible for almost 15 percent of global greenhouse gas emissions, and land for grazing and producing crops for animal feed take up 80 percent all agricultural land. Many people feel that the increase in production of plant- and cell-based meat gives hope for the future.

Prediction 3

The staggering technological advance in recent years has, most people would say, improved people's lives. Automation continues to increase its influence on our economy and society, including reducing employment. Most new jobs are contract work and recent college graduates find it difficult to find work, in addition to starting their working life heavily in debt. Children are experiencing record rates of depression and loneliness. Many feel that this is because of the lack of face-to-face interaction caused by the increased use of smartphones and social media.

Prediction 4

We all take advantage of the increased data activity in our daily lives. The electricity consumption of data centres is enormous and increasing – it may account for 10 percent of all electricity usage by 2030 and produce five times the CO_2 emissions of all air travel. It is not only creating the electricity which will pollute our planet – cooling the data centres will warm the atmosphere, and the disposable minerals in ever-cheaper electronics will pollute the groundwater.

To complete this section: research what scientists think the future might be like. Synthesize your research and the information in this section to write a short note warning your audience about some of the problems they might face.

Communication
Ordering your argument

As you discuss your ideas, it is important to put your arguments in order so that your audience can understand you. You could think of this a bit like coding – as you introduce code into a robot, the order in which you introduce commands is just as important as the commands you use! If you tell a robot to: Turn Left, Turn Off, Step 2 … you will be left with a robot facing left and turned off!

4.8 Ordering your argument

Read the following argument. See if it makes sense to you. Try to reorganize the order of the sentences to help it make sense.

> Technology allows us to overcome new diseases, travel faster, communicate better. It is technology that has allowed us to conquer so many diseases. The future is driven by technology. Don't be afraid of technology, it is our road to the future. It is technology that has allowed us to travel across oceans and even into space. The most important investment we can make for our future, therefore, is in developing more technology. It is technology that allows us to communicate with family and friends miles away, and to learn about and form connections with people from distant lands.

As you reorganize this paragraph, you will find that, for an argument to make sense, it needs to follow a logical order:

1. First, you need to clearly explain what your point, or main argument, is.

2. Second, you need to provide evidence; these are the examples, data, or information you use to support your position.

3. Third, you need to explain what the evidence shows. Don't just list facts and expect your reader to understand why these data are important or relevant.

Year 8 Challenge 4

4.9 Create a puzzle

Choose one of the questions below and write a one-paragraph response. Make sure that you follow the order suggested in Exercise 4.8: Argument, Evidence, Explanation. Write each of these parts on a separate piece of paper, different sticky notes, or on a piece of paper that you can cut up. Then have a partner try to reconstruct your puzzle.

- Is sustainability key for the future? Why or Why not?
- Is equality between men and women important for the future? Why or why not?
- Are plants and animals likely to change in the future? If so, how?

Here is an example of a paragraph organized in a logical way.

> Yes, I think sustainability is key for the future.
>
> Sustainability means using things in a way that leaves them for the future, rather than using them all up.
>
> If we keep using nature as we do now, in the future there will be no clean water, most fish and animals will be dead, and the world will be too hot for most to survive.
>
> So, if we want to have a future, if we want to survive, we need to use nature only in a sustainable way.

4.10 Parts of an argument

Read the short paragraph below. Point out its main argument, its evidence, and its explanations.

> Artificial intelligence will play a key role for humanity in the future. We have created robots that can be used in nurseries and nursing homes (such as Pepper and Zora Bots). Robots can participate in activities of caring and become a part of our family. As we create even better technology, robots will participate more in our society, perhaps one day replacing police and even teachers.

To complete this section: write another note for your time capsule. This time write about your favourite things about the present. Make sure to order your argument logically.

Communication and synthesizing

Synthesizing arguments is an important skill. You will use your ability to synthesize in all areas of your life. Try the following exercises to practice this skill.

4.11 Synthesizing – practise

Work with your team. Take turns fulfilling the role of **synthesizer**. Other members of the group discuss one of the questions below. Each member should try to present a different point of view. The role of the synthesizer is to listen carefully, summarize everyone's contribution, and synthesize it into something new. **Note:** the synthesizer does not need to repeat what everyone said. Instead they should use what others said to create a new, stronger argument.

Questions:

1. Will technology save the human race?
2. Will the future be filled with robots?
3. Will the future require more or less education?
4. What will be the most important jobs in the future?

Active listening

To synthesize the arguments of others you need to *listen actively*. This means listening to understand what the other person is saying – what their argument or position is – and *how* they are saying it (how they are supporting their argument). This is different from just waiting quietly until it is your turn to speak. You need to concentrate to make sure you are understanding what the other person is saying. You need to make the other person feel heard so they share their ideas with you as best they can. You might need to ask questions to clarify certain points. Active listening, in short, is active!

You can also be an *active reader*. Again, rather than passively going through words, active readers are actively trying to make sense of what they read. Active reading includes making notes about what you understood, and writing questions you want to research further.

4.12 Active listening

Work with a partner. Have your partner tell you what they are most hopeful or worried about in the future. Try these tips to be an active listener:

- Lean toward the speaker – but be polite and respect personal space.
- Nod when you understand what they are saying.
- Look at the speaker.
- When the speaker finishes, briefly summarize what they said to you to make sure you understood.
- Ask questions about unclear points, or remark on what you found particularly interesting.

Thinking about your listeners

When you communicate you have two jobs: to be an active listener and to be a thoughtful speaker. Thoughtful speakers think about their audience! How can you make what you say (or write) as clear as possible to your audience? How can you help others to understand you?

4.13 Being a good communicator

Which of these ideas might help good communication? Can you add other ideas to the list?

1. Stating your point at least five times.
2. Explaining the meaning of complicated, specialist, or new terminology.
3. Speaking as fast as possible.
4. Jumping up and down as you speak.
5. Using punctuation well.
6. Using! Lots!! Of exclamation marks!!!!!
7. imho – using text speak.
8. Numbering your arguments.
9. Summarizing your arguments in a memorable conclusion.
10. Using fun, interesting examples.
11. Speaking in a monotone.
12. Writing all your sentences with the same number of words.

4.14 Being a bad communicator

Just for fun: try to give a short (1 minute) speech as poorly as possible. Think about what you are doing to be a terrible communicator!

To complete this section: complete your time capsule. Remember what its aim is. How can you make that aim clear to your audience in the future? Remember to think of your audience! Add any other notes/objects your group think are necessary for your time capsule to fulfil its mission and seal it!

Taking it further

The future is full of possibilities. Take some time to expand your thinking about the future with the suggestions below.

AI (Artificial Intelligence)

- Do you think the future will be led by AI? If so, what will AI be like?

Futurism

- Look into the *Future of Humanity Institute*. This is an organization that researches what the future might be like. If you find anything particularly interesting in their website, perhaps you could send them a letter to thank them for inspiring you, or to let them know what you think.

Geography

- One of our concerns about the future is that where we can live as humans is likely to be quite different from the present. Look into what geographical changes we might see in our future.

Science

- Look into how our environment might change in the future. Can you come up with a list of things you as an individual can do to help our environmental crisis? Can you come up with a list of actions needed by governments or corporations? Draft a letter to a government or corporation stating your views of what they should do and why. State your argument logically: state your argument, then explain your reasons and provide evidence to support your reasons.

Literature

- Literature is full of fascinating descriptions of the future. Some are more optimistic than others. Come up with a list of books or stories about the future with your teacher, or an English teacher, and read a couple of them.

Psychology

- How do you think our psychology as humans might change in the future? Do you think we have changed in the last 100 years?

Foreign languages

- What languages do you think we will speak in the future? Do you think any of our current languages will disappear?

Philosophy

- Do you think humans will still be humans if we are connected to computers in the future?

IT

- Look into developments being made in linking humans to technology. This might include chips we can have implanted to connect us to our bank. Or perhaps machines that help us perform better athletically. Would you connect yourself to the Internet so you can immediately access any information you want through your brain?

What did you learn?

When you complete this challenge, take a moment to reflect over what you have learnt with the table below.

Skill	I get it!	I am starting to get it!	I need to review this.
Analysis: I understand what synthesizing is.			
Communication: I know how to be an active listener.			
Communication: I know how to be a thoughtful communicator.			
Communication: I know how to order my arguments effectively.			
Analysis: I understand what an outcome is.			
Analysis: I understand what an aim is and why outcomes need aims.			

Year 8

Challenge 5
Trade and aid

5.1 Foreign aid

1. Do you think countries have an obligation to help each other?
2. Should every person donate a certain amount to fund international aid?
3. Should international aid be used to buy weapons?

"I don't mind helping you but my own citizens have problems, shouldn't we help our own first?"

"But you know there will be other earthquakes, why should we have to help you every time the earth shakes?"

"Why don't we just trade instead of giving you money?"

"My country needs aid to help us rebuild after the last earthquake."

Challenge overview

International aid is a controversial topic. This means that people hold strong and opposing views on whether it is good.

Some people argue that international aid should be given. Those who hold this view might argue that there is a moral obligation to help others, or that poverty in other countries affects us all through migration and crime. Thus, by helping others we help ourselves. Or they might argue that we all need help at some point.

On the other hand, there are people who argue that international aid is worse than useless. They argue that international aid helps corrupt governments stay in power. Or that those who receive aid get used to being helped rather than helping themselves. Or that countries have a responsibility to their own citizens, not to those outside their borders.

As you can see, there are many arguments for and against international aid. In this challenge, you will be working with a team to make a documentary about foreign aid and trade. By the end of the challenge you can either create a mini-documentary or a vision-board of what your documentary would look like. Your job, as a documentary maker, is to create a captivating story that helps people understand why aid is complicated and helps them decide what should be done.

To complete this challenge, you will:

1. Collect information about the dangers and benefits of aid.
2. Collect information about trade as an option in aid.
3. Choose your documentary's aim and structure.
4. Work with your team to create a documentary vision board.
5. Reflect on what you learnt.

What skills will you develop?

Analysis: The maze of foreign aid
→ You will practise thinking about counter-arguments.

Evaluation: Trade and aid
→ You will learn about trade and fair trade and evaluate these as solutions to foreign aid troubles.

Communication: Comics and other ways of showing information
→ You will learn about visual forms of communication, and review the importance of having a central research question.

Collaboration: Creating as a team
→ You will learn some strategies to help collaboration.

Reflection: You as a consumer and as a team member
→ You will spend some time thinking about what you have learned, and how you worked in a team.

Taking it further
→ Here you will have suggestions to explore this topic further, linking it to other subjects like maths, science, arts, and more.

Analysis
The maze of foreign aid

When looking at foreign aid we could start with the question:

Why is foreign aid so controversial?

> **⚠ Stop**
>
> Take some time to research this question. What answers do you find? Try to take good (clear and concise) notes on your findings. Remember to keep track of your sources.

As you research answers to this question, you will find a number of arguments for and against foreign aid.

Multiple perspectives

Finding arguments on different sides of an issue is a great opportunity to understand an issue from different perspectives. Try to understand the position of people who argue against foreign aid. Are they people who are likely to be helped by foreign aid or are they people who are likely to be asked to donate to foreign aid, for example? Are they in a particular country? What is the logic of their argument? What is their evidence?

The more you understand *why* someone holds the position they do, the better placed you are to decide if you agree or not. Even if you do not agree with a particular position, the better you understand it, the better prepared you are to create arguments against it and to find relevant information. Thus, it is always a good idea to start by trying to understand all sides of an issue.

> **📝 5.2 Researching the other side**
>
> Do you think foreign aid should be given out or not? Choose the side you *disagree* with the most and try to understand as much as you can about it.

Year 8 Challenge 5

> **⚠ Stop**
> Take a moment to think about why it is helpful to present arguments against your position.

Presenting counterarguments

Whatever you are arguing, you should always present and answer arguments that oppose your position.

5.3 Counterarguments

Why would you present arguments against your position? Look at the list below and decide which reasons you agree with.

- Presenting counterarguments shows that you are well informed.
- Presenting counterarguments shows that you are confused.
- Presenting counterarguments gives you the opportunity to show why they are wrong.
- Presenting counterarguments confuses those who oppose you.

How to present counterarguments

When discussing counterarguments you can make use of transitional phrases that highlight the two sides of the debate. For example, you could state:

- *On the one hand, xyz* argues that … *On the other hand, we can see that* …
- *While xyz* argues that, *abc* demonstrates that …
- *Although xyz* believes that, evidence shows that …

5.4 Transitional phrases

Think of other transitional words or phrases to introduce two sides of an argument.

5.5 Listing positives and negatives

List some positives and negatives of foreign aid. Or, for more fun, try to make a maze: from poverty to wellbeing. The positives are bridges to help you cross the maze, the negatives are stumbling blocks that keep a country stuck in poverty.

You could put some of these in your maze:
- Provide education
- Enrich corrupt officials
- Support economic alliances
- Help build roads
- Help reconstruction after a natural disaster

To complete this section: create a list of arguments for and against foreign aid. Work with your team to decide how you could present these in a documentary.

181

Evaluation
Trade and aid

Imagine that, as part of your documentary, you interview a businessperson who presents you with the argument below. Your job for the documentary is to evaluate this argument, helping your viewers understand its strengths and weaknesses.

"I think a strong argument against aid is that it does not encourage the needy to find solutions for their poverty. Rather they become dependent on aid and cannot survive without it.

What if rather than giving countries hand-outs, we help them to trade? They can sell the goods they have to gain money. Entering into trade will encourage people in the poorer country to become creative, to take risks and start new businesses. This is exactly what a country needs to become wealthier.

I met a man once who survived only from money an NGO gave him and argued that aid was necessary and important. He was rather grumpy and inarticulate. I think this is what aid does to people."

5.6 Judging evidence

Work with your team to decide what valid points the businessperson makes.

- Does the argument present valid evidence?
- Is the argument logical?

Then list what points you think are weak.

- Does the argument rely on assumptions?
- Does the argument rely on criticizing individuals rather than ideas? This is called an *ad hominem* logical fallacy, where the person making an argument tries to win by attacking the character of their opponent.
- Does the argument use simplifications?

If you could meet the person who made this argument, what follow up questions would you ask?

Multiple perspectives – a class discussion

One of the challenges of aid and trade is that they don't affect all the population of a country in the same way. Think about how getting involved in trade might be different for:

- elderly populations vs. young populations
- healthy vs. sick populations
- women vs. men
- people in different regions of a country.

Could trade make one sector of a country better off and other sectors worse off? Could aid help some parts of a country but not others?

Fairtrade

Fairtrade is an attempt to make trade better and fairer for the poorest. The Fairtrade Foundation is a charity that grants Fairtrade certification to products that meet its standards. Fairtrade standards include product price, environmental protection, workers' safety and gender balance.

> "For most products sold under Fairtrade terms, a minimum price is set to protect Fairtrade farmers and producers. An additional Fairtrade Premium is paid on top of this, which producers invest democratically in their businesses or communities, providing essentials from fertiliser and farm equipment to water pumps, schools and health clinics."

5.7 Fair Trade

Spend some time researching Fairtrade so you can add it to your documentary. Evaluate the idea of Fairtrade. Think about:

- Does Fairtrade address the *causes* of the problem?
- Could Fairtrade have any unintended consequences?
- Would you buy Fairtrade products?
- Is Fair Trade based on evidence?

To complete this section: summarize what you have learnt about trade and Fairtrade and discuss.

Communication
Comics and other ways of showing information

Comics can be a great way to make information accessible and interesting. Understanding comics, however, requires that you think creatively and critically about a topic.

5.8 Cartoons

Some say that 'a picture is worth a thousand words'. See if you can come up with some words to explain the following cartoons.

What do you think they are trying to show? Discuss them in a group.

"We know you're thirsty, but how about we build you a nice building first?"

5.9 Drawing cartoons

As a group try to create some cartoons about foreign aid. What argument do you want to make? Do you have a team member who is particularly good at drawing? Can other team members research and add text?

Year 8 Challenge 5

Making a point

If you look over the comics in this section again, you will see that each of them makes a point. The point could be to show the power of international aid, or to show a way in which aid can fail. The aim can be to question the generosity of aid donors, or to highlight why trade can fail. A comic without a clear aim, or purpose, will be unsuccessful ... and not very interesting!

5.10 Challenge: analysing cartoons

Find cartoons about issues you are interested in and share them with your team. Discuss what they mean and what question they are asking.

Your documentary, the outcome of this challenge, also needs to ask a question. Without a central question, your documentary will have no point. What question will your documentary ask?

5.11 Planning a documentary

As a team discuss what you want your documentary's question to be. Choices could include:

- Should foreign aid be given to countries that oppress their population?
- Should foreign aid be stopped?
- Who does foreign aid help?
- Is Fairtrade fair?

As you discuss, make sure to:

- give everyone the opportunity to speak; you could ensure this by going around the group in order, so everyone has a turn. You could give everyone a set time to make their point so no one can speak for too long.
- remember that disagreements are not a bad thing. Disagreements can produce new understanding as people explain their position and learn from each other. If there is disagreement in your group, make sure discussion remains polite and respectful. Remember that if someone disagrees with your ideas it does not mean that they disagree with you as a person. Don't take another person's disagreement personally.

To complete this section: choose your documentary's main question.

Collaboration
Creating as a team

You will now be putting your documentary together with your team. You will do this through a 'vision board'. There are many choices to make. For example, you will need to decide on your documentary's structure, the sources of your information, what visuals and sounds you will use, and how you will ensure that you fairly discuss both sides of the issue to present an unbiased work.

5.12 Creating a vision board

Work with your team to create a vision board of what your documentary will look like. On a large piece of paper draw out the structure of your documentary. Put pictures or notes of what different parts will cover. Make notes of any music, cartoons, book quotes, or anything else you want to use. Try to make this board as inspiring as possible. You want others to be able to 'see' your vision when they look at this board.

As you work with your team, you might find it challenging to get everyone's input into the board, or you might find that only a couple of people are doing most of the work. Some of the following activities might help to get everyone *collaborating* together.

Collaboration tickets

Everyone starts with a number of project tickets (two or three). To add an element to the vision board each member has to 'pay in' a project ticket. Every idea costs one ticket. Everyone has to pay in their tickets before any final decisions are made and once you are out of tickets ... you are out!

Clapping for a common vision

To ensure a project is successful it is important to make sure everyone in the team shares the same vision about where the project should go.

Try this: have the team sit down, close their eyes, and imagine the documentary. Then, with your eyes closed, have everyone describe what they imagined (you can go around clockwise in a circle, so everyone knows when to speak). When a teammate shares something that you find exciting and want to do, clap. Spend some time sharing until you are all clapping.

Sharing in order

To ensure everyone's ideas get heard, come up with different orders in which people get to speak. Use a different system every time you are discussing so different people get to speak first each time.

- Speak in alphabetical order by first name.
- Speak in the order of your birth month.
- Speak in the order of your birth date.

The thank you board

Kind words go a long way! On a separate piece of paper make it a habit to write or draw about the good things your teammates do or the good ideas they had. You could stop your work every 30 minutes or so to take a 5-minute (no longer!) 'happy writing time' on this board. As you think about what is going well and as team members feel appreciated, everyone is more likely to work harder and better.

5.13 Reviewing your documentary

Look at the vision board you have put together. Do you think it fairly represents both sides of the issues you are discussing? Try having everyone in your team give their views on the fairness of your documentary.

5.14 Feedback techniques

Walk around your class looking at the vision boards of other students.

Think of yourself, first, as an art critic and each board as a piece of art. Find what is interesting about it, what is beautiful about it. Then think of yourself as a journalist and find what question you think each board tried to answer. Do you think it provides clear answers? Are the answers one-sided?

To complete this section: complete your documentary vision board and, if you are up to the extra challenge, take it further and make a mini-documentary.

Reflection

You as a consumer and as a team member

Take some time to think about what you have learnt in this section. With your teacher's guidance, choose a couple of the exercises below to reflect on what you have learnt about foreign aid and trade and about working in a team.

5.15 Being a team member

Working in a team is fun and is also hard work. Think about your experiences researching and creating a documentary vision board with your team members. What did you learn about yourself? You can start by choosing true or false for each statement below.

- I like to take control of the group.
- I'd rather sit back and let other people decide what to do.
- I ask questions when I don't understand something.
- Sometimes I pretend I understand even if I don't.
- I can explain my ideas to the team clearly.
- I sometimes struggle to voice my ideas or to explain them.

5.16 SWOT

Take a piece of paper and divide it into four. On each square, write one of these letters: S, W, O, T

S is for Strengths: write about your strengths. For example: Are you an active listener who inspires others to share? Are you good at inspiring others with new ideas?	**W is for Weaknesses**: write about areas you need to get better at. For example: Are you afraid of discussing problems? Do you sometimes let others do the work?
O is for Opportunities: write about the opportunities working as a team gives you. For example: You can learn from others. You can try out ideas that are too hard on your own.	**T is for Threats**: write about what can keep you from being a good team member: Is shyness or embarrassment keeping you from sharing your ideas? Is fear of failing making you take over too much of the work?

5.17 Your views on foreign aid

Did your views on foreign aid change as you worked on this challenge? If so, how? If they did not change, why not? Did they stay the same because you did not encounter any new information, or because the information you found supported the views you already had?

5.18 Your country's needs

If you were given 1000 million dollars of foreign aid for your country, what would you do with it? Would you, for example, give everyone in your country an equal share of the money? Or would you give most of the money to a specific area, such as education or fishermen, or to a particular population, such as people who suffer from cancer? Create a list of your country's needs; rank them by what is most urgent and why.

5.19 Your role as a consumer

In this challenge you learnt about Fairtrade. Fairtrade products carry a clear label. Every time you shop you can choose to support Fairtrade by buying products with this label. There are also labels to show that a product is organic, that a product is Rainforest Alliance Certified™, and that a product has carbon footprint certification. Find out about these other certifications, then discuss the following questions with a partner:

- Do you or your family look for any of these labels when you shop? Why or why not?

- Do you think it is your job as a consumer to think about how what you buy affects others and affects our world?

- If you found out that something you buy and love was hurting people or the environment, would you stop buying it?

- Do some research on how the things you consume are made. Do the people that make them get paid a fair wage? Is the environment hurt in the production process?

Taking it further

Foreign aid and trade open the door for you to learn so much more about history, economics, politics and more. Use the suggestions below to expand your learning.

Politics

- Find out how much your country gives or receives in foreign aid. Do you think this money is well spent?

History

- Look into the history of foreign aid. Can aid be used as a political tool? You could investigate the Marshall Plan.

Maths

- Create a graph of the sums of foreign aid given out for different purposes. Or graph how the quantities of foreign aid have changed in the last century.

Economics

- Look into arguments that support free trade. Do you agree with the view that free trade is the best form of foreign aid?

Philosophy

- Do you think we have a moral duty to help those who need it? Is foreign aid a way of helping or a strategy to advance the power of the rich?

Writing

- Write a report on an example of foreign aid: what was it used for? Who did it affect? Did it have all positive effects?

What did you learn?

When you complete this challenge, take a moment to reflect over what you have learnt with the table below.

Skill	I get it!	I am starting to get it!	I need to review this.
Analysis: I understand what a counterargument is.			
Evaluation: I know how to evaluate arguments.			
Evaluation: I understand what *ad hominem* is.			
Collaboration: I have learnt strategies to help me in group work.			
Collaboration: I have learnt more about myself as a team member – what I do well and what I can do to improve.			
Communication: I understand how images and comics can be used to communicate ideas.			
Collaboration: I have learned techniques to give feedback constructively and effectively.			

Challenge 6 Sustainability

Year 8

6.1 Sustainability

What is more important – to be wealthy or to have a healthy environment?

Who should decide how we use the environment?

Should people who pollute be put in jail?

Some statistics on sustainability:

The average beef hamburger takes 2400 liters of water to produce.

In 2016, the world's cities generated 2.01 billion tonnes of solid waste, amounting to a footprint of 0.74 kilograms per person per day.

An estimated five trillion plastic bags are used worldwide each year.

Globally only 9% of plastic ever produced has been recycled, whilst 79% can now be found in landfills, dumps or the environment and 12% has been incinerated.

An estimated 7 million people die every year from air pollution, with almost 90 percent of deaths occurring in countries of low and middle incomes.

Source: https://sumas.ch/sustainability-statistics

Challenge overview

For the past several centuries, a lot of humanity has used natural resources with little concern of these running out. It is only recently that we have begun to understand that if we use up the resources in our planet, that if we pollute our environment, we will run out of what we need to survive. We have begun to understand that we must live in a way that is *sustainable*. This means we need to live in a way that allows nature to replenish what we use. We need to live in a way that does not destroy the environment we enjoy.

We must live as polite guests in our wondrous planet Earth.

There have always been cultures and groups of people who have tried to live in a respectful relation with nature. There are cultures who see themselves as protectors of our environment, rather than as its users. There are cultures that see humans as dependent on the goodwill of our environment, there are cultures that see the environment as the holder of spirits that must be respected and paid tribute to. On the other hand, there are cultural views that hold humans as above the rest of nature, which see nature as a means for human advancement. As you can see, there are multiple perspectives on what nature is and how we should relate to it.

Science has shown us that our environment is in trouble and that we need to change how we relate to nature if we want to save it, and save ourselves. However, there is still a lot of misunderstanding about what we can do to live in a more sustainable way. In this challenge you will learn, and help others learn, how we can live more sustainably. To complete this challenge, you need to create a treasure hunt that others in your school can participate in. As they complete the hunt, students will learn about our environment and sustainability, with each clue guiding them to knowledge about our environment.

To complete this challenge, you will:

1. Create a plan and a timeline for your treasure hunt.
2. Start to think about the questions and images you want to use in your treasure hunt.
3. Find information for your treasure hunt.
4. Think about how you will evaluate if your treasure hunt is a success. Plan how you will let people know about the treasure hunt.
5. Conduct your treasure hunt and enjoy!

What skills will you develop?

Collaboration: Working as a group
→ You will discuss what a team needs to successfully complete a project.

Communication
→ You will practise focusing on your audience and will look at the power, and dangers, of visual communications, reviewing how to evaluate sources for biases.

Research: Sustainability
→ You will learn about vested interests and reflect on the information you find.

Evaluating your outcome
→ You will learn strategies to judge if you were successful or not.

Communication: Plan to action
→ You will learn to share information in a clear and understandable way.

Taking it further
→ Here you will have suggestions to explore this topic further, linking it to other subjects like maths, science, arts, and more.

Collaboration
Working as a group

You will be working in groups to create your 'Sustainability Treasure Hunt'. In order to make a team project work well, you need a few essential ingredients.

6.2 Ingredients for teamwork

Read the short story below. What do you think this group needs in order to get out of the woods?

Five young people find themselves in some ancient woods. They look around. Every side is filled with huge trees. There seems to be a small path heading to the South ... or is it the East? And maybe another one in the opposite direction. The young people look at each other, confused. Are they supposed to go someplace?

One of them yells, 'Let's follow the path. Now!'

Another one yells back, 'No! That is stupid. It was probably made by a bear, I don't want to be eaten!'

'You are both silly!' screams a third person, 'We need to stay here until someone else comes.'

Time passes, a couple of them leave to follow the path. A young person sits reading a comic book. Another one cries, scared, with a friend trying to console him.

The story above shows you a group that has failed in every way. Some of its members are scared. Others might be lost or hurt. They are unlikely to get out of the woods. They are not even sure if they are supposed to get out of the woods! What does a group need to succeed?

Stop

Before you read the list on the next page, can you come up with a list of what a group needs to succeed?

To succeed a group must have:

1. **Respect:** nothing will end a project as quickly as people within the team feeling hurt or disrespected. Team members need to feel able to share their ideas without fear of others making fun of them or ignoring them. A successful team will demonstrate respect by how team members speak and listen to each other. Can you see where respect was lacking in the story above?

2. **A plan:** to get anywhere a group needs to know where it needs to go and how. You cannot get out of the woods if you don't know you are supposed to get out. You need a goal and you need a map! If there is disagreement about where you are going within the group, you might use up all your time arguing or end up going in two different directions. Thus, a clear, agreed upon, plan is necessary.

3. **A timeline:** there is always a temptation to leave things until later – or tomorrow – and before you know it, it is too late to get anything done! Be careful. Start a project by creating a timeline – a plan which states when you will get each part done by. Stick to the timeline and give yourself extra time at the end for unexpected problems and to fix any mistakes.

6.3 Making a plan

With your classmates, establish:

Your goal – what do you want your treasure hunt to be like? What will the purpose of the treasure hunt be?

Your plan – how will you make the treasure hunt happen? Who will do what?

Your timeline – when will each person do what?

How to establish a goal, a plan, and a timeline

- One way to do this is to have each of you write down your views and then compare notes and discuss until an agreement is reached.

- Another strategy might be to appoint a scribe to write down people's views and synthesize a strategy.

- Alternatively, you can each (or in several pairs) present a goal, a plan, and timeline, and the group can then vote on which goal, plan and timeline they want to follow.

To complete this section: make a plan for creating a treasure hunt with your team.

Communication

In this challenge, you will be creating a treasure hunt to help young people learn about sustainability. To prepare this treasure hunt, you will need to create a series of questions you want participants to answer. Through each question you will teach them something about our environment and sustainability. Once again, you must create good questions.

Can you remember what characteristics a good question has?

You need to make sure young people can understand your questions. They should be clear, focused, not leading, and they should also be fun! Think about your audience!

6.4 Thinking about your audience

To practise thinking about your audience, try to rewrite the questions below, as if you were asking them to:

- a classmate
- your six-year-old cousin
- the president of your country
- a university professor.

Question 1: How can you reduce your carbon footprint?

Question 2: What can our country do to become greener?

Question 3: Is being "green" cool?

Note: this is quite a tricky exercise! The important thing is that you keep thinking about how you need to 'translate' or adapt your information for different audiences. Keep this in mind as you write your treasure hunt.

The power of images

To make your treasure hunt accessible to a wide audience you could use images. Images are a powerful way of helping people to understand ideas in new ways. They can catch a person's attention and inspire them to action. They can illustrate what you have written. They can make your project accessible to those who cannot read or those who cannot read your language.

Year 8 Challenge 6

6.5 Images

1. Find images that help you demonstrate sustainability and unsustainability.
2. Look at the images below. Discuss with a partner: how do these images make you feel? How do you think they might make your audience feel?

Citing images

Most images you will find during your research belong to someone. Someone has taken a picture, or drawn a graphic, to illustrate a point. It is their work that you are using. So, like texts, you must cite them.

Why do you need to cite images?

You need to cite images for the same reasons you need to cite texts. First, the person who took the picture or made the image deserves credit for their work. Second, you want your audience to be able to look at the sources of your images. By reviewing your sources, your audience can make sure you used valid information and that you used the information accurately.

Warning – Biases

We discussed the importance of being aware of biases in Challenge 5 of Year 7. Just like texts, images can be biased. A particular section of an image can be cropped out of context. An image can be Photoshopped. Or a picture can be taken from a particular angle to affect the outcome. Be careful and always check and verify your pictures to make sure they are real and that they are reliable – just like you should with all other data!

Stop

Can you explain what a biased source is?

To complete this section: gather images you want to use in your treasure hunt. You can also start to gather other relevant information.

Research sustainability

To create an interesting treasure hunt, you will need to find some interesting information on sustainability. You might want to provide some fascinating facts about sustainability to capture the attention of your participants – or even to get participants!

Finding facts about sustainability

6.6 Possible sources

The Internet

Did you know that if you add '.edu' to your search, you will be given results from educational institutions such as universities? If you add '.org' you will be given results from organizations.

Library

Have you visited your school library? Make sure you take the opportunity to speak with your librarian. Perhaps your class could set up an appointment to have your librarian guide you through the various sources your library has, including databases. These sources might have fantastic information for your treasure hunt.

Interviewing experts

Are there are any local experts on environment and sustainability whom you could interview?

Make a list of the types of sources that might be useful in this project.

6.7 Information finding exercise

You could research the following questions for your treasure hunt. Notice that some questions are harder than others.

With your group, find the information to answer these questions and think of other questions you could add.

Year 8 Challenge 6

- What is the average carbon footprint of a person in your country, the USA, China, and two other countries?
- How much energy comes from renewable sources now in your country, the USA, China, and two other countries?
- For how long do people wear their clothes in today's world? Was this different in the past?
- How many trees are cut down every day?
- How many trees are planted every day?
- How long does it take for plastic to dissolve?
- Can you list at least two renewable sources of energy?
- Why are trees good for the environment?
- What is a carbon footprint?
- What is the carbon footprint of travelling from Delhi to New York? From Florida to Rome? From Manila to Moscow?

Warning – Vested interests

Take care to note where your information is coming from. Be careful of sources that might have a particular interest in the information they share. This is called a 'vested interest'. For example, if you are looking at information on whether cutting trees is good for the environment, do you think a logging company might have a vested interest?

6.8 Reflecting on your actions

As you find information about sustainability you might be surprised to find that some of the things you do, or the things you buy, have a high environmental cost.

For example, you might be surprised to find that your favourite clothes are made of polyester, a plastic, and that every time you wash your clothes you are sending plastic into the oceans! Or maybe you will realize that your family's travels create a large carbon footprint.

Take some time to think carefully about your views on sustainability. Will you be making any changes in your life to live in a more sustainable way? To help you, start by answering the questions below:

- Which of my actions has the highest environmental impact?
- Could any of the products I use be replaced by more sustainable choices?

To complete this section: create a list of questions to use in your treasure hunt. Then design your treasure hunt. Will participants get points every time they get a right answer? Will the winner be the person who collects the most points?

Evaluating your outcome

How will you decide if you have achieved what you want from your treasure hunt?

To evaluate whether your project was successful you will need a clear goal and a measurement.

1. Clear aim

To evaluate any project, you need to go back to your goal or aim. What was the purpose or aim of your treasure hunt? Did you want to teach people about sustainability? Did you want to convince people to change some of their actions? Any of these is a suitable aim. The important thing is to have a clear, and well-defined, aim which you can then evaluate.

2. Measuring success

Once you have a clear aim, it will be easier to measure its success. If your aim, for example, is to get people to your treasure hunt, then you can measure success by the number of people who attend! You might decide that if you can get more than 50 people to attend, you have succeeded. You need to decide on how you will measure success. Will it be by the number of attendees … by how much they learn … by their response to your treasure hunt?

After the project: lessons learnt

Whether your project is successful or not, you can always learn from it and make future projects better. This is an important part of evaluating your project: learning lessons for the future.

Remember: no project is ever perfect. We can always improve. Take time to learn from mistakes but also take time to celebrate what you did well!

6.9 Measuring success

Look at the goals below and try to come up with some measurements of success. You can also try to think of more projects, with other aims and outcomes.

Project name	Project aim	Project outcome	Possible measurements of success
Unnecessary plastic	Encourage people to replace plastic with more sustainable options	Poster showing options to plastic, for example, using metal rather than plastic straws	1. Sale of cloth bags next to poster show 2. Questionnaire given to attendees about whether they will change their consumption habits
Stopping palm oil	Educate people about palm oil	Education booklets	How many people take booklets
Zero pesticides	Educating community about the effects of pesticides	Short videos that can be sent via social media	
Fundraising for trees	Fundraising for a tree planting NGO	Bake sale	

6.10 Evaluating your project

Discuss with your group how you will decide if your treasure hunt is successful. It is important to decide this *before* you complete your project as you might need resources to measure your success during the project.

Getting the word out

To host a successful 'Sustainability Treasure Hunt' you will need to get the word out – you need people to hunt the treasure! Letting others know about your projects and convincing them to join takes some skill. You will need to think about:

- **where** to share about your project. If you want students from your school to participate, for example, would it make more sense to share details about your project in a school bulletin board, or to buy an ad in a national newspaper?

- **when** to share about your project. Don't advertise so early that people forget, or so late that people cannot plan to be there.

- **how** to share about your project. If you create a flyer that is full of typos or that is confusing, many might not take your project seriously and might refuse to participate.

To complete this section: decide how you will measure the success of your treasure hunt and start publicizing it!

Communication
Plan to action

Taking a project from a plan to reality is surprisingly tricky. Lots of unexpected problems and turns can emerge. Sometimes what you had planned will be impossible. To succeed you will need to be creative. You will also need to be resilient and keep going even when things go wrong.

Warning – Always have a Plan B!

Whether you are conducting a research project, or putting together a community show, things can always go wrong. Your initial plan (Plan A), might fall flat. It is, therefore, always important to have an alternative plan (Plan B) – ready just in case! If something is really important, you might even want to have a Plan C!

6.11 Plan B … and C!

Look at the problems below. With your group, spend some time discussing what you would do in each scenario.

Problem	Plan B	Plan C
You saved your 5000-word essay in your friend's computer. The computer crashed!		
You were planning on using plastic straws to demonstrate unsustainable consumption. Your little sister found them and made a sculpture instead.		
You have divided your presentation on pesticides and bee death among your group. One of your team members comes down with laryngitis the day before the presentation.		
You make a video on how palm oil is really not that bad, then realize that the source you used in your research is sponsored by a palm oil factory.		
You are presenting about how much fossil fuels international flights use, when you realize your audience does not understand what fossil fuels are.		

Communication

You can have powerful, fascinating information to share with others, but if you do not share this information in a clear and understandable way your project will not succeed.

Tips for speaking in public

If your project involves public speaking, try these tips:

- Stand up straight and make eye contact with your audience.
- Speak so that people in the back of the room can hear you.
- Memorize and understand what you are saying to your audience, so that you can explain it to them rather than reading from a paper.
- Avoid 'filling sounds' or 'filling words' such as: 'ummm', 'ahhh', 'like', 'so'.
- Record yourself giving the presentation. Watch your video and think about what you could do to improve. Or give your presentation in front of a mirror. Remember, no one is perfect, we can all get better!

Try it as a team!

Present your information on sustainability to each other. Gently discuss what you could each do better.

Always start your feedback to others with something positive!

Let each person start by stating what they think they could do *better themselves*. Teammates should then go second by telling them what they did well. Only after you have pointed out something positive should you discuss what could be improved using the rubric below, or a similar one.

Presentation guidance

- Did the speaker look at the audience?
- Was the speaker's volume adequate?
- Did the speaker read from their notes, or were they able to explain the information with only glances at their notes?
- Did the speaker speak too quickly, or too slowly?

To complete this section: conduct your treasure hunt! Enjoy it, then take some time to reflect on how successful it was.

Taking it further

We are living through a critical environmental crisis. The more we can learn about our environment and how to live sustainably, the better. Take this opportunity to expand your learning by following the ideas below:

Economics

- What would be the economic cost of stopping all international flights to avoid their carbon footprint?
- Can you research what the price or cost of animals and plants that become extinct would be? How could we determine such a price?

Politics

- What governments have been most or least willing to support policies to protect the environment?
- Write a letter to your government about what you think should be done to support your country's environment.

Science

- Look into some of the scientific advances that are trying to collect greenhouse gases from our atmosphere.

Art

- Can you create a piece of art that shows people the importance of taking care of our environment? Alternatively, find a piece of art that shows the power, importance, or frailty of our environment?

Music

- Can you create a piece of music about the environmental crisis which you could share?

History

- When did the environmental crisis start?
- Can you look into how different cultures have related to the environment in the past?

Marketing

- Imagine you are hired to create adverts to promote sustainable activities. Can you come up with a couple of adverts or commercials to promote sustainable choices?

Year 8 Challenge 6

What did you learn?

When you complete this challenge, take a moment to reflect over what you have learnt with the table below.

Skill	I get it!	I am starting to get it!	I need to review this.
Collaboration: I understand that groups need a clear plan, a timeline, and respect to succeed.			
Evaluation: I understand what vested interests are.			
Evaluation: I understand how a project can be evaluated.			
Communication: I understand that images can be biased and should be carefully evaluated.			
Research: I understand that images need to be cited, just like other sources.			
Communication: I understand that images are powerful tools of communication.			
Communication: I have learned and practiced some strategies to improve public speaking.			

Year 8

Challenge 7 Making a difference

This is the last challenge of Year 8, and we think you are ready for something a bit more difficult and a bit more independent. Thus, this challenge has been written to get you to practise for what you will be doing in Year 9. You will think about the topic to start with and then you will be given checklists to use as you prepare your project. This will help you to bring together everything you have learnt in Years 7 and 8.

What you have learnt

Research

Research is like a treasure hunt. You need to know what you are looking for. You need to know what tools to use and how to use them. You need to know how to separate rubbish from jewels, and you need to know how to make something from what you find. Thus, we have worked on:

- Choosing a question – a guide to what our treasure is.
- Choosing research methods – deciding what tools we will use to find information.
- Choosing sources – deciding where we will look for information and whether they are valid and useful places to look.
- Taking notes – sorting through what we find to separate what is useful from what is not.
- Synthesizing information – bringing things together to make your own argument.
- Creating a bibliography – ensuring we give proper credit for where we find information and helping others to review what we found.

Analysis

Analysing is about making connections. You analyse the information you find to understand the causes of problems, the consequences of actions, and how local, national, and global events are interconnected. You have learnt to beware false causalities and unexpected consequences.

Evaluation

You have worked hard to learn how to evaluate sources. You now check every source to see if it is valid and reliable.

Communication and collaboration

Working in a group, communicating with your group, and communicating your ideas and findings to different audiences are tricky things! In the past two years, you have practised ways of working with others to ensure everyone is heard, feels respected, and appreciated. You have practised how to give and take feedback in a positive way. You have tried to put yourself in the shoes of your teammates and your audience to speak and write in ways that are understandable and useful. You have practised creating logical arguments that are supported by valid information which you reference carefully.

Reflection

You have spent time thinking about your strengths and weaknesses as a researcher, team member, and presenter. Everyone has strengths and weaknesses. As you realize what yours are, you can work to strengthen weak areas, and use your strengths to help others. As you learn about various global topics you have spent time thinking about your values: what you consume, how you live, how you treat others. Based on what you have learnt, you might have decided to change some of your habits, such as what you buy.

Perspectives

You have practised seeing all sorts of issues from different perspectives. You have seen, for example, how gender, age, and wealth can affect how we experience problems. You have also seen how problems, and solutions, look very different from a local, a national, and a global perspective.

What skills will you develop?

In this Challenge you will get the opportunity to put into practice what you have learnt. You will choose a way to improve your community, research it, analyse what you find, evaluate your sources and possible solutions, collaborate with your peers, communicate your ideas, and reflect on what you have done.

➜ Making a difference: The challenge
➜ Solving an issue
➜ Presenting possible solutions
➜ Presenting your work

Making a difference The challenge

This challenge is simple and yet difficult. *You need to find a way to help improve your community*.

You will be working in a group of three to five.

Step 1 RESEARCH

All projects need to start from knowledge. You cannot make your community better if:

1. you don't know who your community is
2. you don't know what your community is struggling with.

Thus, as always, *we need to start with research*. We need to start asking questions and look for information to help us come up with a plan!

Step 1a Define the scope of your research

With any question or project, you need to decide what your perspective will be. Will you take a local, a national, or a global perspective? Your perspective will affect what community you are trying to affect. Depending on your perspective your community can be:

- your school
- your neighbourhood
- your city
- your region
- your country
- your continent
- your planet

Step 1b Background research

Once you decide on your community, you will need to start looking at what your community needs. Thus, we have *a starting question*: What issues does your community face?

- Think about where you can find this information.
- There will be more than one place where you can look for information.
- Will you be looking for primary or secondary data?
- Can you split your background research among your team mates?

Step 2 COLLECTING INFORMATION

As you start your research you will need to keep track of the information you find so you and your group can use it as needed.

- What techniques will you use to keep track of the information you find?
- Will you write down everything you find?
- How will you keep track of your sources?

Step 3 NARROWING YOUR FOCUS

Use your background research to decide what *specific* community problem your group would like to address. You will need to put all the information you have together, discuss it and come to a view on what specific issue you want to work on.

- How will you decide as a group?
- How will you ensure that everyone's views and research are considered?

Step 4 RESEARCHING YOUR ISSUE

Step 4a Once your team decides what community issue you want to address, you will need to go back and do some more research to understand this issue in in depth. For example, if you have found many interviews or articles noting that your community is struggling with too much traffic, you will need to understand where that traffic comes from, why there is traffic, and what solutions have been proposed in the past.

Step 4b Finding Sources

Step 4c Collecting information

Step 4d Synthesizing information

As you will note, research is an iterative, or repetitive process.

Start by asking questions about this topic or challenge, research and find information, which helps you make new, and more detailed, more focused, questions, which you then research. Again, as you find more information and continue to clarify your views, you come up with a possible answer or solution to the problem. You might then research whether this solution has been used before, what its consequences have been or might be.

In short, your work will look a bit like this:

Ask question

    Research

        Come up with new questions

           Research

                Come up with a possible solution

                    Research solution

Solving an issue

Each Global Perspectives Challenge asks you to improve an issue. In this case you have chosen an issue your community faces and you are trying to come up with a possible solution.

Clarity

You need a clear aim. If you are not clear on what problem you are seeking to solve, or what question you are trying to answer, your work will be vague, and you are likely to end up lost.

Which of the following provide a clear aim? Which are too vague?

a. Come up with a possible solution for the decrease in bees in your area.

b. Come up with a way to help the environment.

c. Help others understand climate change.

d. Help your family understand what causes global warming.

Analysis

To explain why something is happening, and to decide what should be done about it, we need to understand its **causes**. We need to understand **why**.

In other words, if we have a problem we need to understand what causes the problem so that we are able to propose useful solutions. Without understanding causes, we might end up simply fixing symptoms or even making the problem worse!

What are the causes of the community problem you are trying to solve?

Remember that simply because something comes before something else, it does not mean that the first event has caused the second.

Look at the table below, which explores different possible causes for the same problem. Try to fill in the missing squares.

Problem	Cause	Solution
Too much traffic	People love cars	Adverts to promote cycling and public transport
Too much traffic	Lack of public transport	
Too much traffic	Lack of safety in public transports, so people choose to drive	
Too much traffic	Cars are very cheap	
Too much traffic		Help people find jobs closer to their homes
Too much traffic		Decrease the price of public transport

Evaluation: Rethinking your sources

As you research, always remember to keep a critical eye on your sources.

This means:
- don't believe everything you read
- don't believe everything you hear
- don't believe everything you see.

You need to double check your sources to make sure they are giving accurate, unbiased information.

* Be careful of sources that present **fake** information. It is a good idea to make sure you can find the same information in more than one source, for example, to make sure it is real.

* Be careful of sources that present **biased** information. If your source has a vested interest in selling a particular thing, or in supporting a particular idea, they are unlikely to present information in a fair way.

* Be careful of sources that are out of date. If you find information on traffic in your city in the 18th century, it is unlikely to help you understand what is causing traffic in your city now!

Look at the sources below. Why might they be problematic (match between the columns)?

Column A	Column B
Likely to present biased views	A blog you found online, written in 2002
Data will not be current	A campaign ad for a politician or an interest group
Might have wrong data	A newspaper article

Presenting possible solutions

Global Perspectives Challenges ask you to think about possible ways to solve personal, local, national, and global problems. It is important to note that very few problems have *one* solution. More than one possible solution can exist. It is likely that no solution is perfect. Do not be disheartened if you cannot find the magic way to make problems disappear. Our job as global citizens is to find small (or big) ways to help things improve a step at a time and to keep taking these steps.

Consequences

As you come up with possible solutions to a problem you need to consider the consequences of your proposed solution. Remember that not all consequences are immediate – some take time to appear. Not all consequences are intended either. Sometimes an action creates unexpected and unforeseen ripples. Be careful! We have to try our best to think about what consequences our proposed solutions might have, but remember that the unexpected is, well, unexpected!

Unexpected consequences – at the personal level

The idea of unexpected consequences is also important at the personal level. Think about times when you said or did something and your friends or family reacted in a way you did not expect. Perhaps your compliment was misunderstood as an insult. Or your desire to share food was misinterpreted as you disliking the food. When we realize that actions can lead to unexpected consequences we become more thoughtful about our actions, and we are also more willing to give others the benefit of the doubt when they do something that appears rude or mean at first sight.

Take some time to think about instances where your actions had unintended consequences. Could you have done anything differently?

Your outcome

Your *outcome* is part of your solution to each Global Perspective Challenge. In each outcome you demonstrate some of the skills you are working on in this course.

For each challenge, your outcome will be different. Your outcome will depend on what issue you are working on, whom you are trying to affect, and how you are trying to affect them. For example:

→ If you are researching why there is water pollution in your city, and seeking to affect policy makers, your outcome might be a petition.

Year 8 Challenge 7

→ If you are researching why women in your city do more domestic work than men, and trying to affect your community, your outcome might be a series of videos on social media to raise awareness.

→ If you are researching why there are so many abandoned dogs in your country, and seeking to affect dog owners, your outcome might be a series of posters to place in pet shops.

In this book we have given you suggested outcomes for each challenge but you can, of course, come up with your own!

Can you list all of our project outcomes for the year? Could you also list some of the skills you feel you have learnt in each Challenge?

My Global Perspectives outcomes throughout this year		
Global Perspectives Challenge	Outcome	Skills learnt
Water crisis		
Migration		
Beliefs about food		
Looking at the future		
Trade and aid		
Sustainability		

As you can see, your outcome can be as creative as you wish to make it. But it must be supported by solid research. Your research will support your argument with solid evidence. It is often a good idea to write your research up as a short report along with any other creative outcome, to consolidate your learning and to practise communicating your findings powerfully.

Creative outcomes

To help you come up with some creative outcomes, try to match the options below (there are multiple possible matches):

puzzle with the various parts needed to solve a problem

raising awareness about fake news

an email chain

solutions for environmental change

teaching your community about the power of media

a theatre show

a piece of art or a song

helping immigrants integrate

a video call between community leaders

a collection of real and photoshopped images

213

Presenting your work

Remember that no matter how excellent your research or how clever your ideas to solve issues might be, if you do not communicate clearly, no one will know what you have done. Here are some tips for presenting your work as clearly and powerfully as possible.

1. **Be clear on what you are doing.**

    State simply and clearly what issue you are working on; what your research question is and what you propose as a solution.

2. **Present your evidence.**

    Make it clear to your reader that you have evidence to prove that your solution makes sense.

    Make sure you cite your evidence properly to demonstrate its validity and so your reader can review it.

    Remember to be consistent in the way you cite your sources. If you need to review how to cite sources using MLA, we have provided some help in an Appendix.

3. **Think of your audience.**

    Read over your work trying to see it as your audience will see it. Make sure you use the appropriate tone: formal for academic work, friendly but smart for community work. Always try to be as clear as possible.

4. **Review and edit your work.**

    Have you heard the expression 'Genius is 1 percent inspiration, 99 percent perspiration'? Good work takes time. You need to give yourself time to read over what you have done and make changes, improve it, clarify it, add more information, and correct typos.

Year 8 Challenge 7

Ideas for making a difference:

- What is one thing you wish you could change to make the world better?
- Think about your individual talents – how can you use these to make the world better?
- Review a community newspaper. What seems to be the biggest problem?
- Could you send out a survey to ask the community what they would like to change?

End of Year 8 Bringing it all together

You have now completed Year 8 of Global Perspectives. Congratulations! You have learnt about new parts of the world, expanded your research, analysis, evaluation, communication skills, worked with friends, and learnt a lot about yourself. Take some time to reflect on what you have learnt.

1. What is the most interesting topic you discussed this year?

2. Has your research during the year led you to change your views on any of the topics you have learnt about?

3. What was the hardest part about teamwork?

4. What was the best part about teamwork?

5. What was the most helpful thing you did in your group?

6. What skill do you feel you particularly improved on this year? Some of the ones you could choose include:

    a. Finding resources

    b. Finding useful information in resources

    c. Judging whether resources are biased

    d. Building a clear argument

    e. Using evidence well

    f. Making interesting presentations

    g. Seeing problems from multiple perspectives

7. What other topics would you like to learn about?

8. If you could solve any local, national or global problem, what problem would you solve?

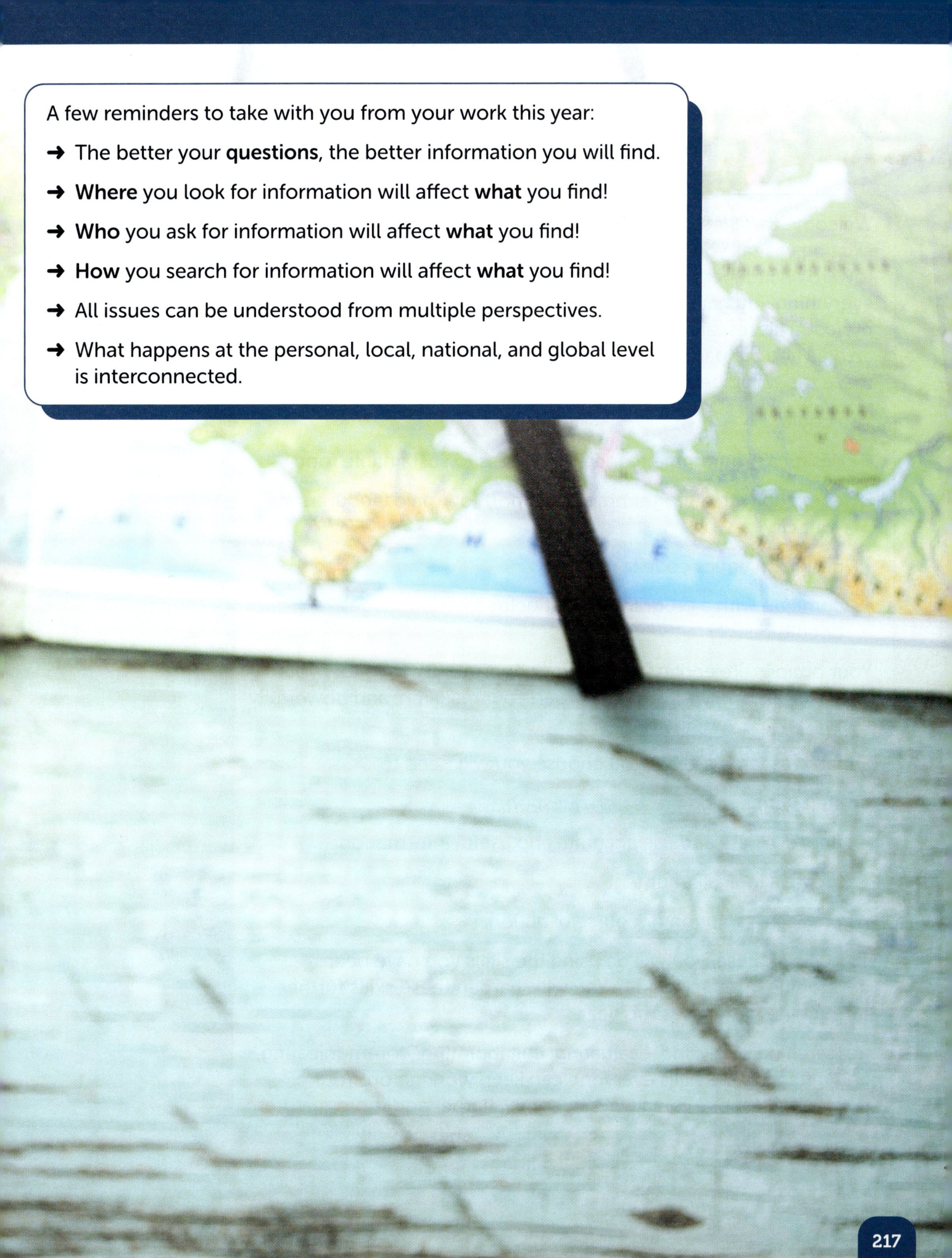

A few reminders to take with you from your work this year:

→ The better your **questions**, the better information you will find.

→ **Where** you look for information will affect **what** you find!

→ **Who** you ask for information will affect **what** you find!

→ **How** you search for information will affect **what** you find!

→ All issues can be understood from multiple perspectives.

→ What happens at the personal, local, national, and global level is interconnected.

Year 9

Welcome to Year 9 of Global Perspectives! This is a particularly exciting year as you will spend a large portion of your time working toward an independent research project. You will be putting everything you have learnt into play to create a fantastic, original project. This research project gives you the opportunity to explore an area you are particularly passionate about, and suggest ways to make the world better in this particular area.

You could:

- design a programme to increase access to sustainable food
- come up with a programme to support low-paid labourers in your city
- design an ethics code for AI
- come up with a programme that helps save languages or cultures.

Your options are endless. This is your opportunity to follow your interests, expand your mind, sharpen your research, and powerfully communicate your ideas.

For any research project you choose you will need to:

- start with a strong research question
- find, evaluate and use accurate and useful information
- create a logical argument
- propose a solution or course of action.

To achieve these, you will be using the skills you have been developing in Years 7 and 8. You will sharpen these skills further through new exercises this year.

Researching, analysing, evaluating, collaborating, communicating, and reflecting are skills everyone can keep working on. Your research questions can always become sharper and more mature.

Your research can always become more powerful. Your evaluations can always become more insightful. And everyone can learn to be better communicators and better team members.

To help you sharpen your skills, this year you will be working through new exercises for each skill, leaving you plenty of space to develop as an independent thinker and researcher.

You will be working on: constructing and using appropriate research questions; finding and using a variety of valid sources; recognizing multiple perspectives; synthesizing and effectively presenting new arguments that build upon links between causes and consequences; recommending possible solutions to various issues; reflecting on your work as a team member and your views on on various Global Perspectives topics; and working well with your peers.

As in previous years, the material for Year 9 is divided into Challenges. Within each Challenge you will find sections that look at different aspects of the topic being discussed and which work on sharpening different skills. The exercises are written so they can be done as a group or individually, following your teacher's instructions.

Note that while the book looks at the same topics as the CAIE curriculum, it might look at different areas or issues within the topics. This is because each topic covered in Global Perspectives is huge and complex. This means you can approach a topic from many different angles. The purpose of this book, and indeed of Global Perspectives, is not to provide you with specific information on a topic, but to give you the skills so you can become an able, independent researcher, a critical thinker and a global citizen.

Year 9

Challenge 1
Disease and health

1.1 Health

- What do you think were the main lessons the Covid-19 pandemic taught us?
- What do you think governments around the world could have done differently during the pandemic?
- What did you learn about germs during the pandemic?

Challenge overview

Our world has recently gone through one of its largest health scares. In 2020 most of our lives changed as governments around the world required us to stay home to try and decrease the rate at which the new coronavirus was spreading. We struggled to figure out how to keep our lives going without the freedoms we had always taken for granted.

Around the world we were all learning about how viruses spread. The pandemic forced us all to look more closely at our hygiene and our customs. As the virus hit areas with high levels of poverty particularly hard, we were reminded that poverty is a problem that makes all other problems worse. For example, hand washing, a critical part of the hygiene needed to fight virus spread, is impossible when you cannot afford water. The pandemic made us realize that this was not just a problem about microorganisms and science; it was also about economics, social customs, and beliefs.

As we restricted travel and exports around the world, for example, we were reminded that we are all interconnected. What happens between us – our personal, local interactions – can affect the wellbeing of countries on the other side of the globe. And what happens in distant lands affects us. The pandemic, in short, made evident how important it is to study issues from various perspectives and to understand how these perspectives are interconnected.

In this Challenge you will be thinking about diseases and how they affect us at home. We challenge you to work with a team to create an information campaign to help teach primary school students about an issue related to disease and health. To succeed, you will need:

- to narrow down your research to a specific question about disease and health
- to think about what information your audience needs to know
- to collate the information you will need
- to think about how to communicate your information to a young audience
- to work successfully with your teammates to design, create, and distribute your communication programme.

What skills will you develop?

Communication 1
→ You will look at how to communicate clearly to catch your audience's attention.

Research
→ You will look at what research methods you will need to gather information.

Evaluation
→ You will think carefully about your sources to avoid *fake news*

Communication 2
→ You will look at how to use terminology appropriately.

Research and reflection
→ You will consider how we draw conclusions from science and reflect on the topic of disease and health.

Taking it further
→ Here you will have suggestions to explore this topic further, linking it to other subjects like maths, science, arts, and more.

Communication 1
Finding a clear focus

To start an information campaign, you need to decide what information you want to share. That is, you need to choose the focus of your campaign. 'Health and disease' is a large topic. Your team will need to narrow down this topic into an issue that can be realistically researched and presented on. To guide your research, you need a clear research question and a clear argument. Without these you will just end up with a list of facts on an issue. Without analysis and evaluation, a list of facts is not very informative.

Example 1 – An information campaign poster made with no research question or argument:

Example 2 – An information campaign poster made *with* a research question and central argument

Exercise

Exercise = moving your body to increase your heart rate. Exercise includes walking and running.

Exercising improves brain performance. Uganda has the fittest population.

Should you exercise?

YES, we should all exercise daily!

Exercise means activity that increases your heart rate
Exercise has several benefits including:

- Increased mental performance
- Helping you manage your emotions
- Protecting you against illnesses

Some forms of exercise you can do include: running, walking, cycling

Your research question should be clear, help you research the issue without leading you toward any one direction, and allow you to present possible solutions. For example, you could ask:

- Should vaping be forbidden in public places? Why or why not?
- Should there be mandatory hygiene rules? Why or why not?
- Should everyone be forced to maintain a healthy lifestyle?

Year 9 Challenge 1

1.2 Choosing a central question

Work with your team to come up with a question for your information campaign. Make sure it meets the criteria mentioned above.

Remember: everyone in your team needs to understand what your campaign is about for it to be successful.

How will you present your information?
- You could create a PowerPoint presentation to share.
- You could create a short movie.
- You could write a short story for children.
- You could write an information booklet.
- You could design a poster, a mural, or a painting.
- A combination of the above, or others?

1.3 Choosing your means of communication

To decide which method of presentation you want to use, try filling out a table like the one below. Once you fill in the table, decide as a team what you would like to do.

Method	Time it would take to create	Difficulty of creating	Appeal to intended audience	Skills this method requires
Mural/Video				

Catching your audience's attention

You will need to think about how to get your audience interested in what you are communicating.

- You could use an image to start.
- You could try to use a catchy song.
- You could start with some fascinating facts.
- You could ask your audience questions to get them engaged.

1.4 Getting your audience's attention

Spend some time with your team thinking about ways to get your audience's attention. Think about adverts or book covers that have caught your attention. How did they do it? Create a list of options your team can use.

Start any research project with a strong research question.

Research Methodologies

What research methods will you use to find information for your campaign?

1.5 Research methods review

As a class, look at the various research methods listed. Explain each one, note if they are quantitative or qualitative, and explain their benefits and drawbacks.

- Interviews
- Surveys
- Focus groups
- Document analysis
- Fieldwork observations

If you need some help, try to match the descriptions with each method.

- Reading documents created by governments, universities, NGOs, community organizations, or other groups or individuals to find facts or to understand particular points of view.

- A series of closed or open questions given to a group of people to collect their views.

- A conversation with an individual where you ask a set of questions. Questions can follow a strict script or go off the script.

- Spending time observing people in a real-life situation to see what they do and try to understand how, and why they do what they do.

- Can provide numerical data, telling us, for example, how often someone does something, how much someone buys, and so on.

Interviews

You could try to find information through interviews. Depending on whom you are interviewing, you will need different interview questions.

To learn about diseases and germs, it might make sense to interview experts. These might be bacteriologists, immunologists, or medical doctors.

To learn what children know about a disease, it makes sense to interview children. If you are going to interview children about their views on germs, however, you should keep your questions simple and focus on their personal experience. On the other hand, if you are going to interview experts, you can ask technical questions.

Preparing for an interview

Preparation is key for success. People are busy and it is impolite to waste their time, showing up without questions or with questions you could easily find an answer to elsewhere. You also don't want to waste your effort, coming out of an interview with nothing to show for it.

1.6 Planning an interview

With a partner, discuss how you would prepare for an interview using the questions below.

- How would you contact experts or community members to ask them if you can interview them?
- How would you make sure your interviewees understand the purpose of your research and give you consent?
- How would you take notes on the interview? Would you work with a partner and have one of you take notes? Would you use a recording device and transcribe the recording once home?
- What questions will you use for your interview? Will you follow a strict plan or make up questions on the spot if new interesting areas or topics emerge?
- How will you thank your interviewees for their time once your interview is over?
- Should you do some research before your interviews?

Each research method has advantages and drawbacks: choose your methods carefully!

Evaluation
Cross-checking data

As you start to draft your information campaign, you will be collating information to share with your audience.

Warning

Always double-check facts and data. Even reputable sources, such as major newspapers, can make mistakes presenting data. Data can be misprinted. Biased sources, on the other hand, might knowingly misrepresent data or provide wrong information, to support their position. It is wise, therefore, to always double-check data and try to find facts in more than one source. *Checking the same information in more than one source is called cross-checking.*

1.7 Cross-referencing

Find an answer to each of these questions in **at least two sources**. Compare what you find. If you find different answers, why do you think that could be?

1. What is the most commonly broken bone in humans?
2. How many colds a year does an average person get?
3. What is the average life expectancy (in a country of your choice)?

Fake news

We live in an era of easy and fast information. This means that it is easy to create information, whether true or false, and to spread it to millions of people in seconds.

If you lived 50 years ago and you wanted to let people know your thoughts about a disease, you might consider writing a small pamphlet and mailing it out, trying to get something published in a newspaper, or even publishing a book and

Challenge:

Was President Trump's inauguration in 2016 well attended? What evidence can you find?

trying to sell it. It would take time and a lot of effort to get your ideas out. Now, you can simply sit in front of a computer, write whatever you want, and put it out on social media – Facebook, Twitter, YouTube, TikTok, Instagram. Within minutes you could have millions of people see what you wrote or said. Many of your viewers could believe you, even if what you wrote was absolute nonsense or full of errors. They would then share what you made, declaring it the truth. You have just created *fake news*.

1.8 Social media

With your teacher's help and supervision, post an interesting, but appropriate, picture on a social media platform and write that you are doing this for your Global Perspectives research class. Ask people to share the image to show the power of social media. See how many shares you get. Perhaps the image will travel beyond your country. To make it more interesting you could post a 'mistaken' fact about germs or diseases with a correction – help spread knowledge!

Fake news and coronavirus

The 2020 coronavirus pandemic demonstrated the dangers of false information. Countless websites emerged claiming all sorts of cures and preventions for the virus. People searching for information about the virus needed to cross-reference the information they found to ensure it was accurate and valid, or they could risk serious injury.

1.9 Finding fake news

Find fake news. Can you work with a couple of classmates to find some of the strangest ideas shared about coronavirus during 2020? Or you could choose to look at fake news on other areas related to health and disease.

Cross-checking

To avoid using, and believing, fake, mistaken, or misguided data, you should always check your data in more than one source. Try to use a variety of different sources: universities, governments, NGOs, and International Organizations (World Bank, the United Nations).

Warning

Cross-checking your data is important, but if you find three bad sources, you will still be in a bad place! If you find three different sources that tell you the Earth is flat … the Earth is still not flat! Be extra careful!

Always double (and triple!) check your data!

Communication 2
Using terminology

For a long time, the idea that microorganisms can cause disease was controversial. Although the notion of such organisms had been around for centuries, it was French scientist Louis Pasteur who established the science of bacteriology through a series of clever experiments. Even with Pasteur's proofs, however, many non-scientists (and scientists!) struggled to believe in the existence of beings they could not see. Even now, when we try to teach young kids about microorganisms, it takes some skill to help them understand that there are things we cannot see which affect us.

Trying to explain an idea to others is a great exercise to help us make sure we understand the idea ourselves.

One of the challenges when discussing health and disease is the need to use and explain scientific terms which some people might not be familiar with. Technical terms can help you communicate more precisely and summarize your ideas. This is useful when you have a word limit, as you will have in your Year 9 research project.

1.10 Terminology 1

Try to rewrite the sentences below more succinctly by using appropriate terminology. Look to the example for guidance.

Writing without relevant terminology	Writing using relevant terminology
The amount of money and resources the people in a country have access to will affect how quickly diseases spread.	A country's *poverty levels* will affect how quickly diseases spread.
Taking off the bacteria from surfaces we are in touch with and rubbing soap and water on our hands help to limit the spread of *dangerous entities we cannot see.*	

Year 9 Challenge 1

In the past, some believed diseases were not *moved or given from one person to another* but rather carried through vapours or miasmas. This is why during the Bubonic Plague doctors covered their noses.	
Most *small things that we cannot see and cause disease when they enter our body,* will *no longer be alive* if we wash them with soap and water, apply a *solution with alcohol to our hands,* or, if in food, cook the food properly.	

1.11 Terminology 2

If you use technical terms, make sure you explain these to your audience. How would you explain the following terms to a young audience with limited scientific knowledge?

Term	Explanation
Micro-organism	
Virus	
Bacteria	
Immunity	

1.12 Telling stories

Write a story for kids about germs. Your goal is to explain how your immune system defends you against germs. Be creative, make it fun, and remember to explain things so that a six-year-old child can understand you. If you have time, try to act out your story with a group of peers.

Use appropriate terminology to make your writing clear and precise, and always think about your audience!

Reflection
Learning from science

Research methods: experiments

💭 How has information changed your behaviour?

Think about how information you have received in the past has impacted the health choices you make. Has learning about the effect of sugary foods on your teeth, for example, led you to eat less sugar?

Are there some unhealthy habits you maintain despite having seen information about their negative impact? Why did the information not lead you to change?

Researching health and disease requires using scientific experiments. Experiments can also be used to learn more about how people behave and how information changes their actions, but to be effective, experiments need to be carefully designed.

When you design an experiment, you have to be clear about what you want to test. For example, you might want to test whether a tomato plant grows better with more or less water.

You are testing the growth of the tomato plant; this is your *dependent variable* – that is, it is dependent on how much water you give the plant.

Water is your *independent variable* – it is what you change to see how the dependent variable is affected. You should make sure that there are no other variables that could affect your experiment. For example, if one of your tomato plants gets water, but also has no soil, that plant is likely to die. Saying that the plant died because it received water, however, would be wrong, as it might have also died because it had no soil.

1.13 Experiment

Can you design an experiment to test the effect of information campaigns on hand washing rates?

Year 9 Challenge 1

1.14 Effective campaigns

Research information campaigns set up to help people make healthier choices. Did they work? Why or why not?

You could try looking at the campaign to put images that show the multiple harmful effects of smoking on cigarette packets. Has it decreased how many people smoke?

> **Challenge:**
> What are the dependent and independent variables in this campaign?

1.15 Health concerns

What do you think is the most urgent health concern for your generation? How could your generation be taught about this concern and the steps it needs to follow for its safety?

1.16 Covid-19 and you

Our world has experienced a health pandemic. How did it affect you? Do you think finding valid, reliable, unbiased information about Covid-19 was easy? How do you think your government could have informed you, and others in your country, better about what was happening?

1.17 Teamwork over the years

Have you found working in teams easier or harder from the time you started Global Perspectives in Year 7 to now? Do you think getting older has had an impact? Can you give Year 7 students three pieces of advice to make their teamwork better and easier?

Creating change sometimes takes more than information.

Taking it further

Science

Look into how microorganisms evolve. What leads to their changes?

Research diseases that have been eradicated. How were they eradicated?

Look into how human health has changed through history, for example, how our average height and weight has changed. Why do you think our health and our bodies have changed? Are there things we can do now to stop or increase future changes?

What do you think are the most interesting medical advancements currently? Are there any medical procedures you are particularly interested in?

Maths

How do we calculate the rate of contagion of any disease? Look into the R number and see if you can explain it to others.

Look at human health averages: what is our average height, weight, speed? Can you compare us to people who lived 50 or 100 years ago? Present your information in the form of graphs.

Language

Words are powerful. Look into how we discuss diseases. What happens when we anthropomorphize diseases? Look up what *anthropomorphize* means!

History

How we have treated diseases in the past is fascinating. Look into how our medical practices have changed. Have we always washed our hands? How has our understanding of what causes diseases changed?

Economics

Should governments provide health services for their populations? What should these services include? Should elective surgeries, such as nose jobs, be included?

Look into the costs of healthcare for different countries. Where is healthcare most expensive? Why? Look at Cuba's healthcare system. Is it unique in any way?

Philosophy

Should medicine try to make humans live forever?

Year 9 Challenge 1

What did you learn?

When you complete this challenge, take a moment to reflect over what you have learnt with the table below.

Skill	I get it!	I am starting to get it!	I need to review this.
Communication and collaboration: I can discuss plans and strategies with my teammates.			
Research: I can explain different research methods.			
Research: I understand the benefits and drawbacks of different research methods.			
Evaluation: I understand what cross-checking data means.			
Evaluation: I understand what fake news is.			
Evaluation: I understand why I need to double-check data I find.			
Communication: I try to communicate clearly, using the correct terminology when appropriate.			
Communication: I know various ways to present information, such as presentations, murals, videos, etc.			
Research: I am beginning to explore social experiments as a research method.			

233

Year 9

Challenge 2 Conflict resolution

2.1 Conflict

- What would happen if all countries got rid of their armed forces?
- Are there any things for which you would be willing to go to war?
- Do you think there will be more conflicts in our world if we have fewer resources to share?

Let's play a game. Imagine you are dropped into each of the following conflict situations. What would you do?

You land in between two lions facing off against each other to decide who will lead the pride

You come across two of your friends discussing whose turn it is to choose what game to play.

You find two people you do not know yelling about who should be served first.

You are in the border between two countries, with soldiers from both sides holding weapons.

Challenge overview

You would probably not act in the same way if faced with battling lions as you would if you came across your friends fighting. In fact, you would probably act differently in each of the situations described opposite. What would your actions be based on? Is each conflict different? Does each one need a different solution?

This challenge invites you to look at conflict, think about why it happens, and come up with a course of action to resolve it.

To complete this challenge, choose a conflict to research. Apply the take away from each section to the conflict you have chosen:

1. Try to understand what caused it.
2. Study the conflict from multiple perspectives.
3. Think about what strategies could have been used to resolve the conflict.
4. Think about whether and how biased information affected the conflict.
5. Try to come up with a creative solution for the conflict.

What skills will you develop?

Analysis: Why conflict
→ You will think critically about what might cause conflicts, sharpening your analytical skills.

Perspectives and conflict resolution
→ You will practise using perspectives to understand problems and learn a strategy to see conflicts from a neutral position, to take in new information and come to an informed conclusion.

Collaboration: Conflict resolution
→ You will think about ways to resolve conflict and learn a couple of games you can use to solve conflicts in teamwork.

Reflection: Outgroup and biases
→ You will reflect on the impact biased information can have on conflicts.

Evaluation: Seeking a solution
→ You will work on devizing creative strategies for conflict resolution.

Taking it further
→ Here you will have suggestions to explore this topic further, linking it to other subjects like maths, science, arts, and more.

Analysis
Why conflict?

In the introduction to this chapter, you were presented with several conflicts and asked what you would do. When you decided what to do, you probably based your decision, at least in part, on what you thought was the reason for, or cause of, the conflict.

For example, if you come across two wild animals fighting for territory and domination, you know you cannot sit them down to talk and resolve their conflict – unless you want to become their lunch! In such a situation one animal must win, and the winner must be determined through physical conflict. Peaceful resolution is not possible.

On the other hand, if you come across your friends having an argument, you are likely to assume a misunderstanding as the cause for the conflict and, therefore, think that it is possible for them to talk through their conflict and find a solution.

To decide whether and how to solve a conflict, therefore, you need to understand why a conflict is taking place. That is, you need to find its cause. This is an important part of analysis.

2.2 Critical thinking: causes of conflict

With your class or a group of peers, discuss why it might be difficult to determine the cause of a conflict.

To understand a problem, look at its causes.

Year 8 Challenge 2

Scarce resources

Do you think conflict is caused because we do not have enough resources for all the humans on this planet? Does this mean that conflict will increase as populations grow?

2.3 Choosing a research method

Come up with a strategy to research if this hypothesis is true:

'The more the human population grows, the more conflict there will be, as resources will have to be shared among more people.'

A **hypothesis** is an idea or **explanation** that you can test through study and experimentation.

Human nature

Some philosophers argue that conflict is a part of human nature because it is in the nature of humans to compete. Humans compete, according to these thinkers, for resources, for reputation, for power.

If there are limited resources, we will compete to have more than those around us. However, even if there are unlimited resources, we will compete to have power over others, to have popularity.

According to this view of human nature, competition is an inherent part of our nature and it will always lead us to conflict. Do you agree?

2.4 Human nature

With a group of your peers, discuss what you think human nature is like.

- Do you think humans will always compete with each other?
- Do you think it is human nature to cooperate?
- Do you think humans are willing to work for the benefit of others, even to their own detriment? Can you think of an example?

2.5 Researching human nature

You can discuss your views on human nature, but is there any way to prove them? Some psychologists and philosophers have proposed experiments to try and test our human nature. Can you think of some possible experiments to test human nature?

237

Perspectives and conflict resolution

Throughout your Global Perspectives course, you have learnt to look at problems from multiple angles. This is a particularly powerful tool to solve conflicts.

Philosophy, perspectives and conflict

The philosopher John Rawls came up with a great *thought experiment* to help us think about a conflict or a problem from multiple perspectives. Try it out!

Imagine you and your friends are having an argument about what to do after school – you are a good swimmer and want to go and swim in the river. Your friend doesn't know how to swim and wants to go to the park. As you walk along the street arguing, you see a veil. This is a magical veil, called the Veil of Ignorance.

You step behind this veil and suddenly ... you don't know who you are. You know nothing about your identity. You don't know if you are young or old. You don't know if you are rich or poor. You don't know if you were born in India or Pakistan, in Brazil or Norway. You don't know if you are an Olympic athlete or someone who struggles to move.

Now try to look at a conflict from this position. Remember, you do not know who you are. You don't know what side of the conflict you are on.

Try it with your personal conflict. Behind the veil you don't know if you know how to swim or not. Would you choose going to the river or to the park if you did not know if you could swim? Why? Did the veil help you to see the conflict from a different perspective?

You can also try it with a national or international conflict. If there is a conflict between two religious communities, for example, if you step behind the Veil of Ignorance, you do not know what religion you belong to. This will give you a *neutral* place from which to think about the problem and try to find solutions.

Year 9 Challenge 2

2.6 A Rawlsian solution

As a class or in a small group, choose a conflict to discuss. This could be a global conflict, such as WWII, or a regional, or even communal conflict. Have everyone in your class step behind the Veil of Ignorance and try to come up with a solution to the conflict. Remember, once you are behind the veil, you don't know who you are, so you want to make sure you find a solution that will make you happy whomever you are!

Personal, national, global

Thinking about conflicts from personal, national, and global perspectives helps us understand why a conflict happened and how we can resolve it.

2.7 Analysing a conflict

Imagine you live in a small village. Your life is calm and fun: going to school, playing by the river on the weekends, spending time with family. People in the village are poor, but life seems stable and calm.

Suddenly things change. A group comes to the village and starts recruiting for their cause. They promise new jobs and better services to whoever joins them. Half of your neighbours agree with this new group. Soon they start flying their flag. A conflict breaks out. The new group is supported by foreign forces, who send them weapons. Your family does not want to participate but they are afraid. Then one day you see one of your neighbours hurt another person while yelling the group's slogan.

What can different perspectives tell you about this conflict?

- Personal perspective
- Local (village) perspective
- National perspective
- Global perspective

To understand a conflict, always look at it from multiple perspectives.

239

Collaboration
Conflict resolution

Resolving conflicts is no small challenge. When people or countries hold different or opposing views, when they are fighting over scarce resources, or when they feel offended, it is challenging to bring both sides together beyond the conflict.

Conflict can also happen when you work in a group. Thus, learning strategies to resolve conflicts can help you in team work.

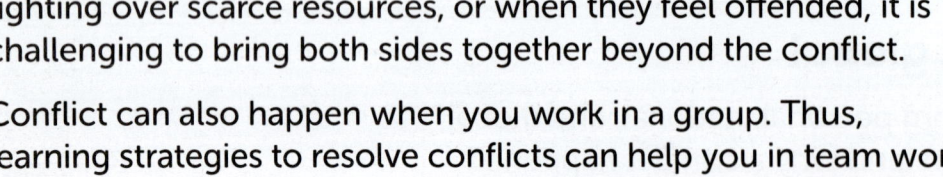

2.8 Problem-solving needs

Imagine you can go 'shopping' for ingredients to resolve conflicts. What would you buy to help resolve a conflict? And why?

Shopping options:

Item	How it would help conflict resolution
Time	
Space	
Competition	
Language translator	
Gentle words	
Truth, however harsh	
Reparations	
Forgiveness	
Forgetfulness	
Fines and payments	
Punishments	
Media	

Language and conflict

When trying to resolve a conflict, words are critical. Try to avoid words like 'everyone', 'always', 'never'. These absolute statements are unlikely to be true and they will build barriers, rather than bridges, between conflicting groups.

Conflict resolution requires careful and thoughtful communication.

Memories

Do you think we should remember conflicts or try to forget them? Think about this with examples from different perspectives.

At a national level: do you think after a civil war, students should learn about what happened in their history classes? Would learning help students to avoid a repetition of the struggle, or would such learning help to maintain flames of animosity between students?

At a personal level: if your team gets into a fight during a Global Perspectives challenge, should you discuss your conflict in the future or try to forget about it?

To resolve a conflict, we need to understand it from various perspectives. We also need to facilitate communication between all the conflicting sides. This might involve overcoming language barriers, cultural barriers, and more.

2.9 Problem-solving strategies

To help overcome a conflict we could design activities that bring both sides together and get them speaking and listening to each other. Can you think of an activity that could do this? After you try and design one, look at the activities below and try one of them. To do this, form groups and then split your group into two. Half of the group is on one side of the conflict and the other half is on the opposing side. You could try this with a fictional conflict

Activity 1: My problem is …

The purpose of this exercise is active listening.

- One side of the conflict should describe what they see as the main issues in the conflict.
- The other side of the conflict *cannot respond* but needs to draw what the other side is saying. Having to draw forces the team listening to concentrate on interpreting and understanding rather than coming up with a verbal response.
- Teams switch sides.

Activity 2 Common experiences

The purpose of this exercise is to help participants on both sides of the conflict find what they have in common.

Divide a large piece of paper into areas such as pets, siblings, school, favourite food. With the help of a facilitator, each side takes turns filling out the sheet. The facilitator points out what both sides have in common – siblings, pets, and so forth. These common areas serve as a basis for communication.

An alternative to this exercise would be to have people move to form new groups when they share something, bringing people physically together. For example, everyone who has a cat stands together … then everyone who likes classical music stands together.

Reflection
Outgroup and biases

Psychologists have argued that humans have a tendency to think of themselves as part of various groups, and to think of those outside their groups as 'outsiders'. This is referred to as social identity theory.

> **2.10 Your community**
>
> What groups do you belong to? Try to think of groups that are local, national, and international.

Identifying with a group is not in itself a problem. Belonging to groups is part of who we are as humans. The problems come when we come to think of those outside our group as enemies; enemies who might hurt us and who must be feared, or as enemies whom we need to attack and work against.

Creating in-groups and out-groups

It is surprisingly easy to create groups and to encourage their members to turn against 'outsiders'.

To demonstrate this to her young students, Jane Elliot, a third-grade teacher in Iowa, decided to run an experiment in her classroom. In 1968, the day after the assassination of Martin Luther King Jr, Jane told her students that blue-eyed children were better. Within minutes she found blue-eyed students mocking their brown-eyed classmates. When she changed instructions, saying that brown-eyed children were superior, the same happened in the opposite direction.

> **2.11 Critical thinking: belonging**
>
> Do you think you could be made to feel part of a group as in Elliot's experiment? Could you be made to turn against another group? In your Global Perspectives teams, how do you make everyone feel part of the team?

Evaluating sources

One of the most dangerous effects of biased sources is that they can help create animosity toward out-groups. This is one of the many reasons why you must carefully evaluate sources in your research, and more generally in your life, so that you are not misguided against others.

A terrible example of the power of biased sources emerged in Rwanda in the 1990s. A series of media outlets, most notably radio stations, started to share highly biased information, creating a strong sense of animosity between different groups in Rwanda, eventually calling for the killing of one of these groups. Biased media was partly responsible for the deaths of about 800,000 people in just 100 days.

2.12 Biased media

Read the transcript below. Highlight areas that demonstrate a bias.

> ... Do not be lazy, let us fight for this Rwanda; do not say that you are fleeing ... They are as young as you are. You are even stronger than they are. Learn the trick to catch them. You may set a trap for them, you may dig a hole in which they can fall ... in a very near future you will be given tools (weapons, arms) in order to go and liberate Rwanda, your mother country.
>
> There is no other way ... [others] steal our country, they destroy it ... Wherever we should go they would call us dogs ... those people are worthless ... they have finished our cassava, why don't they cultivate for themselves or come and work?
>
> *Adapted from*: translation of radio RTLM's transcripts of May 15, 1994, for the United Nations International Criminal Tribunal for Rwanda.

2.13 Belonging and justice

Are there any groups you belong to which present others in a biased way? Can you do something about this?

Biased information can help fuel conflict.

Evaluation
Seeking a solution

There are conflicts that have persisted for so long that few believe they can be solved. Yet creative thinkers look for and find ways to bring people together and overcome conflict in the most amazing ways. One example of this is the West–Eastern Divan Orchestra. This orchestra was started by pianist and conductor Daniel Barenboim and the late Palestinian literary scholar Edward W. Said. The goal of the orchestra is to cross the divide between Israel and Palestine.

To be part of an orchestra, or any musical group, you must listen to your fellow musicians. No instrument is more important – you are playing together, you must listen to each other, respect each other, wait for each other, understand each other. Using this foundation, Barenboim and Said worked to bring people from both sides of the Palestinian/Israeli conflict to listen to each other, to seek to understand each other, to share time and learning, and to learn to appreciate each other. To build together, rather than to destroy.

In this case *music* was used as a means to bring people together. Music gave them a common goal, a common language to communicate in, a shared experience to bond over.

2.14 Assessing an organization
Find out more about the West–Eastern Divan Orchestra. Listen to some of their pieces and interviews. What do you think about their work?

2.15 Art and change
Find other groups that are using the arts as a means to bring peace to situations of conflict.

2.16 Art as a solution

Think about ways in which music has helped you overcome conflicts. Perhaps it has helped you calm down when you were upset. Perhaps you listened to music with people you were struggling to connect with.

2.17 Creative solutions

Come up with other creative solutions to help resolve conflicts. You could look at other forms of art, at means of communication, at sport, at education … Write down your plan and how you think it would help resolve conflict. Share your ideas with a partner or your class.

Reflection

When we discuss conflict, it can be tempting to think only about distant or large conflicts, such as war. But conflict is also something we experience at a personal level. There are people we disagree with. There can be groups we feel excluded from. Your country or city might be divided along religious, political, or cultural lines. Each of us has a choice to make when it comes to building or reducing conflict. What do you do to reduce conflict around you?

2.18 Guiding your future

Write a letter to yourself in the future. Give yourself advice about how to bring peace, rather than conflict, to your life, your country, and the world.

Finishing the Challenge

Go back to the conflict you chose to look at when you started this challenge. Have you used the ideas and exercises presented in these five sections to help you understand the conflict? Try to use your understanding to propose a way to resolve the conflict.

No problem is unsolvable, but some require extra patience and creativity!

Taking it further

Psychology

- To look at why humans enter into conflict, you could research some famous psychological experiments, such as Muzafer Sherif's Robbers' Cave experiment.

Geography

- Look at how the boundaries of countries have changed on the basis of conflict. How have your country's boundaries changed?

Literature

- Write a poem about conflict and/or its resolution. Alternatively, you could look at poetry written during wars. You could also look at novels discussing particular periods of conflict. *A Tale of Two Cities* by Charles Dickens might be worth a look.

Philosophy

- When talking about conflict, the idea of justice is at its core. How do you think justice can be found in a conflict?

Law

- What laws would you create to resolve conflict? Do you think retribution (think 'an eye for an eye') is necessary to reach justice in or after a conflict?

Art

- Create a piece of art about conflict and/or reconciliation. Art can include painting, drawing, collages, dance, theatre and more!

- You could explore some famous pieces of art that have tried to explore and protest against conflict. Look at, for example, Picasso's *Guernica*; Goya's *Third of May*; Antoine-Jean Gros's *Napoleon on the Battlefield of Eylau*.

Politics

- What conflicts are there in your country at present? What are their causes? Could you come up with some ideas to help resolve these conflicts?

Year 9 Challenge 2

What did you learn?

When you complete this challenge, take a moment to reflect over what you have learnt with the table below.

Skill	I get it!	I am starting to get it!	I need to review this.
Analysis: I understand that conflicts can have multiple causes.			
Research: I understand what a hypothesis is.			
Research: I understand how social experiments can be used to research problems.			
Perspectives: I understand why seeing a conflict through multiple perspectives is necessary.			
Collaboration: I learnt some strategies to help resolve group conflict.			
Evaluation: I understand how biased sources can help create conflict.			
Evaluation: I understand why I need to evaluate my sources.			
Reflection: I have reflected on how I can help resolve conflicts.			

Challenge 3
Sports for all

3.1 Sports

- What is your favourite sport to watch? What is your favourite sport to participate in?
- What do you need in order to participate in sports?
- Do you think participating in sport is a human right?
- Should everyone be forced to do a sport?

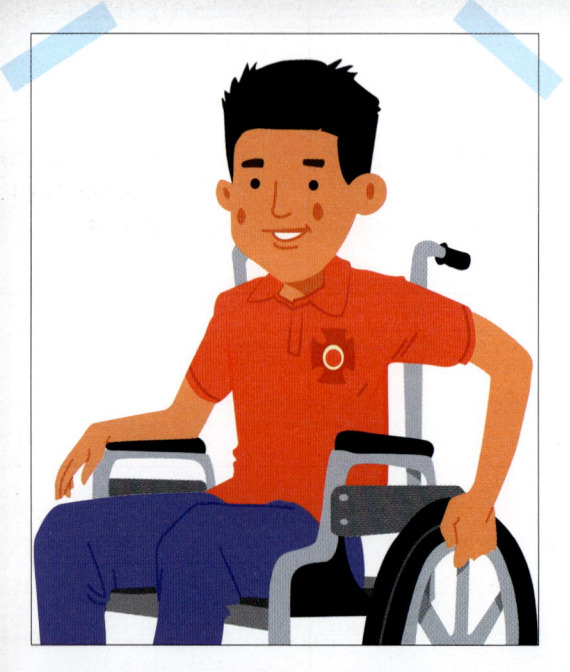

Hola! My name is Tiano. My parents named me Cristiano because they are huge football fans and hoped that I would grow up to be like Cristiano Ronaldo, my dad's favourite player.

However, when I was little, we had a car accident. In the accident my legs were crushed. I have never been able to walk since. Of course, I thought I would never play football again.

Lots of things became difficult, not just sport. My school is in a three-storey building and there are only stairs, no lifts or ramps. My grandma lived on the 10th storey of her building. Once I went to visit her and the electricity went out. I realized I could not leave the building as the lifts stopped working.

Since the accident, everything is harder, but I have found ways to make things work. Everything but football, which I missed.

Then my mom heard of a foundation that runs football games in wheelchairs.

It is not the same as running with your legs, but it is just as exciting!

Challenge overview

In this challenge we will be looking at the power of sports and access to sports for various groups. Your challenge is to research access to sports in your school and think about something you want to change or improve. Present your view to your school board in a way you think will be most effective – we suggest making a model of your school to illustrate any suggestions.

What skills will you develop?

Research: Learning about others
→ You will practise seeing a problem from others' points of view, and choose appropriate research methods to learn about these perspectives.

Analysis: Building your argument
→ You will think about what can cause lack of access to sport, and come up with a course of action to improve access.

Communication
→ You will think about how to best present your argument.

Collaboration
→ You will think about the strengths and weaknesses of your team and learn ways to support teamwork.

Reflection: Skills for the future
→ You will think about the skills you have learnt and how these will help you in your future professional career.

Taking it further
→ Here you will have suggestions to explore this topic further, linking it to other subjects like maths, science, arts, and more.

Research
Learning about others

3.2 Research plan

Imagine you and a small group of peers have been hired to design a new city. What would you put in this city? You have been asked to look in particular at green spaces and sports access. How would you decide what the city needs?

When you complete your discussion, think about how successful it was. Did you feel heard? Did you carefully listen and consider your classmates' ideas? How could a discussion like this be improved in the future?

Designing a city, a school, or any public space is an exercise that requires you to think about different points of view.

3.3 Different needs

Think about what the different people below might want a city to have:

- A mother with two small children.
- An older gentleman who likes quiet spaces.
- A young couple who enjoy going out to restaurants.
- A student preparing for exams.
- A father and businessman who uses a wheelchair.
- A young man who has two large dogs as pets.
- A family with a blind daughter.
- A doctor who has to work night shifts in her hospital.

As you might note, each of these individuals has different needs and wants for their city. To build a city that is accessible and enjoyable for different people, it will be important to take each of their needs and wants into account.

How can you, as a city planner, access different perspectives?

Year 9 Challenge 3

3.4 Applying research methods 1

With your team, discuss what *research methods* you could use to learn about the needs and wants of different people in your city.

3.5 Problem solving

Fill in the table below with what different populations in your city might need.

Population	Needs	How city can fulfil needs
Children	Areas to run and play	Open green areas and playgrounds
People with limited mobility	Areas with flat grounds	Flat walkways in parks

3.6 Applying research methods 2

Create a research tool to gather information about how different members of your school view sports and sports access. Will you use quantitative or qualitative research methods? Why?

Perspectives in your school

Your challenge in this chapter is to research access to sports in your school and to think about something you want to improve. To start your research, think about what different points of view about sports there might be in your school. How will you research these perspectives? (Again, think about research methods).

Warning – Self-selecting populations

When trying to learn about different perspectives we have to realize that sometimes our population is *self-selecting*. This means that they will answer in a particular way because of what group they are a part of. For example, you will not find anyone at your school who will say that they have chosen not to attend your school because it lacks a certain sport – because they won't be at your school! Similarly, if you, for example, go to an all-girls school, you will not be able to ask boys how they feel about being unable to attend the school.

To understand an issue, you need to see it from the perspective of others.

251

Analysis
Building your argument

3.7 Summarizing arguments

Imagine you are making a presentation to your school's teachers and parents about how sports could be more inclusive. Can you start by presenting a summary of the arguments in this article?

Playing sports at any level – club, intramural, or interscholastic – can be a key part of the school experience and have an immense and lasting impact on a student's life. Among its many benefits, participation in extracurricular athletic activities promotes socialization, the development of leadership skills, focus, and, of course, physical fitness. It's no secret that sports helped to shape my life. From a very early age, playing basketball taught me valuable lessons about grit, discipline, and teamwork that are still with me to this day.

Students with disabilities are no different – like their peers without disabilities, these students benefit from participating in sports. But unfortunately, we know that students with disabilities are all too often denied the chance to participate and with it, the respect that comes with inclusion.

...

US laws require schools to provide equal opportunities and not give anyone an unfair head start. So schools don't have to change the essential rules of the game, and they don't have to do anything that would provide a student with a disability with an unfair competitive advantage. But they do need to make reasonable modifications (such as using a laser instead of a starter pistol to start a race so a deaf runner can compete) to ensure that students with disabilities get the very same opportunity to play as everyone else.

Arne Duncan, U.S. Secretary of Education

Year 9 Challenge 3

Thinking about causes

What can limit a person's access to sports? To decide how you want to improve sports access in your school, you have to be clear about what *causes* lack of access. For example, students with physical disabilities might not be able to participate in some sports. Are there other causes that can limit access to sport?

3.8 Thinking about causes

With your team, try to list some reasons that might keep a person from participating in sports. Think about different areas that might impact on this problem: economic, cultural, personal, environmental, political and so on,

Thinking about consequences

Thinking about the needs of others can help us avoid creating projects that negatively impact them. If your school was planning on building an underground pool accessible only through a steep staircase, for example, what do you think the consequences of that pool might be for different students' sports access?

Presenting a solution

A teacher in your school has asked you to present a list of possible solutions to help increase access to sports. It is important to clearly state what you think needs to be changed, and how and why. In other words, you want to clearly explain your suggested course of action.

3.9 Linking causes to solutions

Using the list you created in Exercise 3.8, fill in a table like the one below.

Group	What limits their access to sports?	How can access be improved?
Deaf students	Deaf students cannot hear the gun at the start of a race	Gun can be replaced/combined with a visual cue such as a laser or a flag
Students with sight loss		

A course of action is a suggested solution based on our understanding of what causes a problem.

Communication

3.10 Presenting your views

Once you have decided how your school could improve sports access, your group will need to decide how to present this information. This will be your outcome.

Think of various ways in which you can present your information. Which might be easiest? Which might be most effective? Which might be fastest?

Building your argument

You need to ensure that your argument for improving sports access is clear. Think of your argument as made up of different parts – a bit like pieces of a puzzle. Presenting each part clearly, with appropriate reasons and evidence, will help your audience (or readers) understand you. The parts need to be presented in a logical order: just like a puzzle has an order. If you simply 'throw' all the parts of your argument at your audience in any random order, you will not get very far!

Think about the various possible ways you can structure, or organize, your argument. What do you want to tell your audience first, and why? What is the *last* thing you want to tell them? Do you have evidence to support what you are arguing? When are you showing your audience this evidence?

3.11 Ordering an argument

Another student wants to discuss the following sections in his argument for improving sports access. In what order do you think they should present these sections? Why? Is there anything else you would add?

- Reasons sports *for all* are needed
- Reasons sports are important
- Reasons sports help create equality
- Reasons the school policy is mistaken
- Reasons the school policy can change
- Ways in which the school can change

What is a logical order? Think of this a bit like getting dressed. There are some things you need to do first. If you put on your shoes and then put on your socks … you will have cold feet and dirty socks! When you present your argument, if you want to convince your audience that our school needs to change its sports policy, then you first need to tell them what that sports policy is and why it is mistaken.

Access to international sports

Sports play a large part in human history. Sports can bring us together across national boundaries and unite us in global aspirations. Humans have participated in organized sports for centuries, but we are still figuring out how to make access to sports fair and inspiring.

3.12 Research practice sports

Take some time to research some of the following:

Research the Olympics. Where did they start and why? Why do we continue to support the Olympics? What does the Olympic flame stand for?

Research the Paralympics. When were they established and why?

Research Title IX in the USA and how it has affected different sports.

Perspectives: national and international links

Sports are an interesting example of how the national and the international interact. If your country wants to participate in international sporting competitions, it will need to fulfil the requirements of international organizations. If your country, for example, requests a certain religious outfit for a sport, this outfit must be approved by international organizations.

3.13 International laws

Research international laws that countries must accept to participate in international sporting events.

Do you think some of these laws might limit the access of some countries to sports? How?

3.14 Critical thinking – Sport as a path out of inequality

One argument in favour of sport is that it can help bridge social gaps. On the sports field, the argument states, there are no rich or poor, there are no skin colours, there is no religion, there are only athletes. Do you think this is true? Is it equally true, or false, for all sports?

Present your argument in an organized and clear way.

Collaboration

As you work with your team on your argument and how to best present it, you need to think about how you will distribute the work that needs to be done.

One strategy would be to split the work in equal parts and assign each part to a group member at random. Or you could try to do all parts of the project together, collaboratively. Which strategy do you think might be more efficient? Which strategy do you think may be more enjoyable?

If you split your work, with each team member doing one part, how will you bring all these parts together?

These are not easy questions. One of the keys of good teamwork is to help the members of your team feel valued for what they bring to your group. Perhaps you could try to let each team member do what they are best at. Take some time to think about what each member contributes to your team. Individuals' contributions can take many shapes. Some team members might be:

- full of ideas
- good at thinking critically about ideas, finding blind spots or assumptions
- great at finding resources
- detail-oriented and can create great bibliographies
- great at asking questions
- great at gathering data
- great at analysing information
- great at evaluating ideas
- great at sharing ideas
- good at writing reports/presentations
- good at making things look/sound good – with graphics, fonts, videos, etc.
- good at setting out a plan and a schedule
- good at dividing the work into manageable parts
- good at bringing humour to the work
- good at calming others when they are stressed
- good at listening to the ideas of others
- good at encouraging others
- good at seeing things in new ways
- great at being patient with others.

3.15 Reflecting on your strengths and weaknesses

Take some time to think about what you bring to a group. You can use the list above for inspiration. What are you particularly good at?

List the top three skills you bring to a group. How have you learnt to do these things? Could you write a quick guide to help others do them as well as you do?

What about weaknesses? What are the two things you find the hardest? How do you think you could improve? Could you ask your teacher for help? Find tutorials online? Practise with your team?

Challenge:

It might be interesting for your team to list/discuss how you perceive each other's strengths. You might find you are seen as stronger than you realize!

3.16 Thanking your team

Take a few minutes to think about what each of your team members brings to your group. Some might be more obvious than others. Find something positive to say about each person in your group. Write them each a quick thank you note, thanking them for what they have brought to your project.

Note: Never underestimate the power of gratitude. By thanking your teammates, you will brighten their day. You will help build up their confidence, which will make them more willing to try to help your group work in new ways. You will also help to strengthen team dynamics. By taking the time to write thank you notes, you will have to reflect carefully on what each of your teammates has done, which is a wonderful way to become more thoughtful and reflective. Finally, research shows that gratitude is one of the best roads to happiness.

If you want to be happy, be grateful!

Teams work best when we try to be grateful for what others contribute.

Reflection
Skills for the future

As you work with your team to create a proposal to improve your school's sports provision, you are actually developing a number of skills that will be helpful beyond this Global Perspectives course. These are skills that will help you in all future academic work, as well as in your future professional life.

3.17 What skills?

With a partner, discuss and make a list of the skills you have learnt in the various Global Perspectives challenges. Don't be modest! Feel free to list all the things you have learnt!

3.18 Writing your CV

When you apply for a job, you are often asked to write a CV or resumé. This is a short document where you list your relevant skills and experiences. Try to use the experiences and skills you have developed through Global Perspectives to write a CV you could use to look for work.

David Marcelo
Oxford, UK

Skills:

- Communication: able to share my ideas clearly and successfully with others.
- Writing: able to write succinctly and clearly and to change my style to suit my audience.
- Research …
- Critical thinking ….
- Collaboration …

Experiences

- Researched and wrote a proposal to improve sports access for Hurt Hill School.
- Designed an information campaign to teach primary-aged children about antibiotic resistance.

Time Management

One of the skills future employers will look for is time management. No one wants to work with people who are always late, or who never complete their projects on time.

3.19 Interview

Imagine you are in a job interview and are asked to discuss how well you manage your time. Can you use your work on this course as evidence of having this skill?

Creativity

Another skill valued by employers is creativity. Like all other skills, creativity grows through practice. It is important to practice thinking and communicating in new ways. Try it with sports!

3.20 Creativity

Look at the logos for different sports. Try to redesign some of these logos to make them more inclusive.

3.21 Fun interview

In your future professional career, you will be invited to interviews, where you can discuss what you can do and why you want the job. Like anything else, interviewing well takes practice. Work with a partner and imagine one of you is hiring a project manager. A project manager is someone who makes sure a project gets done, breaking the project into pieces, assigning work to different people, checking deadlines, ensuring high quality work is completed. Interview your partner. Ask them questions to see if they would be a good project manager. Your partner needs to use what they have done in Global Perspectives as evidence of their project management skills.

Fun twist: before finishing the interview, ask your partner to demonstrate their sense of humour or creativity – see what they come up with! Then switch: it is your turn to be interviewed!

Work hard: the skills you are learning now will help you for the rest of your life!

Taking it further

History

- Research how access to sport has been affected by ideas of race. Are there sports where People of Colour (POC) are under-represented? Can you find historical explanations for this?
- Research your country's sport history. What sports is your country particularly good at? What medals and awards have you won? Are there any particularly memorable sporting events in your country's history?

Engineering

- Making equipment that allows athletes with different handicaps to participate in sports is an exciting challenge. Research the wheelchairs designed to help athletes who are unable to use their legs to participate in basketball and tennis. Or research the special sleds designed for ice hockey. Look at how they are built to withstand various forces and to allow movement. You could try and design some new equipment to help diverse athletes improve their sporting experience.

Geography

- Another way access to sport can be limited is geographically. Plot access to a sport on a map. You might find that some sports are only available in certain regions – perhaps, for example, because they need water or snow.

Economics

- Some sports are more expensive than others. This creates an economic barrier to access. Should financial aid be provided to help improve sports access? Why or why not?

Literature

- Find works of literature that discuss the lives of different athletes who overcame challenges to access their sports. What can we learn from them?

Maths/Physics

- Investigate the forces used in different sports. How fast can elite cricket players throw a ball? How fast must a gymnast turn to avoid falling when tumbling.

Year 9 Challenge 3

What did you learn?

When you complete this challenge, take a moment to reflect over what you have learnt with the table below.

Skill	I get it!	I am starting to get it!	I need to review this.
Research: I know how to choose research methods.			
Communication: I understand my argument needs to be presented in a logical order.			
Analysis: I understand what a course of action is.			
Reflection: I can understand how some of my GP skills will help me in my professional career.			
Reflection: I know some of my strengths and weaknesses as a team member.			
Collaboration: I understand the importance of being grateful for my team members.			
Perspectives: I understand why we need to understand the causes and consequences of a problem through multiple perspectives.			
Reflection: I have reflected on the importance of sports.			

Year 9

Challenge 4
Languages

4.1 Languages

- What language do you think is the hardest to learn? Which is the easiest?

- How many languages do you speak? Do you know anyone who is bilingual? Trilingual? A polyglot (someone who knows several languages)?

- Think about movies or cartoons. Do they tend to link heroes and villains with particular languages? Why?

Challenge overview

Imagine if we woke up tomorrow and all languages had been forgotten. Somehow all humans spoke the same language: a language created by computers. What would such a universal language be like? Could there be one language that can express all human experiences and all emotions, from all the cultures of the world?

There are some words that exist only in one or a few languages. *Sobremesa*, Spanish, refers to the enjoyment and conversation that takes places after a meal is over but when people are still sitting together. *Age-otori*, Japanese, means looking worse after a haircut. Can you think of words in your language that cannot be translated into another language? Could a universal language ever cover all these different ideas?

Imagine you were put in charge of deciding the future of the world's languages. You can choose to impose a universal language in the world.

Or you could choose to let people keep their languages but create a *lingua franca*. A lingua franca is language that is adopted as a common language by people who speak various other languages. This is the language that would be used for business and government transactions, for example. You could require that everyone learns at least two languages. Would you let some languages fade out of existence or would you put in place policies to ensure that all languages survive?

In this challenge, we invite you to think about why languages are important, what their personal, local, national and global consequences are. Your challenge is to create a *language guide*. This can be a written guide, or a video guide. In this guide you will present information on a language: where it came from, where it is used, interesting words, etc., and suggest how this language can be supported.

What skills will you develop?

Research 1: Getting started
→ You will practise your research skills, finding information in multiple sources and citing this information properly.

Research 2: Finding out your community's languages
→ You will review what research methods are most appropriate for different purposes.

Analysis: Understanding why language is important
→ You will think about the importance of languages and practise finding the central argument of sources.

Evaluation
→ You will practise making and evaluating claims for clarity, logic, and use of evidence.

Reflection
→ You will reflect on your interest in languages and how local, national, and global interests can clash. You will also think about patterns in global languages and make predictions.

Taking it further
→ Here you will find suggestions to explore this topic further, linking it to other subjects like geography, science, arts, and more.

Research 1
Getting started

When asked to create a project on a topic you are unfamiliar with, it is a good idea to start with some preliminary research. This is research that helps you to start to understand the topic.

You will need this research to discover what you find particularly interesting in a topic, what you want to research further. This preliminary research is often the first step to coming up with your own research question.

4.2 Preliminary research

Start by finding out about languages around the world. Try to come up with broad background questions that will guide you as you explore this topic. These are not research questions to lead a research project with, but initial questions to help you become familiar with a topic. If you need help, we have listed some initial questions below:

- How many languages are there in the world?
- What is the most spoken language in the world?
- What is the least spoken language in the world?
- What is the oldest language?
- What is the most popular language to learn?

4.3 Fun research challenge

Finding information is an important skill. You can get better at all skills with practice. Try the following game to practise your research skills. Break into teams to try and answer the questions below. To win, your group needs to find the most answers in under 15 minutes *and* provide a list of sources! Ready? Go!

1. List two fictional languages.
2. What is the most linguistically diverse country in the world?
3. What is the oldest language in the world?

4. Who created Esperanto?
5. What is SilboGomero?
6. What languages are spoken in the International Space Station?
7. What is the world record for the most languages spoken?
8. What is the longest word in English?
9. Can you list three obsolete English words?
10. What languages are spoken in your country (you might not be able to list them all! Try to get as many as you can before the time is up).

Advice: As you worked through this exercise you might have noticed that it was a good idea to write your sources as soon as you found them, rather than try to go back after you are finished to complete your reference list. This is an important point to learn: write down your sources as you use them. This will make your life much easier!

Choosing a language

In this challenge, you are asked to choose a language to learn about. But how can you choose to learn about a language if you don't know about the language to start with? This is another reason why initial research can help: it can help you find new things to learn about. While doing your initial research you might learn, for example, that there are some languages spoken only by a few people. This can lead you to discover languages in your country with only a few speakers. Suddenly a whole new world of discovery is before you!

4.4 Creative questions

What questions can you use to find languages you have never encountered before? How about these questions?

- What language has the most vowels?
- What language has the longest words?
- What languages have Latin roots?

Start your research with an open mind to explore new ideas.

Research 2
Finding out your community's languages

How could you find out what languages are spoken in your community? Would a qualitative or a quantitative method be better to get this research?

4.5 Write a questionnaire

Design a questionnaire to find out what languages are spoken in your community. Write questions to help you understand what languages people speak most often, where they speak different languages, and if they think languages are important and why. You might want to include some open-ended questions in your survey.

Ethics: obtaining consent!

With any research tool you use, make sure you include a short introductory paragraph where you state what you are doing and why, and also note what you will do with the information you gather. Make sure people consent to participate before you collect any data.

4.6 Peer feedback

Exchange your questionnaire with a peer. Give each other some feedback. Check to make sure your questions are clear, focused and non-leading. You want to help your peer improve their work. When receiving feedback, remember that we can all improve!

Make survey and interview questions clear, relevant, and non-leading.

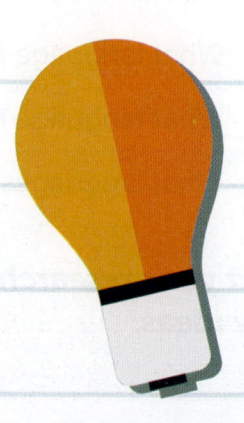

Year 9 Challenge 4

4.7 Reviewing a questionnaire

A group of students put together this questionnaire to find out about languages and education. What do you think they did well? What do you think could have been done better?

Hello, we are 9th grade students from The Woods High School. We are gathering data on language to understand our community better. We would be grateful if you could voluntarily fill out the survey below. We will keep all information safe and anonymous. We will use this information to advocate better language education.

Age ☐   Gender ☐

Highest education level achieved (choose one):
None ☐   Primary ☐   Secondary ☐   University ☐   More ☐

Neighbourhood you live in: _____

Do you think schools should teach in more than one language?   • Yes / • No

What do you think should be the main language used in schools? (Fill in the blank): _____

How many languages do you speak?
1 ☐   2 ☐   3 ☐   4 ☐   or more ☐

Where did you learn your languages?
Home ☐   School ☐   Language School ☐   Travelling ☐   Other ☐

Do you think learning languages is important? Why?
_____
_____

Why do you think it should be mandatory to learn languages?
_____
_____

Challenge:

If you are conducting a survey to learn what languages are used in your community, how would you get the survey to the community? How would you convince community members to participate in the survey? What if part of our community does not speak English?

Analysis
Understanding why language is important

If all human languages disappeared, could we communicate through maths?

Why are languages important? To understand the importance of languages we could think about what effects or consequences they have.

4.8 Predicting consequences

Think about the scenarios below: what would be the consequences for individuals, countries, and the world, if languages changed as suggested?

Scenario 1

What about if we simplified languages? Rather than having words like good, better, best, enjoyable, pleasant, agreeable, pleasing, pleasurable, delightful, great, nice … how about if we simply have one word 'notbad'? Would this make communication easier between persons? Between countries? Could simplification help decrease conflict?

Scenario 2

Why do we need thousands of languages? Wouldn't life be easier if the whole world spoke, say, Swahili? We agree and decide to make Swahili the only language spoken, written and read in the world. What effects could this have?

Scenario 3

What if we used technology to help: every person is fitted with an instantaneous translator as soon as they born. This allows them to understand all other languages in the world. Would this help us communicate more? Would it increase travel? Increase connections between people? Between countries?

To argue that languages should be protected, taught, or prohibited, we need to understand *why* languages matter. It is always important to go back and review the **causes** and **consequences** of an issue. These are often *why* and *how* questions. Why are languages threatened?

Year 9 Challenge 4

Why are languages important? How do languages disappearing affect us? How did the languages we now speak emerge? Without this analytical understanding we cannot build a good argument.

4.9 Finding the main argument

Read the article below and find *why* it argues languages are important. Why does the article claim languages matter?

> **Challenge:**
> See if you can find other articles that support the same claim.

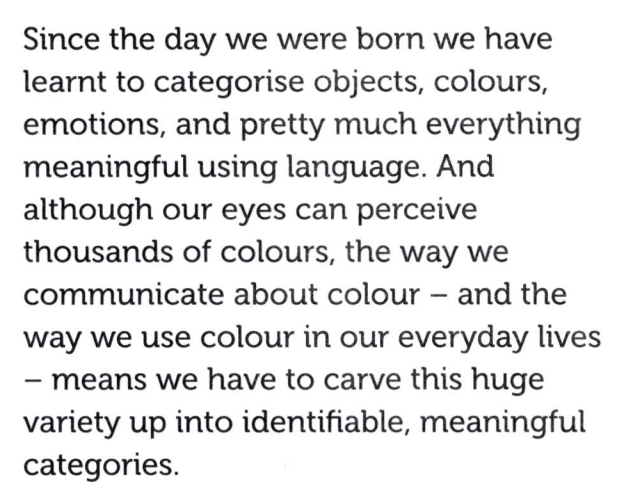

Since the day we were born we have learnt to categorise objects, colours, emotions, and pretty much everything meaningful using language. And although our eyes can perceive thousands of colours, the way we communicate about colour – and the way we use colour in our everyday lives – means we have to carve this huge variety up into identifiable, meaningful categories.

Painters and fashion experts, for example, use colour terminology to refer to and discriminate hues and shades that, to all intents and purposes, may all be described with one term by a non-expert.

Different languages and cultural groups also carve up the colour spectrum differently. Some languages like Dani, spoken in Papua New Guinea, and Bassa, spoken in Liberia and Sierra Leone, only have two terms, dark and light. Dark roughly translates as cool in those languages, and light as warm. So dark colours, like black, blue, and green, are glossed as cool colours, while lighter colours, like white, red, orange and yellow, are glossed as warm colours.

The Warlpiri people living in Australia's Northern Territory don't even have a term for the word 'colour'. For these and other such cultural groups, what we would call 'colour' is described by a rich vocabulary referring to texture, physical sensation and functional purpose.

But this isn't just something that happens with colour, in fact different languages can influence our perceptions in all areas of life. And in our lab at Lancaster University we are investigating how the use of and exposure to different languages changes the way we perceive everyday objects. Ultimately, this happens because learning a new language is like giving our brain the ability to interpret the world differently – including the way we see and process colours.

Adapted from: https://theconversation.com/the-way-you-see-colour-depends-on-what-language-you-speak-94833

Evaluation
Make your case

Making an argument is a skill that takes practice. It is not just about presenting information. It is about presenting information clearly, logically, and persuasively. It is about presenting accurate and valid information in a way that demonstrates how that information supports, or provides evidence for, the claims you are making. You have to make sure your audience understands what you are arguing, and why the evidence shows your argument is correct.

Start with a clear argument

Your argument is the position you have come to after carefully assessing all the information you found through your research. It states what *you* think. Your argument shows your *evaluation* skills. It shows that you can use carefully selected information to come to a conclusion. If you find that you write your entire report and have not stated a clear argument, it is likely that your report is lacking a crucial element: your own voice.

Example:

Clear argument: *Bilingual education should be mandatory in our country*. Here, the author has made a clear claim, now they need to explain their reasons and provide evidence to support these.

Unclear claim: *Bilingual education means two languages are taught*. Here the audience knows the topic, but they have no idea what the author thinks about the topic.

4.10 Make an argument

Write a clear claim, or argument, about each of the following:

→ Mandatory language learning in schools

→ Forbidding the use of certain languages

→ A new law that states all road signs must be in multiple languages

Support your arguments with evidence

You will not win your case by simply stating your opinion. You need to explain to your audience *why* you think as you do and present them with *evidence* to support your reasoning.

Acknowledge and address counterarguments

There are always counterarguments. These are reasons why your claim is not perfect. That is OK, as long as you show your audience that you have thought about possible counterarguments and have provided answers.

4.11 Evaluate an argument

Read the article below and discuss it with a partner. Do you think the article makes its argument well? Discuss whether:

→ it states a clear claim

→ it presents reasons to support its claim

→ it supports its argument with evidence

→ it addresses counter arguments

→ it presents information in logical order.

Should bilingual education be mandatory in Country X?

Our generation is growing in a world that is increasingly multi-lingual. It is no longer enough to learn a little bit of foreign languages in secondary school. To have the opportunity to succeed in the 21st century we need bilingual education. Bilingual education should be mandatory in all schools.

Bilingual education means teaching everything in two languages to help children become fluent in two languages. Studies show that exposure to languages at a young age helps cognitive development: helping the brain respond more flexibly to changing circumstances and improving focus. Other studies have shown that brain aging is slower in bilingual adults.

Besides the health benefits, bilingualism helps bring people together by ending language barriers. Diverse communities, with populations from many cultures who speak different languages, can sometimes struggle to live together. Bilingual education can help ease tensions and build friendships as children grow up learning to speak each other's languages. A language helps us to think. If we learn the language of our neighbours we can better understand how they think. This is why bilingual education should be mandatory, especially in multicultural communities.

Your argument is the position you support after carefully evaluating the evidence you found.

Reflection
A call to action

Look at the data below. Based on what you see, how many languages do you think there will be on our planet 200 years from now? How about 1000 years from now? What patterns in the data, or what information, leads you to make these predictions?

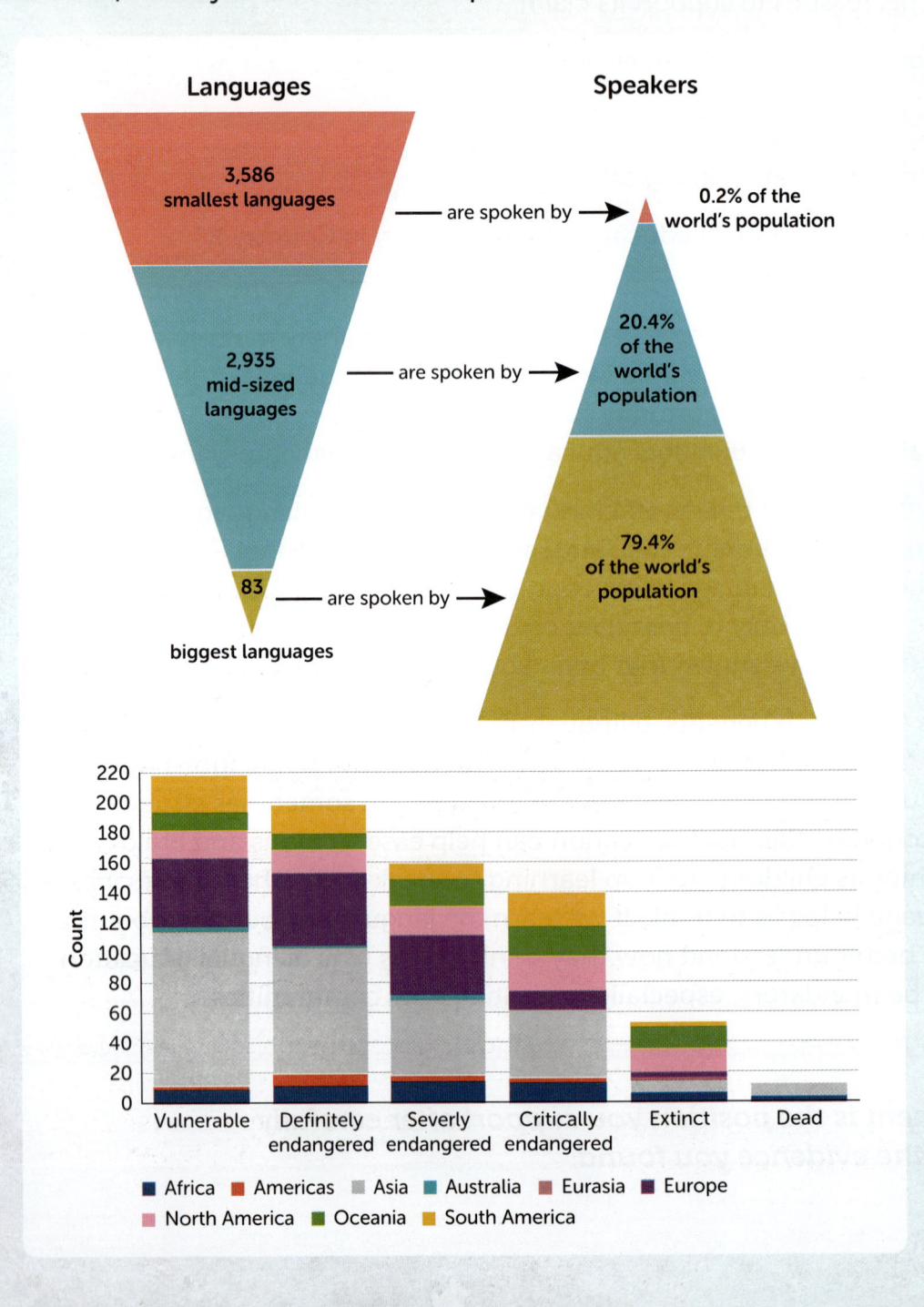

Languages

- 3,586 smallest languages — are spoken by → 0.2% of the world's population
- 2,935 mid-sized languages — are spoken by → 20.4% of the world's population
- 83 biggest languages — are spoken by → 79.4% of the world's population

Speakers

Stacked bar chart — Count by endangerment category:
- Vulnerable: ~220
- Definitely endangered: ~200
- Severly endangered: ~160
- Critically endangered: ~140
- Extinct: ~55
- Dead: ~15

Legend: Africa, Americas, Asia, Australia, Eurasia, Europe, North America, Oceania, South America

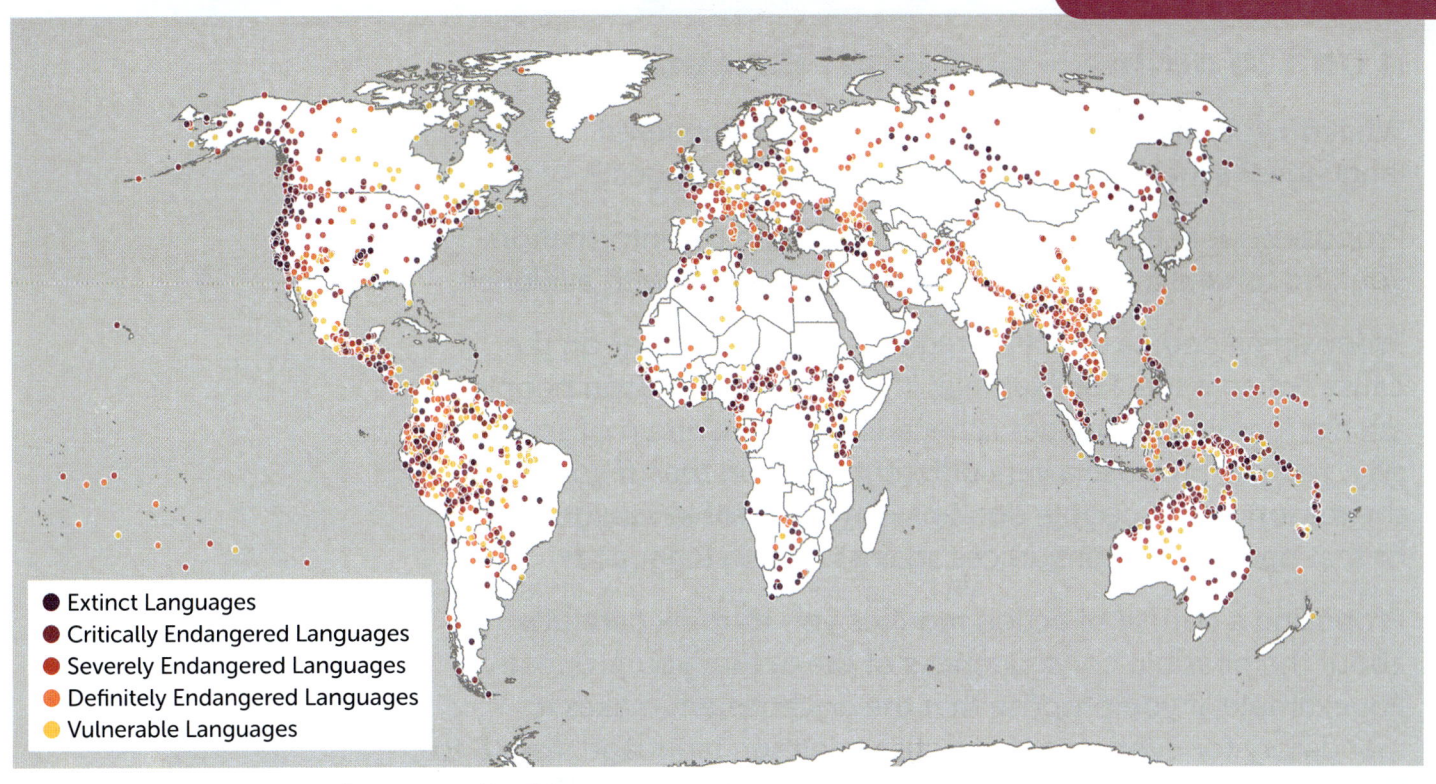

- Extinct Languages
- Critically Endangered Languages
- Severely Endangered Languages
- Definitely Endangered Languages
- Vulnerable Languages

Source: NavinoEvans/Wikimedia Commons

This UNESCO chart depicts hundreds of endangered and vulnerable languages by continent. Thousands more are predicted to disappear by the end of the century.

4.12 Personal interests, national policies

The clash of the personal, the national, and the global.

If one of your languages was among those listed as soon to be extinct, how would you feel? Do you think the feelings of those who speak minority languages should be considered when a country makes its language policy?

Languages once again show us how perspectives can affect each other. While an individual might want to maintain their language and want the government to help the language survive by, for example, being taught in school at a national level, some might argue that it makes little sense to spend money on a language spoken only by a few. At a global level, some languages are becoming increasingly important, and are becoming a global lingua franca. Some argue that countries should spend their resources teaching their population a global lingua franca, such as English. But is it fair to have languages disappear because they are not popular? What about the unique knowledge that each language holds? What about the individual stories that will disappear with that language?

A call to action – and what it needs

What do you think should be done about endangered languages? What course of action would you suggest?

Proposing an action requires you to evaluate the information you find to take a clear position you can support with evidence.

Proposing a course of action requires you to be clear on the causes of an issue. For example, if you think the reason people are not learning languages is because they are afraid of sounding silly, you will propose a very different solution than if you think the reason is that people don't have money for language classes or that people have prejudices against certain languages.

Proposing a course of action requires you to think carefully about the possible consequences of the action you propose. For example, if you propose that the government makes it mandatory for *everyone* to practise a foreign language from 8 to 9 a.m., you need to consider that there will be no police or train drivers or airplane pilots between 8 and 9 a.m.!

4.13 Suggesting a course of action

Look at the various issues with languages below. Come up with a possible solution.

Issue: Immigrant children who do not speak the main language of their new country

Proposed action:

Issue: Most information on the Internet is in English.

Proposed action:

Issue: Coding languages are becoming a necessary part of education.

Proposed action:

4.14 Solutions and causes

You need to make sure your suggested solution addresses the causes of a problem. To give you practice, try to fill out the following table. You can make a similar table for any topic in Global Perspectives.

Problem	Cause	Solution
Local language is disappearing	Everyone uses English to use the Internet	Create website in the local language
Local trees are being cut down	Wood is being burnt to provide heat	Find other sources of heat such as solar power
Local language is disappearing	There are only a few local language speakers left	
Local language is disappearing	Schools make it mandatory that children speak only the local language	

Evidence to support your solution

When you suggest a solution, you will need to provide evidence to support your understanding of the problem, and to demonstrate that your proposed solution makes sense. Remember that evidence can come in many forms: graphs, photos, books, newsletters, interviews, blogs, videos, documentaries, magazine articles, information from governments and NGOs, etc.

4.15 Finding diverse evidence

Try finding evidence to support the view that a community of your choice is a multilingual community – a community that uses multiple languages.

Challenge: Go back through the sources you found and evaluate, or judge, them for quality. How do they build their argument? Do they use valid evidence to support what they are arguing?

Stop

Can you explain the difference between a fact and an opinion?

4.16 Changing your views

After working on languages in this Challenge, have your views on languages changed? Are there any new languages you want to learn?

Taking it further

Linguistics

- Learn more about sounds and languages. Find a sound that you don't use in your language and see if you can learn to make it.
- Research initiatives to document world languages that are endangered. Find out how these projects work: how do you make a dictionary of a language that has not been written down before?

Music and language

- Listen to music in another language. Have you been moved or inspired by another culture's music even if you cannot understand the lyrics? Use a translation tool to understand the lyrics. Does this change how you feel or react to the music?

History

- Research the evolution of a language. You could look at your own language or choose a different language. It might be particularly interesting to research the native languages of your country. What is the oldest language in your country? What is the youngest?
- Not all languages have been voluntarily adopted. Look into how languages were imposed during colonialism and conquest. How did people who were forced to adopt new languages react? See if you can find historical records of how languages were imposed.

Science

- Look into how language learning takes place in the brain. The neuroscience of language learning is fascinating. You could also look at how language is lost through degenerative brain diseases.
- Look at how our body physically creates sound. Are there particular muscles needed to make certain sounds? Can these weaken if they are not developed in early years?

Geography

- Create a map of languages. Can you colour a map by the languages spoken? Can you add strings to show how languages spread?
- Find the countries with the greatest linguistic diversity. What else sets these countries apart from others?

Civics

- Set up as pen pals with someone in a different language. Use technology to help you overcome the language barrier and see if you can teach each other some new words!

Year 9 Challenge 4

What did you learn?

When you complete this challenge, take a moment to reflect over what you have learnt with the table below.

Skill	I get it!	I am starting to get it!	I need to review this.
Research: I can find information in multiple sources.			
Research: I know how to cite information correctly.			
Research: I understand the benefits and drawbacks of different research methods.			
Analysis: I know how to find a central argument.			
Analysis: I understand I need to start my work with a clear position or central argument.			
Evaluation: I understand that good arguments are supported by evidence, and acknowledge counterarguments.			
Analysis: I understand how to use data to make predictions about the future.			

Challenge 5
Writing your report

Year 9 is a particularly fun year in Global Perspectives as you get to choose your own Challenge to explore!

In discussion with your teacher, you will be responsible for writing a *research report* that carefully follows the syllabus guidance.

Think about your research report as an exciting opportunity to look more deeply into something you are fascinated by. Think back over your years of studying Global Perspectives. Were there any instances when you wished you had more time to explore a particular idea or question? Well, this is your chance! This is also your opportunity to show off all the skills you have learnt, demonstrating how well you can research, analyse, evaluate and communicate information.

It is important to note that this is *your* project. This is an individual project and not something others can help you with. Therefore your teacher:

- cannot undertake any research for you
- cannot correct, edit, or make notes on your report before you submit it
- cannot write any part of the report for you.

It is important to carefully read the syllabus instructions before you start, to make sure you:

- understand what you are supposed to do
- understand how you are supposed to do it.

Make sure you:

- write your report on one of the Global Perspectives topics (you can choose any issue you are interested in within the Global Perspective topics)
- provide all the components the syllabus requests
- stick to the word count.

In the following pages you will be given some hints and tips for the different parts of your research report. You will also be reminded of some possible pitfalls.

Remember: enjoy the process! This is a great opportunity to deepen your knowledge in something you are interested in. Don't let worries about the work take the fun out of it. You can do it!

Choosing your topic

The freedom to choose your own topic is one of the most exciting, *and one of the most intimidating*, aspects of Global Perspectives!

Remember: you need to choose your topic from one of those listed in the Global Perspectives curriculum.

Now, where do you start?

Emotions

One suggestion is to follow your emotions. You will need to spend quite a bit of time working on your report, so you should make sure that it is something you are deeply interested in.

Issues that you are passionate about will inspire you to learn more about them so you can figure out how to change them. If you get upset at animals being mistreated, for example, you will want to learn why this is happening and how to stop it! If you want to stop plastic pollution, you will want to learn why it happens and what its consequences are, to try and convince others to use less plastic. Find something you are deeply interested in, so that your interest can drive your research and encourage you to find possible solutions.

Free thinking!

Remember the power of free thinking when looking for a topic. Write down *all* your ideas. Anything you are interested in, anything that might be fun, anything that might be easy, anything that makes you upset ... just write it all down to find inspiration.

Starting your research

A good project requires a good research question. Creating a good question takes some skill!

Remember what makes a good question:

- It needs to be focused.
- It needs to be clear.
- It cannot be leading (in other words, it cannot hint at what the answer should be).
- It needs to be realistic: not something too large to research or on an area where you can't find information.

A good question for your research report will lead to analysis and evaluation:

Analysis: A good question cannot be answered only with your opinion. It needs research to understand the causes and consequences of a problem.

Evaluation: A good question leads you to take a position or present an argument. Your report will not be successful if you simply present information without evaluating, or judging, what is the correct way to act in response to the issue you are analysing.

5.1 Question for the project

Which of the following questions lead to analysis and evaluation?

Example: Do I like bananas?

This question is too constricted or small. I can easily answer this question with YES/NO without doing any research to consider WHY I do or do not like bananas. So, it does not lead to analysis. Also, I don't have to answer whether liking bananas is good or bad, or what should be done about my liking bananas. The question does not lead to evaluation.

- Is water necessary?
- What is the composition of fossil fuels?
- Should the world stop using fossil fuels?
- How can education for young children be improved?
- Why does the use of pesticides matter?
- Is palm oil useful?

Pitfalls

- Be careful about choosing questions that are too large to manage. If your focus is too large, you will find yourself overwhelmed.
- Be careful about choosing questions that are too constricted or small. If your questions are too constrained, you will struggle to find sources for your research.

5.2 Judging questions

Match each question with a description:

Column A	Column B
Natural disasters affect the poorest people hardest. Why?	Too broad
What can we do to help the poorest survive natural disasters?	Too confusing
How did the poorest people living in Pompei feel when Mount Vesuvius erupted in 79 AD?	Does not lead to evaluation, simply to description
Why is it bad not to help the poorest after a natural disaster where everyone is hurt?	Impossible to research
How do natural disasters affect the poor?	Too narrow
	Leading

Remember, coming up with a good research question takes work. You might need to go back to a question and sharpen it, rewrite it or refocus it. You might also ask a question, then do some research and find a new area that is more interesting, leading you to change your question slightly.

Finding and using sources

Finding good sources will be crucial to answering your research question well. Good sources are sources that are relevant, up to date, and reliable.

In your project report you will be expected to carefully *evaluate* your sources. You need to explain how you evaluated them to ensure they were useful, current, and valid. Pay particular attention to possible biases in sources and discuss what these biases might be.

There are numerous sources you could use, including:

- books
- journal articles
- newspapers
- encyclopaedias
- information published by NGOs and IOs such as the United Nations and the World Bank
- blogs and websites
- podcasts and vlogs.

5.3 Finding sources

Demonstrate your growing research skills by finding information about each of the questions below in a newspaper, a blog, a book, and a relevant website.

- What are the most common crimes in your country?
- What are some arguments against wind power?
- Should animal rights be expanded?

Remember to look carefully at where your information came from. Are you citing newspapers known for a particular bias? Are the websites you use well known and respected? Are the authors of your sources experts in the area or are they simply opinionated citizens? Why are their views important? If in doubt, try to find at least one other source that can corroborate or confirm the information you are citing from a source. If possible, cross-checking your information is always a good idea. If you can find the same data cited in at least three distinct sources, you can make a case that it is likely to be valid information. (Be careful, this does *not* prove that the information is true, it simply proves that you have tried to test your sources).

5.4 Cross-checking data

Use more than one source to help you answer the question, 'Can insects become the main human food of the future?'. Use your sources to cross-check any data you use. If a source states, for example, that insects make up 99 percent of creatures on Earth, make sure that you find the same data elsewhere to verify that it is valid. When you write your report, it is also a good idea to cross-check your data to ensure it is valid and accurate.

In your report, explain that you have paid attention to who wrote the sources you are using, and why they wrote them. Could the authors be biased? Could they have a vested interest? You want to show that you thoughtfully evaluate your sources.

5.5 Checking authors

Discuss with your peers: How can you check who the authors of your sources are? For example, why might you be concerned who the authors are employed by? If you use blogs, podcasts, or vlogs in your research, make sure you pay particular attention to who made them, and why.

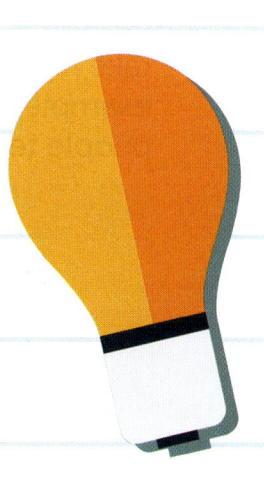

You could also find primary data by conducting your own research. Your research could include:

- interviews
- surveys
- questionnaires
- focus groups
- observation
- experiments.

If conducting your own research, keep three points in mind:

1. Safety: Make sure you are safe. It is best never to conduct research on your own, try to pair up with a friend. Never go to an interview without telling an adult where you are going. You need to obtain your parents' or guardians' permission before conducting any research outside school grounds and you should always let others know where you are, who you are with, and how to contact you.

2. Ethics: You must inform anyone whose data you collect what you are doing, what you are doing it for, and what you will do with their information. You must make sure people agree to take part in your research and you must make it clear to them that they can always change their mind and stop participating. It is your duty as a researcher to try and avoid causing any harm to people who participate in your research. This might require you to keep interviewees anonymous, or to avoid asking certain questions.

3. Quality: Ensure your data is useful by carefully preparing questions and ensuring you have the necessary means to take notes or collect responses. If you are interviewing, for example, don't rely on your memory to remember what people tell you. Take careful notes you can review.

5.6 Testing different methods

Write a questionnaire and an interview script to find information on what your community thinks should be done for children who do not have enough food. You will need to think about who you would use each method with. For example, you might want to interview charity leaders and homeless families. Would your questions be the same?

You will also need to consider what questions are best for an interview, and what questions are best for a questionnaire. Would you ever ask the same questions in a questionnaire as in an interview?

5.7 Numeric sources

Remember that images and graphs are powerful means of communication. Can you find numerical data on your topic, or on how many books people read?

Analysis

Choosing your perspective

As you begin your project, remember to choose the perspective from which you will be conducting your research. Global Perspectives requires you to look at your topic from a national and a global perspective. You are then required to suggest a local or national course of action to help solve the issue.

- Make sure you discuss the issue from both a national and global perspective.
- You should also discuss how these two interact or affect each other.
- When choosing a national perspective, you do **not** have to choose your own country's perspective, or the perspective of the country you live in. You are free to choose any country.

5.8 Global and national

Work with peers to fill in a Venn diagram for one of the questions below. Note how the national and international perspectives are different, and also note where they overlap.

How does food production affect climate change?

Should television be used to help us learn about other cultures?

Should bilingual education be mandatory?

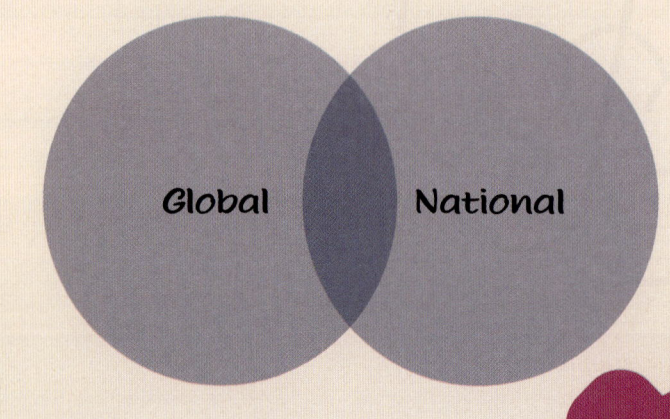

Remember that finding sources is only the beginning of your research. Once you find a relevant source, you need to carefully read it to look for useful information. You can find information that helps you to understand:

- the causes of an issue, for example, 'Why so many people are unemployed in my country', or 'Why are video games so popular?'
- the consequences of an issue, for example, 'What consequences does unemployment have for the people of my country?', or 'Why does it matter if more young people play video games for multiple hours a day?'.

5.9 Why, and So what?

Look through your sources and try to use them to answer the questions: 'Why?' and 'So What?'

Why – Why is the problem you are investigating happening?

So What? – Why does this problem matter? Whom does it affect? How? When?

Remember
Not all sources are equally good! Some might have old data, some might be inaccurate (with wrong data), and some might present a biased perspective.

5.10 Evaluating a source

You must always evaluate your sources. Are they clear? Are they relevant? Are they up to date? Are they accurate? Are they unbiased? What do you think of the source below?

A quick note on fossil fuels

While it is true that fossil fuels are not quite clean, it is also true that we are daily improving in our technology. We now need less fuels to power better and more powerful machines. Alternative sources of energy are not as efficient as fossil fuels and, therefore, are a wasteful investment. Wind stops, the sun goes down. Fossil fuels always burn. We must be wise and stick to what works.

Source: Robert Frump, President of Oil-makers of the 21st Century

Reflection

An important part of Global Perspectives is helping you to become a more thoughtful actor in your local, national, and global community. As you have worked through the materials in this course, several times you have been asked to reflect on what you have learnt.

As you complete your report, you have another opportunity to think about what you have learnt. This is an opportunity to think about how you have changed, and to think about yourself as a scholar, a citizen, and a researcher!

To realize how you have changed, it might be worth **starting** this project by writing down what you think about the issue, before you do any research. You could write down a few questions and write your answers. Keep these someplace safe so you can read your answers again after you complete the project. What questions would you ask yourself? Perhaps:

- Why did I choose this issue?
- What do I think is most interesting about this issue?
- If money or time was not a problem, how would I solve this issue?

After you complete the report you could try to answer these questions again, and also answer:

- What surprised me the most from my research?
- Was the solution to the problem I proposed before I started my research a good solution?

5.11 Assessing skill development

Use the list below to check how your skills have changed.

Skills	Have not changed	Have learnt some skills	Have learnt a lot of skills
I know how to find sources of information.			
I know how to cite sources.			
I know how to evaluate sources.			
I know what a biased source is.			
I know how to create a plan.			
I know how to split a project with teams.			
I know how to solve conflicts in a team project.			
I know how to analyse an issue by finding its causes and consequences.			

Also spend some time thinking about how your research skills have grown during your time as a Global Perspectives student. Are you better at finding sources? Are you more careful about what sources you choose? What is the most important piece of advice you would offer younger Global Perspective students?

5.12 Reflecting on your learning

Can you think of three ways in which you have changed as a result of studying Global Perspectives?

Can you list three things you have learnt through this course?

What is the most important skill you have learnt by doing Global Perspective Challenges?

If you could change anything about the course, what would it be?

5.13 Creative reflection

Try to make a drawing about a topic you have particularly enjoyed learning about.

Communication
Writing your report

How you structure your report is up to you. You can be creative and have fun. There are, however, several areas you need to make sure you cover:

→ Make sure the issue you are discussing, and the question you are seeking to answer, are clear.

→ Make sure you clearly discuss your issue from a global and a national perspective.

→ Make sure you include a discussion of the sources you chose, why you chose them, and how you evaluated them.

→ Make sure you analyse your issue: what are the causes of this issue? What are the consequences? Ensure you provide evidence, from your sources, to support your views on causes and consequences.

→ Make sure you propose a course of action for this issue. This course of action, or possible solution, can be focused at the local or the national level. How will the solution work? How would you measure its success?

→ Makes sure you show how your suggested course of action addresses the causes or consequences you analysed.

→ The conclusion should include your personal reflection. What have you learnt from this report? How has research impacted your personal perspective?

When writing, remember to think about your audience. Try to read your report as if you were your audience. If you were a Global Perspectives teacher, how could a student show you that they have carefully researched an issue? How could they show you that they thought carefully about the resources they used and made sure they did not include 'fake news' as real information?

Think of this as a formal report. You want to ensure your language is clear, concise, and accurate. Give yourself plenty of time to edit your report. Very few people can write a perfect report on their first try! Most people need to write, edit, review, and write again. That is fine. Just make sure you give yourself the time you will need to edit and rewrite as needed.

5.14 Editing writing

Look at the paragraph below. Can you help this student edit their writing to make it clearer?

> Education can be a powerful tool against violence. In particularly, education can help students avoid being radicalised. Education can help students from being attracted to extreme ideologies. It can do this by helping them think critically about the ideologies proposed. Students who are used to critical thinking will ask why an ideology states what it does or does not. They will seek evidence to support what the ideology claims. Once they find a lack of evidence, they are unlikely to believe the ideology. Education can also give students confidence to stand against extreme ideologies. Students confident in their own abilities are less likely to fall under the spell of preachers and teachers who claim to know the only true way (Johnson, page 5). There is no magic weapon against radicalisation, but education is an important tool we should not discount.

5.15 Mapping your report

Remember, writing a report requires planning and organizing. Take some time to write down the different parts your report will cover. You might reorganize these as you write and edit your work, but starting with a clear plan can only help you.

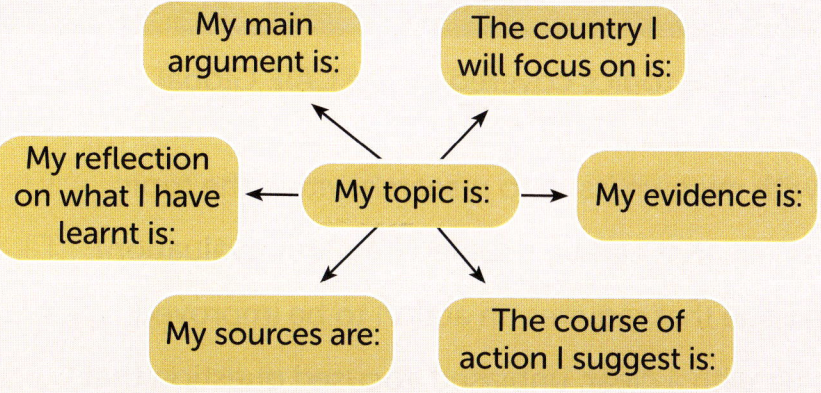

- My main argument is:
- The country I will focus on is:
- My reflection on what I have learnt is:
- My topic is:
- My evidence is:
- My sources are:
- The course of action I suggest is:

Remember to cite all your sources. Follow the citing style your school has chosen, and make sure you are consistent. Anyone who reads your report should be able to know what information you found and in what sources, and be able to find these sources themselves by using your reference list.

Note: Once again, remember to enjoy the process. You are learning and sharpening skills that will help you for the rest of your life. You are learning to see your world in a thoughtful and critical way. Enjoy!

Year 9 Reflection

After you complete your research project, or before, you might want to take some time to reflect with the questions below.

1. What is the most interesting topic you learnt about in Global Perspectives?
2. What did you learn about yourself by working as part of a team in different challenges?
3. Did you find working on the Challenges or writing your research report harder? Why?
4. What was your favourite part of Global Perspectives?
5. What skill do you think you have advanced the most in by working on this course? research/analysis/evaluation/collaboration/communication?
6. If you could solve any local, national or global problem, what problem would you solve?
7. Do you see yourself as a person with a global perspective?

Global Perspectives Year 9 report checklist

Topic – I have chosen one of the topics covered by the CAIE Global Perspectives curriculum. ☐

Issue – I have come up with my own issue to research within the topic. ☐

Issue – I have chosen an issue that can be debated (requires evaluation). ☐

Issue – I have chosen an issue that requires an action to be improved. ☐

Research – I have come up with a clear, unbiased, focused question that can be realistically researched. ☐

Research – I have come up with a question that leads to analysis and evaluation. ☐

Research – I have found a variety of sources with valid, relevant, and current information about my issue. Sources can include: scholarly articles, newspaper and magazine articles, government websites, NGO websites, blogs, videos, and podcasts. ☐

Research – I have taken good notes from my sources, and carefully noted where I found my information, creating a list of references. ☐

Research – I have carefully evaluated my resources, thinking about who wrote them and why, paying particular attention to possible biases, and have noted this evaluation in my report. ☐

Perspectives – My report discusses my issues from a national and a global perspective. ☐

Perspectives – I clearly show the global relevance of my issue. ☐

Perspectives – I clearly show the national relevance of my issue, using two or more national examples. ☐

Analysis – My report clearly explains the causes and consequences of my issue. ☐

Course of action – My report clearly proposes a (single) course of action to help improve or solve the issue I am writing about. This course of action is national or local in its scope. ☐

Conclusion – My conclusion clearly states how I have answered my research question. ☐

Reflection – In my conclusion, I reflect on what I have learnt, and how my own perspective has changed through my learning. ☐

Writing – My writing is clear, succinct, and professional. ☐

Writing – My research report is no more than 1000 words (excluding references). ☐

Writing – Sources are carefully cited in my report. ☐

References – My research report has a list of references. ☐

Economic appendix

A short guide to basic economic ideas

To understand many Global Perspective Challenges, it is useful to understand some basic classical economic ideas.

The basic economic problem

I want more!

The basic economic problem states that there are not enough resources to satisfy all human needs and wants. In other words, even if we use everything our planet has, we will not be able to produce everything every person on the planet needs and wants. Someone will always want or need more.

Thus, we face two important limitations:

SCARCITY – there are simply not enough resources in the world for all of us to get everything we want or need.

CHOICE – since we are limited in what we can have, we have to make choices. To have more of one thing, we have to have less of something else.

Scarcity and *choice* apply at all levels of the economy. As an individual, you only have so much time (your resource) and so many things you need and want to do. If you *choose* to spend all your time sleeping, you will not have time to eat or study. If you study for 23 hours a day, you will have no time to eat, play, and sleep! To do more of one thing, you have to do less of something else. The same applies to countries. If a country wants to spend more money on education, it will have less to spend less, for example, on roads.

With limited resources and unlimited needs and wants, we constantly have to choose **what** to produce and for **whom**. The world simply cannot produce everything it wants, and it cannot give it to everyone.

When you propose a change – for example, if you argue that fewer trees should be cut down – you are arguing for a different balance on what should be produced and for whom.

What resources do we have in our planet to create things with? According to traditional economic theory there are four types of resources:

1. Land – this refers to all our natural resources.
2. Capital – this refers to money *and* to machines, physical tools, plants and equipment used to produce goods.
3. Labour – this refers to the people who can work.
4. Entrepreneurship – this refers to the motivation and creativity of people to create new goods and services.

Questions to ponder:

Do all countries have the same amount of each resource?

Are some resources more valuable than others?

What do you think a country should choose to produce, since it has limited resources?

How does a country's choice of what to produce affect different parts of its population?

Will limited resources and endless wants/needs lead to conflict?

Writing appendix

To succeed in Global Perspectives, as in other academic fields, you will need to express your research findings clearly, citing your evidence properly. Here are some suggestions to help your writing.

Introduction

Your introduction is a powerful part of any essay or report. It is here where you can catch the attention of your reader and clearly *state what question drives your work and how you have answered it*. Often, we are not quite clear what we are doing until we have done it, so it might be worth writing your introduction once you finish the rest of your paper!

Using evidence

As you write your report, it is important to use evidence to support your argument. If you are arguing, for example, that your country should stop using pesticides, you need to use evidence to *demonstrate why* pesticides are bad or unnecessary. Make sure you:

- avoid simply re-stating what others have said. You need to be presenting your own argument.
- avoid simply listing facts. You need to *explain* to your reader why the facts you are using *are evidence*, and how they prove that your argument is correct.
- cite all the information you use so your readers can check your data. You also need to cite your sources so writers and researchers get fair recognition for their work.

Look at the examples below. Which makes a clear point? Which simply repeats what others have said? Which cites sources properly?

Example 1

Pesticides are damaging our bee populations. Bees are necessary for plant pollination. Without bees, we will have no food. One third of the food we eat relies on bees for its pollination. Without bees we might soon face food shortages. If some plants disappear without pollination, entire food chains might collapse.

Example 2

In the UK there are 25 types of bees. Bees pollinate one third of our food. Einstein said "If the bee disappeared off the surface of the globe then man would only have four years left to live."

Guiding your readers

Remember that those who read your work will often know less than you about the issue you are writing about. Always think about your audience. Give them enough background information to understand what you are arguing. Make sure each point you are making is clear. Don't just throw information at your readers: *tell* them what you are arguing and how the information supports your point.

Using your conclusion

Your conclusion is another powerful part of your essay. Use your conclusion to remind the reader what you have argued, what problem you focused on and what solution you proposed. Also use the conclusion to reflect on what you have learnt through your research. This is your opportunity to make sure the reader has understood your argument, and can see how much you have reflected on the material.

Editing your work

No one creates perfect, clear work on their first try. Give yourself plenty of time to revise and edit your work. We strongly suggest that you complete your work at least a day or two in advance. Then take a nice long break and re-read your work *out loud*. You will be surprised by how many oversights or errors you find!

MLA guide

Citing your sources properly is *very important*. Citing your sources means that you are giving fair credit to the people whose work you are using to build your argument. Citing your sources also means that anybody who reads your work can go back to check your sources to make sure you used them accurately. They might also want to check to see if you used current, unbiased sources.

For Global Perspectives you can use any citation style. Your school might have a preferred style. What is important is to remain consistent. Whatever style you choose, you must use the same style in all parts of your work.

One of the styles you can choose to use is MLA. Below is a brief MLA style guide.

	In text citation	
Book with one author	(Surname, page number)	Author surname, Author first name. *Title*. Publisher, Year.
Article from a scholarly journal in a database	(Surname, page number)	Author surname, Author first name. "Article Title." *Journal Title*, Version, Number, Publication date, Page Numbers.
Website	(Surname or website if no author)	Author surname, Author first name. "Title of article or individual page." *Title of website*, Name of publisher, Date of publication, URL or DOI.

Source: https://guides.lib.uw.edu/c.php?g=341448&p=4076094

Learning objectives and exercises

Research: Learning to ask questions, find information, and record findings.

Learning objective	Relevant exercises
• Learning to ask relevant, clear, focused, non-biased and non-leading questions	
• Learning to find information in a variety of sources, including books, magazines, videos, websites, videos, and podcasts	
• Understanding and using different research methods to find information	
• Collating, selecting, and synthesizing information	
• Recording information and sources effectively	

Analysis: Understanding an issue by studying its causes and effects. Using multiple perspectives to help you understand an issue.

Learning objective	Relevant exercises
Understanding an issue from different perspectives	
Using graphical or numerical data to understand an issue and/or as evidence	
Explaining the causes and consequences of an issue	
Suggest possible solutions for an issue	
Understand how local, national, and global perspectives are linked	

Evaluation: Judging the quality of sources, arguments, and possible solutions

Learning objective	Relevant exercises
Evaluating sources to see if they are clear, relevant, current, and non-biased	
Evaluating an argument for clarity and effective use of relevant and valid evidence	

Reflection: Thinking deeply about our work as teammates and researchers, as well as about our personal learning.

Learning objective	Relevant exercises
Think about my work in a team: what I have done and what I could do better	
Think about what I find most challenging and most enjoyable about teamwork	
Think about how my views on various Global Perspectives have changed as I learn more about them	
Think about what skills I have developed as I work on Global Perspectives challenges	

Collaboration: Learning to work in a team to achieve shared goals

Learning objective	Relevant exercises
Learn how to assign tasks to successfully complete a Global Perspectives Challenge	
Support my team with new ideas, new strategies, and techniques to resolve conflict and support communication	

Communication: Learning to listen to others and to communicate our ideas effectively

Learning objective	Relevant exercises
Share our ideas clearly, logically, using relevant, properly cited, evidence to support our arguments	
Actively listen and support my peers with relevant questions and suggestions	

Index

access aspects 155, 248–261
active listening 85, 94–95, 174–175
agenda selection 124–125
AI 176, 218
aid, trade and 178–191
aim discussions 167, 200, 222–223
alternative education models 77–79
analysis 6, 13, 116–117, 206, 210–211, 216
    conflict resolution 235–236
    diplomacy and traditions 40–41
    education 69, 74–81
    employment 101, 106–113
    food beliefs 151, 158–159
    globalization 48–57
    human differences 24–27
    languages 263, 268–269
    migration 85, 89–96, 137–141
    MLA guide 299
    report writing 280, 286–287
    sports for all 249, 252–253
    trade and aid 179–181
    water crisis 124, 128
animals, human differences 24–25, 27–28, 30–31
anthropology 44
argument aspects 24–25, 72–79, 252–255, 269–271
art 44, 82, 98, 114, 134, 148, 162, 204, 246
artificial intelligence (AI) 176, 218
asylum seekers 85, 88–94
audience aspects 196, 214, 221–223, 229, 297
author source checks 283

background research 208–209
Bear Grylls 150
behavior aspects 230–231
biases 36–37, 85–95, 124–126, 142–143, 156–157, 197, 242–243
blogs 27, 143
Boolean modifiers 127
borders and migration 88, 136–137, 141–145
bullseye 21

cartoons 184–185
causation 74–75, 79–81, 137–142, 145–148, 210–211, 253, 287
child labour 110–111
citations 39, 132–133, 197, 283, 291
civics 98, 276
clarity aspects 20–21, 37, 210, 214, 270
closed questions 224
collaboration 6, 15, 117
    conflict resolution 235, 240–241
    disease and health 231
    education 73, 81
    employment 101–103, 105
    food beliefs 151, 160–161

    globalization 55–56, 64–65
    MLA guide 299
    report writing 286–287
    sports for all 249, 256–257
    sustainability 193–195, 203
    trade and aid 179, 186–189
    water crisis 123, 125–126, 129–131
collaboration tickets 186
comics 184–185
communication 6, 15, 117, 207, 216
    debates 28–29, 85, 94–95
    diplomacy and traditions 33, 42–43
    disease and health 221–223, 228–229
    food beliefs 157
    future perspectives 165, 172–175
    globalization 47, 64–66
    migration 85, 94–95, 137, 146–147
    MLA guide 300
    report writing 290–291
    sports for all 249, 254–255
    sustainability 193, 196–197, 201–203
    trade and aid 179, 184–185
    water crisis 123, 129–133
community languages 266–267
comparative perspectives 104–105
computers, human differences 16, 27, 30
conflict resolution 234–247
consent aspects 266–267
consequences 76–81, 140–148, 158–160, 212–213, 253, 287
constructive feedback 125
consumer roles 188–189
coronavirus/Covid-19 pandemic 66, 148, 220, 227, 231
counter-arguments 181, 270–271
creativity skills 213, 259, 289
citing sources 118–119
critical thinking 72–73, 106–107, 112–113, 137–141, 144–145
cross-checking sources 227, 283
cross-referencing information 226–227
cultural traditions 32–45, 154–158, 192–193
customs and traditions 33–36, 220

data analysis 47, 54–57, 90–91, 106–110, 251
data interpretation 47, 54–57
data surveys 59–61
debates 28–29, 85, 94–95
dependent variables 230–231
diplomacy and traditions 32–45
disease and health 220–233
diversity 250–251, 264
documentaries, trade and aid 179–181
drafting videos 80–81

301

economics
    appendix 294–295
    disease and health 220, 232
    employment 92, 109, 114
    food beliefs 158
    globalization 52–53, 62, 66
    guide to 294–295
    migration 138–139, 143–144
    sports for all 260
    sustainability 204
    trade and aid 181, 190
    water crisis 125, 134
editing work 214, 296
education 44, 68–83
emotions 97, 144, 279
employment 100–115
engineering 134, 260
environmental change/concerns 52–53, 125, 138, 144, 154–159, 192–205
equality and education 74–75, 80, 83
ergo propter hoc 137, 139
ethics 47, 62–63, 97, 266–267, 284
evaluation 6, 117, 206, 211, 216
    conflict resolution 235, 243–245
    disease and health 221, 226–227
    education 69–73
    employment 111–113
    future perspectives 165–167
    languages 170–171, 263
    migration 85–91, 95, 137, 142–143
    MLA guide 299
    report writing 280, 287
    sustainability 193, 197, 200–201
    trade and aid 179, 182–183
evidence aspects 26–27, 111, 227, 270–271, 296
examinations, education 83

fact aspects 69–75, 198–199
Fairtrade 179, 183, 185, 189
fake news 221, 226–227
feedback 65, 105, 125, 207, 266–267
fiction 165, 169
    see also literature
fieldwork 101, 107, 224
fines and penalties 122, 158
flash fiction 169
focus 20–21, 37, 124–125, 209
food beliefs 150–177
forced labour 108–111
foreign aid 178–191
foreign languages 176, 263–276
free thinking 18–19, 71, 124, 279
future perspectives 113–114, 164–177, 258–259, 263

gender aspects 69, 71, 74–77, 80–81
geography 66, 98, 134, 176, 246, 260, 276
girls school attendance 69, 71, 74–77, 80–81

globalization 46–67
global perspective overview 8–11
goal analysis and evaluation 112–113
graphs 54–57, 60, 90–91, 108–110
gratitude, displaying 187, 257
group creation 242–243
guide to economics 294–295
guide to writing skills 296–297

headline evaluations 89
health 154–155, 220–233
history 44, 82, 148, 162, 190, 204, 232, 260, 276
human traits 16–31, 237

ICT 44
imagery 196–197
immigration see migration
inclusiveness 74–75, 80, 83
independent variables 230–231
inequalities 74–75, 80, 83, 255
information collection 38–39, 198–199, 209, 251, 282–285
information and communications technology (ICT) 44
information cross-referencing 226–227
information presentation 184–185, 201–203, 212–216, 222–223, 252–255, 274–275, 278–291
information sharing 42–43, 193, 201
information sources 38–39, 126–127, 142–143, 282–285
information synthesizing 170–174, 206, 209, 298
in-groups 235, 242–243
interacting/interconnected perspectives 11, 75, 220, 286–287
inter-cultural communication 157
international aid 178–191
international sports links 255
Internet 55–57, 66, 104, 126–127, 198
interviews 62–63, 97, 198, 225, 259

journalism 114

key skills overview 6–7

languages 55–60, 66, 98, 148, 176, 232, 240–241, 262–277
laws 30, 148, 246, 255
leading questions 20
libraries 198
lingua franca 263, 273
linguistics *see* languages
listening skills 85, 94–95, 174–175
literature
    conflict resolution 246
    diplomacy and traditions 45
    employment 114
    future perspectives 165, 169, 176
    globalization 66
    migration and refugees 98
    sports for all 260
    trade and aid 184–185
    what makes us human 31

local perspectives 8–15, 216–217, 292–293
    conflict resolution 239–242
    disease and health 220
    education 75–77
    employment 104
    food beliefs 150
    globalization 57, 60–62
    human differences 22
    languages 263, 266–267, 274, 286–290
    making a difference 206–207
    migration 85, 142, 144–145

magazine surveys 61
mapping reports 291
marketing 44
maths 78, 82, 114, 134, 162, 190, 232, 260
media 61, 89–91, 95–98, 184–185, 200
memories 241
menu planning 150–177
migration 84–99, 136–149
milk teeth 35
minimum wage 104–105, 115
MLA (Modern Language Association) style citations 133, 298–300
multiple perspectives 9–15, 137–141, 144–145, 180–181, 238–239
music 204, 244–245, 276

national perspectives 9, 11–15, 206–207, 216–217, 292–293
    conflict resolution 238–239, 242
    education 75–79
    employment 104
    food beliefs 151, 158–159
    globalization 53, 58, 62, 66
    human differences 22
    languages 263, 273–275
    migration 85, 141–145
    report writing 286–290
    sports for all 255
    traditions 32–45
newspapers 61, 89–91, 96
New Year customs 35, 39
note organization 40–41
Nowruz celebrations 39
numerical data analysis 54–57

open questions 154–155, 224
opinion evaluation 69–71
opposites 19, 47, 52–53
orchestras 244–245
outcomes 80, 165–166, 197, 200–201, 212–213, 254–255
out-groups 235, 242–243
overlap 11, 75, 286

paid work 100–115
pandemics 66, 148, 220, 227, 231
participation, sports 248, 252–253, 255
partner drawing 147

penalties 122, 158
perfect education 71
personal goals 112–113
personal perspectives 8, 10–15, 212–213
    conflict resolution 239
    food beliefs 155
    globalization 60–61
    languages 263, 273–275
    migration 144–145
    report writing 286–287
    sustainability 199
philosophy
    conflict resolution 238–239, 246
    diplomacy and traditions 44
    disease and health 232
    employment 114
    future perspectives 176
    migration 148
    trade and aid 190
    water crisis 134
    what makes us human 30
photography 148
physics and sports 260
plan creation 195
plan to action 193, 202–203
policy aspects 137, 141–147
politics
    conflict resolution 246
    diplomacy and traditions 44
    globalization 66
    migration 98, 138, 144, 148
    sustainability 204
    trade and aid 190
    water crisis 125, 134, 138, 144
pollution 122–127, 133, 192
poster creation 47
post hoc game 137, 139
power of social media 227
power of words 88–91, 103
predictions, globalization 61
preliminary research 264–265
primary data 58, 284
problem solving 75–81, 210–211, 244–245
propaganda 87–88
psychology 97, 144, 176, 246
public speaking 203
pull/push factors 138–139

qualitative and quantitative research 152–153, 266–267
quantifying work 107
questionnaires 151, 154–155, 266–267
question selection
    disease and health 224–225
    employment 105–106, 111–112
    food beliefs 154–157
    globalization 58–61
    human differences 20–21
    languages 263–267

    report writing 280–285
    sustainability 198–199
    traditions 36–37
    water crisis 123–127

Rawls, John 238–239
reflection 6, 207, 216, 292–293
    conflict resolution 235, 242–243, 245
    debates 29
    diplomacy and traditions 33–35, 43
    disease and health 221, 230–231
    education 73, 77, 81
    employment 101, 107, 113–115
    future perspectives 165, 168–169
    globalization 63, 65
    languages 263, 272–275
    migration 85, 96–97, 145
    MLA guide 299
    multiple perspectives 15
    report writing 288–289
    sports for all 249, 258–259
    sustainability 199
    trade and aid 179, 188–189
    water crisis 130, 134
refugees 84–99
    see also migration
religion 31, 45, 82
report writing 278–291
research 6, 116–117, 206–209
    diplomacy and traditions 33, 36–39
    disease and health 221, 224–225
    education 69–70, 73–75, 77, 80, 82
    employment 101–114
    food beliefs 151–160, 165
    future perspectives 165, 170–171
    globalization 47–63
    human traits 18–21
    languages 263–267
    migration 85–91, 96–97, 137–143, 146–148
    MLA guide 298
    report writing 280–285
    sports for all 249–261
    sustainability 193, 198–199
    trade and aid 179–181
    water crisis 122–135
resource scarcity 234, 237, 240, 294–295
restaurant planning 150–177
reviewing work 214, 267
rivers, water crisis 122, 134

sampling 151, 157, 159
scarce resources 234, 237, 240, 294–295
science 66, 123–125, 133–134, 148, 162, 176, 204, 230–232, 276

scope of research 208
SDG (Sustainable Development Goals) 74
search engines 126–127
searches, media evaluation 91
self-selecting populations 251
shark fin soup 158–159
social media 227
sociology 44, 82, 114, 148, 162
sources
    report writing 282–285
    survey questions 58
    traditions 38–41
    water crisis 126–127, 142–143, 282–285
    year group summaries 117, 206, 209, 211, 216
sports for all 248–261
Strengths, Opportunities, Weakness's and Threats (SWOT) analysis 188–189
summarizing skills 54–57, 123, 128–129
surveys 58–61, 82, 266–267
survival, languages 268–269, 272–273
sustainability 192–205
Sustainable Development Goals (SDG) 74
SWOT analysis 188–189

team work *see* collaboration
telegrams 129
terminology usage 221, 228–229
text analysis 72–73, 89, 92–93
thought experiments 268–269
time aspects 50–51, 66, 259
time capsules 164–177
trade and aid 178–191
traditions 32–45, 154–155, 157–158
treasure hunts 170, 193–205

unbiased questions 20, 37, 124–125
unpaid work analysis 106–107

variables, disease and health 230–231
Venn diagrams 75, 286–287
vested interests 199
videos 80–81
vision boards 179, 186–188

wages 92, 104–105
wars 141, 234, 241, 245–246
WaterAid 122
water crisis 122–135
what makes us human 16–31
words, power of 88–91, 103
work *see* employment
writing skills 98, 131–133, 146–147, 258–259, 278–291, 296–297

Yousafzai, Malala 75

304